McDougal Littell
Wordskills

Yellow Level

James E. Coomber
Concordia College
Moorhead, Minnesota

Howard D. Peet
North Dakota State University
Fargo, North Dakota

McDougal Littell
A HOUGHTON MIFFLIN COMPANY
Evanston, Illinois • Boston • Dallas

ISBN: 0-395-97988-9

Copyright © 2000 by McDougal, Littell & Company
Box 1667, Evanston, Illinois 60204
All rights reserved. Printed in the United States of America.

7 8 9 10–HWI–03

CONTENTS

To the Student

Why study vocabulary? Increasing the number of words that you know helps you read, write, and speak better. You'll understand more of what you read with less reliance on the dictionary, and you'll be able to express yourself more accurately. This doesn't mean using twenty-dollar words to amaze others. It just means using the right words to say exactly what you mean.

How to Use This Book

You may notice something unusual about this vocabulary book. Definitions are not given with the word lists. Instead, you are given something more powerful—strategies for determining the meanings of words yourself. You'll find this information in Unit 1. Then, in the following units, you will master new words using a five-step process:

1. First you will infer the word's meaning through context clues.
2. Second you will refine your understanding by studying the word's use in a reading selection.
3. Then your understanding of the word will be reinforced through a variety of exercises.
4. Next you will relate the word to other words in the same family.
5. Finally you will use the word in writing and speaking.

The words in this book are ones you are likely to encounter in your reading or in college entrance exams. Some you may already know; others may be completely unfamiliar. As you study these words, try to move them into your "active vocabulary," the words you understand well enough to use in your speaking and writing.

A Personal Vocabulary-Building Program

You can apply the vocabulary skills in this book to learning any new words that you encounter. Here are several tips that will help you.

1. Keep a vocabulary notebook. Jot down the new words you encounter. Record the essential information for each word: correct spelling, part of speech, pronunciation, definition.
2. Review the words in your notebook. Take a few minutes each day to study them. Set a realistic goal of learning a certain number of new words per week.
3. Study the words actively. Active study means that you use as many senses as possible in studying the word. Listen to yourself say the word. See it in your mind's eye. Then use the word as soon as possible in speech or in writing. In general, if you use a word twice, it is yours.
4. Invent your own memory devices. Try to associate the word with other similar words you know. Create a mental image that relates to the word and helps you remember its meaning. One student remembered the meaning of the word *pretentious*, "showy, flaunting," by picturing a small boy playing make-believe, *pretending* to be a king.

There is one final reason for studying vocabulary, one that we hope you discover for yourself as you use this book: Words are fascinating! They are as surprising and alive and insightful as the people who use them.

Strategies for Unlocking Word Meaning

What happens when you encounter an unfamiliar word in your reading? If you have a dictionary at hand, you can look up the word. If you don't have a dictionary, you still have two excellent strategies that can help you make sense of the word: **context clues** and **word parts analysis.** You will be using these strategies in every unit of this book. With practice, you can master these strategies and improve your reading skills.

Part A   Determining a Word's Meaning from Context

Skilled readers often use context clues to determine a word's meaning. **Context** refers to the words or sentences before or after a certain word that help clarify what the word means. There are several types of context clues you can look for, including **definition and restatement, example, comparison, contrast**, and **cause and effect.**

Definition and Restatement

Sometimes a writer will directly define a word, especially if the word is a technical term that may be unfamiliar to readers. Here is an example:

Students of the clarinet and other wind instruments must perfect their *embouchure,* the correct positioning of the tongue and lips on the mouthpiece of the instrument.

More often, a writer will restate the meaning of a word in a less precise form than a dictionary definition.

He was a *hirsute* individual, with long hair streaming down his back.

The meaning of *hirsute*—"hairy"—is suggested in the last part of the sentence. Definition and restatement are often signaled by punctuation (note the comma in the examples) and by certain key words and phrases.

Words Signaling Definition and Restatement		
which is	or	also known as
that is	in other words	also called

Example

The context in which a word appears may include one or more **examples** that unlock the meaning of an unfamiliar word, as in the following sentence:

The motel we stayed at provided all the *amenities,* such as clean sheets and towels, a television, and a swimming pool.

The list of examples following the phrase *such as* helps reveal the meaning of *amenities*—"features that add to one's comfort." The following words often signal examples:

Words Signaling Examples		
like	for instance	this
including	especially	these
such as	other	these include
for example		

Comparison

Another type of context clue is **comparison.** The writer compares the word in question with other, more familiar words. By noting the similarities between the things these words describe, you can get an idea of the meaning of the unfamiliar word.

Like other reference books in the library, the *thesaurus* is a helpful guide for writers.

Although the sentence does not tell us the exact function of a *thesaurus,* it does reveal some things about it through comparison — that it is a reference book to be found in a library and that it serves as a guide for writers. Comparisons are often signaled by these key words:

Words Signaling Comparisons		
like	resembling	also
as	likewise	identical
in the same way	similarity	related
similar to		

Contrast

Context may also help reveal the meaning of a word through **contrast,** as in this example:

You may think him *intransigent,* but he is really quite flexible.

In this example the structure of the sentence indicates to us that *intransigent* is the opposite of the word *flexible.* The words *but...really* imply a contrast, not a similarity. The following key words and phrases signal contrasts:

Words Signaling Contrasts		
but	on the other hand	dissimilar
although	unlike	different
on the contrary	in contrast to	however

Cause and Effect

Another type of context clue is **cause and effect.** The cause of an action or event may be stated using an unfamiliar word. If, however, the effect of that action is stated in familiar terms, it can help you understand the unfamiliar word. Consider the following example:

Since a special treatment has made this fabric *impervious* to moisture, the fabric is now suitable for a raincoat.

In this sentence, the cause—a treatment rendering a fabric *impervious* to moisture—leads to the effect—suitability for rainwear. Therefore, *impervious* must mean "incapable of being penetrated or affected by." Certain key words and phrases may signal cause and effect:

Words Signaling Cause and Effect		
because	consequently	when
since	therefore	as a result

Inference from General Context

Often the clues to the meaning of an unfamiliar word are not as obvious as the preceding examples. You will need to **infer,** or draw a conclusion about, the word's meaning. In some cases, the entire sentence may suggest or hint at the meaning of the word. When no specific clues are given, read the whole sentence carefully to get some sense of the meaning of the word. Consider this example:

Come enjoy the *salubrious* climate of California.

You may know that the climate of California is generally considered to be good. You can infer that someone inviting you to California and the using the word *enjoy* would be praising the climate. Therefore, even though no synonyms or added information is given, you might guess that the word *salubrious* means something like "beneficial." There is one caution, of course, about such guessing — when possible, you should check your guesses by using your dictionary.

In some cases a single piece of information several sentences away from the unfamiliar word may unlock the meaning. Study the following example:

In this section of the country, spring is the most *ephemeral* of seasons. Summer is usually mild and starts in June. Later, Labor Day marks the changing colors of fall, and the first real snowfall comes in early December. The remainder of winter is long and brutal. Spring, on the other hand, lasts only a few days, vanishing almost before you know it has come.

The clue to the meaning of *ephemeral* is found in the last sentence. The detail *lasts only a few days, vanishing almost before you know it has come* suggests that *ephemeral* means "short-lived, fleeting."

Sometimes the supporting details in a paragraph must be examined together to help you infer the meaning of an unfamiliar word. Consider the example below:

The contractor is clearly *culpable* for the collapse of the bridge. He was seldom on the job to check the progress of the work. Records show that he authorized the use of inadequate materials in order to cut costs. Furthermore, examination of the footings disclosed that they were not up to specifications.

The series of details that follows the unfamiliar word *culpable* helps you draw the conclusion that *culpable* means "deserving blame."

Determining Meaning from Context Each of the following sentences contains an italicized word you may not know. Look for context clues to help you determine the meaning of the word and write the definition in the blank.

1. I thought him *mendacious,* but he turned out to be quite honest.

   _____

2. My mother is a defense lawyer and a worthy *adversary* for any prosecuting attorney.

   _____

3. The announcer had a *mellifluous,* honey-like voice.

   _____

4. Chico is *disputatious,* arguing all the time.

   _____

5. No government official has *plenary* power; instead a system of checks and balances prevails.

   _____

6. The trouble with *garrulous* people is that they just talk too much.

   _____

7. His lips curled in *disdain* as he mocked my idea.

   _____

8. His size would suggest that he is a *glutton,* but he actually eats very little.

   _____

9. Like a truck, the *ponderous* lineman rolled over the opposing players.

   _____

10. She tried to *dissuade* me, but I stuck to my plans.

   _____

11. Other *notorious* figures, such as Al Capone and Machine Gun Kelley, were finally sent to prison.

   _____

12. Front-page news stories aggravated the situation and served only to *instigate* more violence and rioting.

_____

13. The sentence was severe because the judge felt that the criminal had shown no *compunction* for committing such a terrible crime.

_____

14. Pam is an *assiduous* worker who never wastes time and often works late.

_____

15. After *dissipating* his inheritance on extravagant living, the young man found himself bankrupt.

_____

Number correct _____ (total 15)

Understanding Context Clues Use a dictionary to define any unfamiliar words and then write a sentence for each of the words below. Use a different type of context clue for each sentence. After the sentence, label the method you used to define each word, choosing from one of the following ways: **definition and restatement; example; comparison; contrast;** and **cause and effect.**

astute   coerce   immutable   meticulous   sanction

1. _____

_____

2. _____

_____

3. _____

_____

4. _____

_____

_____

5. _____

_____

_____

_____

Number correct _____ (total 5)

Part B   *Determining Meaning Through Word Analysis*

Word analysis is another way to determine a new word's meaning. If you know what each part of a word means, you can often understand the complete word.

Prefix   a word part that is added to the beginning of another word or word part

Suffix   a word part that is added to the end of another word or word part

Base word   a complete word to which a prefix and/or a suffix may be added

Root   a word part to which a prefix and/or a suffix may be added. A root cannot stand alone.

Examine the word *unalterable*. It is made up of the prefix *un-*, the base word *alter*, and the suffix *-able*.

un ("not")+alter ("to change")+able ("having the quality")
unalterable=not able to be changed

Now look at a word with a root instead of a base word. *Revocable* is made up of the prefix *re-* ("again or back"), the Latin root *voc* ("to call"), and the suffix *-able* ("having the quality of"). Therefore, something *revocable* can be "called back or cancelled."

Prefixes

The following chart contains prefixes that have only one meaning.

Prefixes That Have a Single Meaning		
Prefix	**Meaning**	**Example**
bene-	good	benefit
circum-	around	circumvent
col-, com-, cor-	with, together	collapse, compile
contra-	opposed	contradict
equi-	equal	equidistant
extra-	outside	extralegal
hemi-	half	hemisphere
hyper-	over, above	hypercritical
inter-	between, among	international
intra-	within	intracellular
intro-	into	introvert
mal-	bad	maltreat
mid-	halfway	midday
mis-	wrong	misspell
non-	not	nonworking
pre-	before	predawn
post-	after in time or space	postpone
retro-	backward, behind	retroactive
sub-	under, below	subzero

Some prefixes have more than one meaning. Study these common prefixes listed in the following chart.

Prefixes That Have More Than One Meaning

Prefix	Meaning	Example
ab-, a-	not	abnormal
	away	absent
	up, out	arise
ad-	motion toward	adopt
	nearness to	adjoin
ante-	before, prior to	antecedent
	in front of	anteroom
anti-	against	anticensorship
	prevents, cures	antidote
	opposite, reverse	antimatter
be-	around, by	beset
	about	bemoan
de-	away from, off	derail
	down	decline
	reverse action of	defrost
dis-	lack of	distrust
	not	dishonest
	away	dispatch
em-, en-	to get into, on	embark
	to make, cause	enfeeble
	in, into	enclose
il, im-, in-, ir-	not	immature
	in, into	investigate
pro-	in favor of	prolabor
	forward, ahead	propel
re-	again	replant
	back	repay
semi-	half	semicircle
	twice in a period	semiannual
	partly	semiconscious
super-	over and above	superhuman
	very large	supertanker
trans-	across	transatlantic
	beyond	transcend
un-	not	unhappy
	reverse of	unfasten

Suffixes

Like a prefix, a suffix has a meaning that can provide a strong clue to the definition of a whole word. Suffixes can also determine the part of speech of a word. Certain suffixes make words into nouns; others create adjectives, verbs, or adverbs.

Once you know suffixes and their meanings, you can form new words by attaching suffixes to base words or roots. For instance, the suffix *-ous* ("full of") can be added to the noun *fallacy* ("an error") to form the adjective *fallacious* ("having many fallacies or errors.)" Note that the *y* from *fallacy* is changed to an *i* before the *-ous* suffix is added. For information about spelling rules for adding suffixes, see the **Spelling Handbook,** pages 208–215.

Noun suffixes, when added to a base word or root, form nouns. Become familiar with the following common noun suffixes.

Noun Suffixes That Refer to Someone Who Does Something

Suffix	Example
-ant	commandant, occupant
-eer	auctioneer
-er	manager
-ician	beautician, statistician
-ier	cavalier
-ist	geologist, somnambulist
-or	counselor

Noun Suffixes That Make Abstract Words

Suffix	Example
-ance	vigilance
-ancy	vagrancy, vacancy
-ation	imagination
-cy	accuracy
-dom	freedom, kingdom
-ence	independence
-hood	womanhood, brotherhood
-ice	cowardice, prejudice
-ism	realism, federalism
-ity	sincerity
-ization	civilization
-ment	encouragement, commitment
-ness	kindness, fondness
-ship	ownership, worship
-sion	decision
-tude	gratitude, solitude
-ty	frailty

Adjective suffixes, when added to a base word or root, create adjectives—words that are used to modify nouns.

Adjective Suffixes

Suffix	Meaning	Example
-able	able to, capable of being	readable
-acious	full of	vivacious
-al	relating to	musical
-ant	that has or does	triumphant
-ful	full of	harmful
-ible	able to	convertible
-ic	pertaining to or like	heroic
-ical	pertaining to	economical
-ish	pertaining to or like	waspish
-ive	pertaining to	descriptive
-less	without	senseless
-like	like	lifelike
-ly	like	scholarly
-most	at the extreme	topmost
-ous	full of	furious
-ular	pertaining to	cellular

Verb suffixes change base words to verbs. The following chart lists four common verb suffixes.

Verb Suffixes

Suffix	Meaning	Example
-ate	to make	activate
-en	to become	lengthen
-fy	to make	simplify
-ize	to become	crystallize

Adverb suffixes change base words to adverbs—words that modify verbs, adjectives, and other adverbs. The following chart lists the most common adverb suffixes.

Adverb Suffixes

Suffix	Meaning	Example
-ily, -ly	in such a manner	quickly, readily
-ward	toward	skyward
-wise	like	clockwise

Roots and Word Families

A word root cannot stand alone but must be combined with other word parts. A great many roots used in our language originally came from Greek or Latin. These roots generate whole families of English words. A **word family** is a group of words with a common root. For example, all of the words in the following word family are derived from the Latin root *miss,* meaning "to send."

dismiss	missile	permission
emissary	mission	remiss
emission	missionary	transmission

By learning word roots you develop your vocabulary because you can recognize roots in many related words. The following two charts show some common Greek and Latin roots.

Useful Greek Roots

Root	Meaning	Example
anthrop	human	anthropology
aster, astr	star	asterisk
auto	self, alone	automobile
bibl	book	bibliography
bi, bio	life	biology
chron	time	chronology
crac, crat	govern	democracy
dem	people	epidemic
gen	birth, race	generation
geo	earth	geoscience
gram	write	grammar
graph	write	paragraph
hydr	water	hydrogen
log	word, reason	dialogue
logy	study of	geology
meter, metr	measure	barometer
neo	new	neophyte
nom, nym	name, word, law	synonym
ortho	straight, correct	orthodontist
pan	all, entire	panorama
phil	love	philosopher
phobia	fear	claustrophobia
phon	sound	phonograph
psych	mind, soul	psychology
scope	see	telescope
soph	wise, wisdom	sophisticated
tele	far, distant	television
theo	god	theology
therm	heat	thermometer

Useful Latin Roots

Root	Meaning	Example
capt	take, hold, seize	capture
cede, ceed, cess	go, yield, give away	proceed, recession
cred	believe	credit, credence
dic, dict	speak, say, tell	dictate, dictionary
duc, duct	lead	induce, conductor
fac, fec, fic	do, make	factory, defect, fiction
fer	carry	transfer, ferry
ject	throw, hurl	eject, inject
junct	join	junction, conjunction
miss, mit	send	dismiss, admit
mot, mov	move	motion, move
par	get ready	prepare, repair
pon, pos, posit	place, put	component, deposit
port	carry	porter, portable
puls	throb, urge	pulsate, compulsory
scrib, script	write	description, scribe
spec, spic	look, see	spectacle, conspicuous
stat	stand, put in a place	statue, stature
ten	stretch, hold	tendon, tenant
tract	pull, move	tractor, retract
ven, vent	come	convention, event
vers, vert	turn	versatile, invert
vid, vis	see	video, vista
voc, vok	call	vocation, invoke
vol	wish	volunteer, malevolent
volv	roll	revolve, involve

Determining Word Meaning Through Prefixes and Suffixes Draw lines to separate each of the following words into three parts—prefix, base word, and suffix. Determine the meaning of the prefix and suffix. Then, by adding the meanings of the prefix and suffix to the base word, write the meaning of each complete word.

1. abnormality: _____

2. antimagnetic: _____

3. dehumidify: _____

4. disquietude: _____

5. nondiplomatic: _____

6. hyperactivity: _____

7. illegalize: _____

8. predetermination: _____

9. reemployment: _____

10. semicircular: _____

Number correct _____ (total 10)

Determining Word Meaning Through Prefixes, Suffixes, and Roots Each of the following words consists of a Greek or Latin root and a prefix or suffix. Use your knowledge of roots, prefixes, and suffixes to put together the meanings of the word parts, and write a definition for each word. You may check your definitions with a dictionary.

1. convocation: _____

2. chronicler: _____

_____

3. demographics: _____

_____

4. hydrology: _____

5. inscription: _____

6. monotheism: _____

7. philanthropist: _____

8. progenitor: _____

9. renominate: _____

10. volition: _____

Number correct _____ (total 10)

Number correct in Unit _____ (total 40)

UNIT 1

Part A Target Words and Their Meanings

The twenty words that follow will be the focus of this first unit. You will find them in the reading selection that follows as well as in the exercises in this unit. Some of these words may be unfamiliar to you, but you will become better acquainted with them—and better able to use them in your reading and writing. For a guide to the pronunciations provided for these words and others found in this book, refer to the **Pronunciation Key** following the Glossary.

1. arbitrary (är′ bə trer′ ē) adj.
2. circumstance (sur′ kəm stans′) n.
3. comprehend (käm′ prə hend′) v.
4. concentration (kän′ sən trā′ shən) n.
5. conform (kən fôrm′) v.
6. consent (kən sent′) n., v.
7. constitute (kän′ stə tōōt′, -tyōōt′) v.
8. despotism (des′ pə tiz′m) n.
9. diffuse (di fyōōz′) v. (di fyōōs′) adj.
10. obligate (äb′ lə gāt′) v.
11. posterity (päs ter′ ə tē) n.
12. precede (pri sēd′) v.
13. proclaim (prō klām′, prə-) v.
14. prone (prōn) adj.
15. subdivision (sub′ di vizh′ ən, sub′ di vizh′ ən) n.
16. subsequent (sub′ si kwənt, -kwent′) adj.
17. susceptible (sə sep′ tə b'l) adj.
18. tyranny (tir′ ə nē) n.
19. unalterable (un ôl′ tər ə b'l) adj.
20. uniform (yōō′ nə fôrm′) adj., n.

Inferring Meaning from Context

For each sentence write the letter of the word or phrase that is closest to the meaning of the word or words in italics. Use context clues to help you determine the correct answer. (For information about how context helps you understand vocabulary, see pages 1–5.)

_____ 1. The king's rule was *arbitrary*; no one understood how or why he made his decision.

a. easygoing b. responsible c. without reason d. helpful

_____ 2. Although she overcame the unfavorable *circumstances* of her upbringing to become famous, she never forgot the poverty and hardships of her youth.

a. conditions b. schools c. decisions d. fashions

_____ 3. I find chemistry easy to learn and remember, but I can barely *comprehend* physics, as evidenced by my low final grade.

a. complete b. understand c. teach d. like

_____ 4. The last two decades have witnessed a migration of people from rural to urban areas, thus increasing the *concentration* of people in the cities.

a. freedom b. density c. discipline d. scattering

_____ 5. A fear of being different leads many teen-agers to feel pressured to *conform to* the expectations of their peers.

    a. disagree with   b. challenge   c. ignore   d. act in agreement with

_____ 6. We were relieved when the coach gave his *consent* for us to play basketball in the gym on Saturday mornings.

    a. permission   b. restriction   c. opinion   d. disapproval

_____ 7. When the rebels took power, they announced their intent to *constitute* a new government.

    a. eliminate   b. think about   c. imitate   d. establish

_____ 8. The government of that country is an example of *despotism*; the president will not tolerate any opposition to her rulings, and her word is absolute law.

    a. democracy   b. tyranny   c. indulgence   d. disorder

_____ 9. Because the poisonous gas from the leaking railroad car had become *diffused* throughout the neighborhood, an emergency was declared and residents were evacuated.

    a. scattered   b. contained   c. functional   d. diluted

_____ 10. I promised the police officer that I would fix my noisy car, so I feel *obligated* to buy a new muffler as soon as possible.

    a. happy   b. reluctant   c. compelled   d. little desire

_____ 11. Taking care of our natural environment will ensure a better life for us now and for *posterity*.

    a. our ancestors   b. the wealthy few   c. future generations   d. our neighbors

_____ 12. Moral decay *preceded* and contributed to the Fall of Rome.

    a. came after   b. came before   c. curbed   d. vanished

_____ 13. Many people do not realize that when Abraham Lincoln *proclaimed* that slaves should be freed, his declaration applied only to slaves in Confederate states.

    a. concealed   b. wished   c. denied   d. announced officially

_____ 14. Medical researchers are still trying to understand why some people are *prone to* certain diseases, such as cancer and diabetes, while others are more resistant to them.

    a. in favor of   b. opposed to   c. resistant to   d. inclined to

_____ 15. A developer has bought a piece of farm land at the edge of town and plans to build *a subdivision* on it, which will result in thirty new homes.

    a. a shopping center   b. smaller farms   c. a housing development   d. an industrial complex

_____ 16. At first we thought Mr. McLean was unpleasant, but in *subsequent* meetings we have found him to be friendly.

    a. later   b. organized   c. previous   d. unimportant

_____ 17. Gloria is so _susceptible to_ allergies during the summer that her physician has suggested that she consider getting allergy shots.

a. easily affected by   b. pleased by   c. immune to   d. suspicious of

_____ 18. The senator passionately attacked all forms of _tyranny_, arguing that all people must be given a voice in their own government.

a. law   b. dictatorship   c. democracy   d. taxation

_____ 19. Mr. Smith's decision to sell the lake cottage was _unalterable_; no one could persuade him to change his mind.

a. indefinite   b. inconsistent   c. unchangeable   d. routine

_____ 20. At one time, speed limits on interstate highways varied considerably because each state set its own limit. To prevent confusion, speed limits have now been made _uniform_ in all fifty states.

a. the same   b. public   c. proper   d. lower

Number correct _____ (total 20)

Part B   Target Words in Reading and Literature

You should now have a general idea of the meaning of each target word. Refine your understanding by examining the shades of meaning the words have in the following excerpt.

Our Basic Liberties: Freedom of the Individual

Sam J. Ervin, Jr.

Too often we take political freedom for granted. But, as former Senator Sam Ervin explains, freedom did not just happen. He points out that the United States Constitution was written to guarantee political freedom.

The men and women who made America believed that governments derive their just powers from the **consent** of the governed. Moreover, they [the people who made America] had absorbed the lessons taught by the history of the struggle of the people against **arbitrary** power for the right to be free from **tyranny**. Hence, they **comprehended** some eternal truths respecting people and government.   5

They knew that those who are entrusted with powers of government are **susceptible** to the disease of tyrants, which George Washington rightly diagnosed in his farewell address as "the love of power and **proneness** to abuse it." For this reason, they realized that the powers of public officers   10 should be defined by laws which they as well as the people are **obligated** to obey.

They likewise knew that Thomas Hobbes had **proclaimed** an **unalterable** principle when he said: "Political freedom is political power divided into small fragments." They also knew the truth **subsequently** embodied by Daniel   15

Webster in this aphorism[1]: "Whatever government is not a government of laws is a **despotism**; let it be called what it may."

For this reason, they realized that liberty cannot exist except under a government of laws, i.e., a government in which the conduct of the people is controlled by certain, constant, and **uniform** laws rather than by the arbitrary, uncertain, and inconstant[2] wills of those who occupy public offices, and in which the laws accord to the people as much freedom as the commonweal[3] permits.

They knew, moreover, the political truth afterwards phrased by Woodrow Wilson in these words:

Liberty has never come from the government. Liberty has always come from the subjects of it. The history of liberty is a history of the limitation of governmental power, not the increase of it. When we resist therefore the **concentration** of power, we are resisting the processes of death, because concentration of power is what always **precedes** the destruction of human liberties.

For these reasons, they realized that the powers of government should be **diffused** among different repositories,[4] that "local processes of law are an essential part of any government conducted by the people," and that "no national government . . . can be as closely in touch with those who are governed as can the local authorities in the several states and their **subdivisions**."

To preserve for themselves and their **posterity** the blessings of freedom, they framed a Constitution which created a government of laws **conforming** to these eternal truths, and which they intended to last for the ages and to **constitute** a law for rulers and people alike at all times and under all **circumstances**.

---

[1] aphorism: a short sentence expressing a wise observation or a general truth
[2] inconstant: not constant, changeable
[3] commonweal: the public good
[4] repository: a container in which things may be placed for safekeeping, in this case the local and state authorities and organizations that govern

Refining Your Understanding

For each of the following items, consider how the target word is used in the passage. Write the letter of the word or phrase that best completes each sentence.

_____ 1. Ervin uses the word *arbitrary* (line 4) to describe power that is a. not determined or limited by rules b. based on democratic principles c. temporary and unenduring.

_____ 2. George Washington warned that all public officials need to guard against a "*proneness* to abuse" power (lines 9–10). A modern example of this might be a. a high government official taking a bribe b. public discussion of national priorities c. the failure of many citizens to vote in elections.

_____ 3. If laws are to be *uniform* (line 20), they must a. be written by one person b. not restrict any activities c. be applied in the same way to everyone.

_____ 4. "*Concentration* of power" (line 28) threatens liberty because a. public officials are evil and need to be restrained b. it increases the speed and efficiency of government bureaucracies c. when one person has too much power, the temptation to abuse power is too great.

_____ 5. Ervin's use of the word *posterity* (line 36) suggests that the writers of the Constitution were concerned about the a. past b. present c. future.

Number correct _____ (total 5)

Part C   Ways to Make New Words Your Own

By now you are familiar with the target words and their meanings. This section presents reinforcement activities that will help you make these words part of your permanent vocabulary.

Using Language and Thinking Skills

Finding the Unrelated Word Write the letter of the word that is not related in meaning to the other words in the set.

_____ 1. a. consent b. approval c. disagreement d. permission

_____ 2. a. understand b. comprehend c. misinterpret d. perceive

_____ 3. a. inconstant b. stable c. unalterable d. firm

_____ 4. a. inclined b. likely c. prone d. reluctant

_____ 5. a. ensuing b. previous c. latter d. subsequent

_____ 6. a. pursue b. follow c. precede d. chase

_____ 7. a. proclaim b. obligate c. commit d. bind

_____ 8. a. susceptible b. impenetrable c. inclined d. receptive

_____ 9. a. circumference   b. condition   c. situation   d. circumstance

_____ 10. a. concentration   b. compression   c. diffusion   d. density

Number correct _____ (total 10)

Practicing for Standardized Tests

Synonyms   Write the letter of the word that is closest in meaning to the capitalized word.

_____ 1. PRONE: (A) likely   (B) unexpected   (C) appropriate   (D) friendly
(E) supportive

_____ 2. UNIFORM: (A) contrasting   (B) shallow   (C) formal   (D) unusual
(E) unvarying

_____ 3. DIFFUSE: (A) calm   (B) explosive   (C) murky   (D) dense   (E) spread out

_____ 4. SUBSEQUENT: (A) under   (B) following   (C) inferior   (D) orderly
(E) preceding

_____ 5. CONFORM: (A) display   (B) obey   (C) refuse   (D) understand   (E) rate

_____ 6. SUBDIVISION: (A) house   (B) job   (C) ladder   (D) part   (E) operation

_____ 7. TYRANNY: (A) storm   (B) freedom   (C) despotism   (D) defense
(E) government

_____ 8. CONSTITUTE: (A) compose   (B) disassemble   (C) govern
(D) conform   (E) falsify

_____ 9. ARBITRARY: (A) helpful   (B) subjective   (C) sensible   (D) lawful
(E) necessary

_____ 10. POSTERITY: (A) rear   (B) backwardness   (C) descendants
(D) ancestors   (E) advertising

Number correct _____ (total 10)

Word's Worth: tyrant

Words, like old Western movies, have their good guys and their bad guys. Some words, however, are undeserving of their negative associations. For example, the words *tyranny, tyrant,* and *tyrannical* are all derived from the Greek word *tyrannos,* meaning "one who has seized power." The tyrants of ancient Greece were not the cruel, unjust, authoritarian rulers that one thinks of in today's use of the word. In fact, because tyrants had oppressed the aristocrats, they often came to power as champions of the common people. Some were even elected by the people instead of taking power in a coup. The rule of one tyrant, Peisistratus of Athens, is regarded as a golden age. The tyrants dealt very harshly with the aristocrats, however, and it was the aristocrats who recorded history. The aristocrats overlooked no opportunity to give their enemies a bad name so that today anyone called a tyrant is definitely a bad guy.

Spelling and Wordplay

Word Maze Find and circle each target word in this maze.

```
C O N C E N T R A T I O N A X U W G P S
C I W P N T Y R A N N Y Y H B W M C D U
F O R Z T V G E U W C J W L D I A E P B
D M H C R C K Q N B O A F T E L S H R S
D I F F U S E O Z M N D R X J P I Y O E
Y A D M S M T A O R F D E B O U E C C Q
N B X L T N S P G O O J O T I D P T L U
P O S T E R I T Y F R I I P A T S J A E
K X Y S V N E M A I M S K R V G R X I N
C P N O K N S M N M K L O O P I A M T
L O P R E C E D E U C M L N U Z D L R U
C O X M O R W E A L S E K E F I X E B Y
A S U B D I V I S I O N S T R U B J Q O
D U R L Q F C I X E P O X I M O R L E S
B S P V S B C O N S T I T U T E O O A Z
N C T R A M D I E L B I T P E C S U S G
J R C O M P R E H E N D A D E I B Q P R
Q E U N A L T E R A B L E G T H A M V X
```

arbitrary	consent	posterity	subsequent
circumstance	constitute	precede	susceptible
comprehend	despotism	proclaim	tyranny
concentration	diffuse	prone	unalterable
conform	obligate	subdivision	uniform

Part D Related Words

A number of words are closely related to the target words you have studied. Use your knowledge of the target words and of word parts to determine the meanings of these words. (For information about word parts analysis, see pages 6–12). Learning these related words expands your vocabulary and helps you learn the target words more thoroughly.

1. antecedent (an′ tə sēd′ ′nt) adj., n.
2. arbitrator (är′ bə trāt′ ər) n.
3. comprehensible (käm′ prə hen′ sə b'l) adj.
4. comprehensive (käm′ prə hen′ siv) adj., n.
5. concede (kən sēd′) v.
6. conformity (kən fôr′ mə tē) n.
7. constitution (kän′ stə tōō′ shən, -tyōō′-) n.
8. despot (des′ pət, -pät) n.
9. diffusion (di fyōō′ zhən) n.
10. fusion (fyōō′ zhən) n.
11. infuse (in fyōōz′) v.
12. nonconformist (nän′ kən fôr′ mist) n.
13. obligation (äb′ lə gā′ shən) n.
14. obligatory (ə blig′ ə tôr′ ē, äb′ lig ə-) adj.
15. proceed (prə sēd′, prō-) v.
16. recede (ri sēd′, rē′ sēd′) v.
17. transfusion (trans fyōō′ zhən) n.
18. tyrannical (ti ran′ i k'l, tī-) adj.
19. uniformity (yōō′ nə fôr′ mə tē) n.
20. unison (yōō′ nə sən, -zən) n.

Turn to **Words with the "Seed" Sound** on page 216 of the **Spelling Handbook.** Read the rule and complete the exercises provided.

Understanding Related Words

True-False Decide whether each statement is true or false. Write **T** for True and **F** for False.

_____ 1. Rulers who are *tyrannical* give their subjects a great deal of freedom.

_____ 2. Something that undergoes *fusion* is broken into smaller units.

_____ 3. German is not *comprehensible* to someone who has not learned the language.

_____ 4. A *comprehensive* study of a problem focuses on only one aspect of the problem.

_____ 5. If a coach says that a Saturday practice session is *obligatory*, then members of the team are free to decide whether or not they should attend.

_____ 6. A *despot* usually shares power whenever possible.

_____ 7. When you *concede* defeat, you admit that you have lost.

_____ 8. A person who owes money to someone else has an *obligation* to that person.

_____ 9. An *arbitrator* is a person selected to make a judgment or give a decision.

_____ 10. The rules for electing officers are usually outlined in the *constitution* of an organization.

_____ 11. The automobile was the *antecedent* of the horse and buggy.

_____ 12. If you walk into a business office and everyone is either in a three-piece suit or a dress, you are seeing *conformity* in action.

_____ 13. A *nonconformist* always seeks to fit in with the crowd.

_____ 14. When a crowd claps in *unison*, everyone claps together.

_____ 15. A rash and inconsistent person will exhibit *uniformity* in his or her daily life.

Number correct _____ (total 15)

Analyzing Word Parts

The Latin Root *fus* The related words *diffusion, fusion, infuse,* and *transfusion* are all derived from the Latin verb *fundere,* "to pour." Many other words, such as *profuse,* also come from this root. The five words shown here, along with the meanings of their prefixes, are listed below.

diffusion: *dis-* "apart"   profuse: *pro-* "forth," "out"
fusion: no prefix   transfusion: *trans-* "across"
infuse: *in-* "in"

Match each of the following words with its appropriate definition. Write the letter of the definition in the blank. Use your dictionary to check your work.

_____ 1. fusion
_____ 2. infuse
_____ 3. profuse
_____ 4. transfusion
_____ 5. diffusion

a. the act of taking blood from one person and transferring it to another
b. a blending or melting together
c. a scattering; a spreading about
d. given or poured forth
e. to put into; instill; impart

Number correct _____ (total 5)

The Latin Root *cede* The target word *precede* and the related words *antecedent, concede, proceed,* and *recede* all contain the root *cede,* from the Latin *cedere,* meaning "yield" or "go." These words are listed below, with the meanings of their prefixes.

antecedent: *ante-* "before"   proceed: *pro-* "forward" or "ahead"
concede: *con-* "with" or "together"   recede: *re-* "back"
precede: *pre-* "before"

Write the word that best completes the meaning of each of the following sentences.

_____ 1. When the flood waters _?_ , people living in low-lying areas will return to their homes.

_____ 2. Does the preamble _?_ the Constitution?

_____ 3. If Jacques Cousteau's new wind ship is successful, the conventional sailboat will be referred to as the _?_ to his newly designed craft.

_____ 4. When his cart is loaded with groceries, Father will _?_ to the checkout counter.

21

_____ 5. Pinned to the mat and unable to move, Shane must _?_ defeat to his opponent.

Number correct _____ (total 5)

Number correct in Unit _____ (total 70)

The Last Word

Writing

Many high-school students like to think of themselves as *nonconformists*. They are proud of their independence in thought and action. However, the adolescent years are also a time of great *conformity*. Peer groups often pressure young adults to dress alike and act alike, sometimes leading individuals to actions that go against their better judgment. Write a paragraph in which you define yourself as a conformist, a nonconformist, or a blend of both. Be sure to use examples to illustrate your points.

Speaking

What talent, skill, or personality trait do you have that might one day benefit *posterity*? Will future generations listen to your musical compositions or read your novels with admiration? Will your descendants tell fond stories about your wacky sense of humor? Will people be sitting in houses that you built or using the invention that made you famous? Describe one thing about yourself that may be remembered by posterity. Be sure to use specifics so that your audience can appreciate what makes you memorable.

Group Discussion

In the United States, there has always been a tension between individual liberty and responsibilities to groups, including the community, the state, and the nation. This tension usually becomes apparent whenever income taxes are discussed. At one extreme, some people believe that no citizen should be made to pay income taxes, for such taxes infringe on our individual liberty to keep the money that we earn by our labor. At the other extreme, some people want taxes to be increased so that government can provide more and better human services, such as health care, education, and housing. These people argue that our responsibilities to other members of society are more important than individual liberty.

Divide into groups of five. Each group should discuss the issue of income tax as it relates to liberty and responsibility. Should the government have the right to tax income? If the government does have that right, should taxes be increased to provide more services? Where taxation is concerned, how can we draw the line between individual liberty and group responsibility?

UNIT 2

Part A Target Words and Their Meanings

1. adapt (ə dapt′) v.
2. alien (āl′ yən, -ē ən) adj., n.
3. array (ə rā′) n., v.
4. classify (klas′ ə fī′) v.
5. diminutive (də min′ yoo tiv) adj., n.
6. enigma (ə nig′ mə) n.
7. evoke (i vōk′) v.
8. fragility (frə jil′ ə tē) n.
9. frigid (frij′ id) adj.
10. infinite (in′ fə nit) adj.
11. interior (in tir′ ē ər) adj., n.
12. merge (murj) v.
13. mingle (miŋ′ g'l) v.
14. parasite (par′ ə sīt′) n.
15. perennial (pə ren′ ē əl) adj., n.
16. persistent (pər sis′ tənt) adj.
17. sprawl (sprôl) v., n.
18. stunted (stunt′ əd) adj.
19. tenuous (ten′ yoo wəs) adj.
20. undulate (un′ joo lāt′) v.

Inferring Meaning from Context

For each sentence write the letter of the word or phrase that is closest to the meaning of the word or words in italics. Use context clues to help you.

_____ 1. Rather than resisting change, she must learn to *adapt to* new conditions.
a. be opposed to b. expect c. adjust to d. welcome

_____ 2. While exploring a Martian valley, Captain Kirk discovered his first *alien* life-form—a furry, purple creature with four protruding eyes.
a. distasteful b. belonging to the imagination c. belonging to another world d. forgettable

_____ 3. The florist created an interesting *array* of several types of dried flowers to decorate the banquet table.
a. kind b. picture c. collection d. garden

_____ 4. The electronic sorting machine could *classify* the eggs according to size.
a. group b. count c. photograph d. break

_____ 5. The child was so *diminutive* he had to stand on a stool to wash his hands.
a. small b. fearful c. uncoordinated d. lazy

_____ 6. The mathematics problem that Ms. Underhill posed was a real *enigma*; we spent several hours after school trying to figure out the answer.
a. inspiration b. mistake c. puzzle d. time-waster

_____ 7. Paul's insult *evoked* an immediate response—Patti slapped him as soon as the last word was out of his mouth.
a. produced b. resulted from c. avoided d. brought back memories of

23

_____ 8. The *fragility* of antique china dishes is obvious; handle them carefully.
   a. delicacy   b. beauty   c. cheapness   d. expense

_____ 9. On one *frigid* day in 1964, temperatures dropped to a record-breaking -96° F in Oymyakon, Siberia.
   a. unalterable   b. very cold   c. subsequent   d. pleasant

_____ 10. To the men who first explored it, the tundra seemed to occupy *an infinite* expanse that spanned immeasurable distances.
   a. a strange   b. a slight   c. an endless   d. an uninhabited

_____ 11. During a tornado, stand against *an interior* wall, away from the windows.
   a. an inner   b. an outer   c. a paneled   d. a subdivided

_____ 12. In Pittsburgh, the Monongahela and the Allegheny rivers *merge* to form the Ohio River.
   a. join   b. run   c. separate   d. go underground

_____ 13. Martin Luther King, Jr., envisioned a day when poor and rich children, white and black children could *mingle* together without prejudice.
   a. fight   b. go separate ways   c. conform   d. mix

_____ 14. One of the most common *parasites,* the flea, probably could not survive without dogs, cats, and other susceptible mammals that sustain it.
   a. organisms that live off of others   b. poisonous insects   c. organisms that nurture others   d. sighted insects

_____ 15. Finding enough blood donors has become *a perennial* problem for health organizations; many people won't take the time to give blood.
   a. a rare   b. an occasional   c. an easily solved   d. a continuing

_____ 16. Mr. Borden sometimes irritated his customers by being very *persistent* in trying to sell his products, but his effort usually paid off.
   a. messy   b. dishonest   c. half-hearted   d. determined

_____ 17. Exhausted from work, Carmen *sprawled* on the sofa, much to the annoyance of her brother, who wanted to sit there and watch television.
   a. jumped   b. sat stiffly   c. studied   d. spread out

_____ 18. Because of the constant winds and low temperatures at high elevations, evergreen trees near the timberline often appear *stunted,* for they are unable to grow to the size one would expect at lower elevations.
   a. green   b. uniform   c. healthier   d. not fully developed

_____ 19. Although the fibers of a spider web are *tenuous* and delicate-looking, the web is an amazingly durable construction.
   a. tough   b. dangerous   c. sticky   d. thin

_____ 20. Joe studied the motion of the worm as it *undulated* along the path.
   a. reacted excitedly   b. sped   c. hid   d. moved in a wavelike manner

Number correct _____ (total 20)

Part B Target Words in Reading and Literature

You should now have a general idea of the meaning of each target word. Refine your understanding by examining the shades of meaning these words have in the following excerpt.

Tundra

Rachel Kilsdonk

Have you ever wondered what the vast expanse of northern Canada is like? This author describes the tundra—the large, flat plains of the Arctic.

You couldn't find a better word for it if you tried . . . tundra. It **evokes** vast distances of **infinite** loneliness and **frigid**, singing winds, mystery and **alien** beauty, the **tenuous fragility** of communities of plants, animals, and insects. But the tundra is not a silent, empty wasteland; it's an exciting world of unexpected beauty, one of this planet's last remaining wilderness reserves, the   5 most promising source of oil, copper, asbestos, nickel, and sulfur in Canada's mineral-rich history, and something of an **enigma**.

To begin with, there's no definite line where it starts up north. It **merges** with the **stunted** trees and swamps of the taiga[1] and northern evergreen forest, running northwest from the southern shores of Hudson Bay to the Mackenzie   10 Delta. It **sprawls** across the top of the continent, covering nearly a third of Canada's 3,851,809 square miles from the western mountain ranges, across the rich, fuel-bearing rocks of the **interior** plains—the so-called Barren Lands— over the glacier-worn plateaus of the Canadian shield and the **undulating** plains

---
[1] taiga: the far northern forest

of the Hudson Bay lowlands, through northern Quebec and Labrador to the 15
Atlantic. It clings thinly to the rocks of the Arctic lowlands until its **persistent**
lichens and mosses finally give up their struggle to clothe lands buried all year
by thick polar ice.

Over this one-and-a-half million square miles, various kinds of tundra **adapt** to
varying soil depths and types: there's alpine tundra above the tree line on high 20
plateaus; shrub tundra, **mingling** with the wind-torn black spruce on the edge of
the taiga; sedge tundra as you go farther north; and, finally, moss and lichens
merging with the ice cap.

Much about these rolling, treeless plains continues to baffle science,
particularly the permafrost[2] and the peculiar cycles of plants and other forms of 25
life the tundra supports. When its **diminutive**, slow-growing plants are trampled
upon, they may never grow back again. The mass of dainty mosses, strange
lichens, tiny sedges, heaths, and dwarf shrubs shelter an amazing **array** of
annual and **perennial** flowers. They grow and blossom during the short
summer—hundreds of square miles of bright yellow arctic poppies, purple 30
saxifrage and crocus, the pale primrose and dryas, masses of yellow arnica,
pink lousewort, golden cress, spines of sweet wintergreen, the dainty white
bells of the heather.

And among these flowers thrives a population of bees, tiny flies, midges,
minute **parasite** wasps, big and little spiders, butterflies and a host of fragile 35
moths. Many of these creatures have not yet been described or **classified.**

---

[2] permafrost: permanently frozen subsoil

Refining Your Understanding

For each of the following items, consider how the target word is used in the
passage. Write the letter of the word or phrase that best completes each sentence.

_____ 1. Kilsdonk's use of the word *infinite* (line 2) suggests a loneliness that is
a. impossible to comprehend   b. alterable   c. small but intense.

_____ 2. The *alien* beauty (line 2) of the tundra can be explained by the fact that
it   a. resembles the landscape of other countries   b. makes people feel
distant and afraid   c. bears little resemblance to other landscapes.

_____ 3. The tundra is described as an *enigma* (line 7) because   a. it is a place of
scientific study   b. it is dangerously cold   c. its size and diversity make
it difficult to understand.

_____ 4. The description of the Hudson Bay lowlands (line 14) as *undulating*
suggests that these plains are   a. unusually flat   b. rolling   c. filled
with moving waters.

_____ 5. Because tundra can *adapt* (line 19) to various soil conditions, there are
a. different kinds of tundra   b. tundra that can survive in most regions
of the world   c. fewer and fewer regions of tundra.

Number correct _____ (total 5)

Part C *Ways to Make New Words Your Own*

By now you are familiar with the target words and their meanings. This section presents a variety of reinforcement activities that will help you make these words part of your permanent vocabulary.

Using Language and Thinking Skills

True-False Decide whether each statement is true or false. Write **T** for True and **F** for False.

_____ 1. When you judge a person by *interior* qualities, you pay attention only to his or her physical appearance.

_____ 2. The *fragility* of glass requires that you handle it with care.

_____ 3. When two companies are combined into one, they *merge*.

_____ 4. A student who gives up after doing poorly on his or her first math test is *persistent*.

_____ 5. An American living in Germany may be described as an *alien*.

_____ 6. By wearing a coat in northern winters, you are showing your inability to *adapt* to the seasons.

_____ 7. A *perennial* flower blooms for only one year.

_____ 8. Eskimos have learned to adapt to *frigid* temperatures.

_____ 9. If placed beside a monkey, an elephant appears *diminutive*.

_____ 10. *Parasites* exist by living off their hosts.

_____ 11. A basketball player who is seven feet tall is a victim of *stunted* growth.

_____ 12. Your dresser can hold an *infinite* number of blue jeans.

_____ 13. When a single thread holds a button to a coat, the connection is *tenuous*.

_____ 14. When a lake's surface *undulates*, the lake is perfectly still.

_____ 15. An *enigma* is easily solved.

Number correct _____ (total 15)

Practicing for Standardized Tests

Analogies Each item below consists of a related pair of words followed by five pairs of words. Write the letter of the pair of words that best expresses a relationship similar to that of the original pair. For a detailed explanation of analogies, see page 54.

_____ 1. SPRAWL : SOFA ::   (A) play : chess   (B) pass : football   (C) sit : chair   (D) sing : songbird   (E) rule : kingdom

_____ 2. EVOKE : MEMORY ::   (A) listen : hearing   (B) desert : dessert
(C) please : pleasantry   (D) extract : tooth   (E) oppose : agreement

_____ 3. GLASS : FRAGILITY ::   (A) cash register : business   (B) consent :
disapproval   (C) sun : coldness   (D) writer : pen   (E) steel : strength

_____ 4. BUSINESSES : MERGE ::   (A) fields : plant   (B) winters : freeze
(C) cars : collide   (D) agreements : negotiate   (E) responses : ask

_____ 5. HUGE : DIMINUTIVE : :   (A) outstanding : ordinary   (B) slender :
tenuous   (C) gentle : quiet   (D) unalterable : stubborn   (E) large :
medium

_____ 6. MINGLE : PARTY : :   (A) rest : job   (B) dream : future   (C) exercise :
gym   (D) slam : door   (E) compromise : argument

_____ 7. ENIGMA : DETECTIVE : :   (A) riddle : puzzle   (B) misunderstanding
: comprehension   (C) hands : clock   (D) sickness : doctor   (E) scissors :
paper

_____ 8. FLEA : PARASITE : :   (A) sidewalk : pavement   (B) despot : tyrant
(C) snake : reptile   (D) dog : Chihuahua   (E) stranger : friend

_____ 9. ADAPTABLE : INFLEXIBLE : :   (A) powerful : strong   (B) agreeable
: acceptable   (C) helpful : constructive   (D) reachable : attainable
(E) forgettable : memorable

_____ 10. ARRANGE : ARRAY : :   (A) walk : run   (B) announce : proclaim
(C) reap : sow   (D) learn : teach   (E) rain : flood

Number correct _____ (total 10)

Word's Worth: parasite

The word *parasite* is derived from the Greek roots *para,* meaning "near" or "beside," and *sitos,* meaning "bread," "grain," or "food."   The ancient Greeks coined the word *parasitos* to describe people who ate at the tables of priests or public officials.   However, in English usage the word gradually gained a powerful negative connotation, suggesting a person who shamelessly flatters the rich to gain material benefits.   In the first dictionary of the English language, published in 1755, Samuel Johnson defined a parasite as "one who frequents rich tables and earns his welcome by flattery."   Around the same time, biologists extended the use of *parasite* to describe an organism that is completely dependent on another organism.

Spelling and Wordplay

Crossword Puzzle Read each clue to determine what word will fit in the corresponding squares. There are several target words in the puzzle.

ACROSS
1. Strange
7. Abbr. for *modus operandi*
10. To bring to mind
11. Adjusts
14. 2d person singular of *to be*
15. 3.14159265
16. Leg joints
17. A mystery
21. Public hotel or restaurant
22. Abbr. Royal Air Force
24. Not down
26. Indefinite article meaning "one"
27. To spread through
30. Abbr. Old English
31. Frees oneself of
33. A group
34. Not sweet
35. A beam of light
36. Wager
37. Abbr. Short Stop
38. Ginger — — —
39. Abbr. Los Angeles
43. Extremely cold
45. To move in waves
48. Abbr. Lieutenant
49. To categorize
50. To compete
51. An exclamation expressing surprise, anger, triumph, etc.
52. Foreign
54. Without end
55. Huge or great

DOWN
1. Constant
2. Level
3. Abbr. Company
4. Abbr. United Kingdom
5. Abbr. Low Efficiency
6. Abbr. Radium
7. To make evident
8. Not shut
9. Abbr. United States Ship
12. Abbr. Dark
13. Slender or flimsy
15. Ma's partner
18. Mischievous children
19. To unite or combine
20. Condition of being easily breakable
23. On, in, near, or by
25. Determined
26. A display
28. Small rug used at a door
29. Prefix meaning "in"
32. Coloring agent
40. To mature
41. Abbr. *Anno Domini*
42. Advertisements
43. Fire-making stone
44. Abbr. Royal Air Force
45. Abbr. Underwriters' Laboratories
46. Chemical symbol for sodium
47. Objective case of "we"
48. Falsehoods
49. A tin — — —
50. By way of
51. A word of greeting
53. Abbr. Low Voltage

Part D Related Words

A number of words are closely related to the target words you have studied. Use your knowledge of the target words and of word parts to determine the meanings of these words. (For information about word parts analysis, see pages 6–12).

1. adaptable (ə dap′ tə b'l) adj.
2. adaptation (ad′ əp tā′ shən) n.
3. adapter (ə dap′ tər) n.
4. alienate (āl′ yən āt′, -ē ən-) v.
5. classification (klas′ ə fi kā′ shən) n.
6. enigmatic (en′ ig mat′ ik, ē′ nig-) adj.
7. finite (fī′ nīt) adj.
8. frigidity (frə jid′ ə tē) n.
9. infinitesimal (in′ fin ə tes′ ə məl, in fin′-) adj.
10. infinity (in fin′ ə tē) n.
11. persist (pər sist′, -zist′) v.
12. persistence (pər sis′ təns, -zis′-) n.
13. stunt (stunt) n., v.

Understanding Related Words

Sentence Completion Write the word from the preceding list that best completes the meaning of the sentence.

1. To achieve worthwhile goals in life, you must _____ in your efforts, even in the face of obstacles and disappointments.

2. You cannot plug in this appliance without an _____ .

3. The international problem of malnutrition is difficult to solve because the world's resources are _____ .

4. As a professional singer, she was remarkably _____ ; she could vary her style to sing opera or popular ballads.

5. Scientists who study Antarctica must protect themselves from the harsh and unrelenting _____ of its climate.

6. If Rod acts sullen and rude, he will _____ his friends.

7. Botanists do not always agree on the _____ of new plants.

8. Darwin's theory of evolution originated as an attempt to explain the _____ of animals to their natural environment.

9. Aesop's tale of the tortoise and the hare shows that _____ can be more important than natural ability.

10. The professional wrestler liked to brag about the time he threw three opponents out of the ring; that was obviously his favorite _____ .

Number correct _____ (total 10)

Turn to **Words Ending in y** on page 208 of the **Spelling Handbook**. Read the rule and complete the exercises provided.

Analyzing Word Parts

The Latin Root *vok* The target word *evoke* contains the root *vok* and comes from the Latin word *vocare,* meaning "to call." By analyzing the word parts of *evoke* (*e-* + *vok*), you can determine that it means "to call out." A number of words contain the *vok* root. Some of these words are listed below, along with their meanings.

convocation:	*con-* ("together") + *vok* + *ation* ("quality of") = assembly; meeting
revoke:	*re-* ("back") + *vok* = to withdraw, repeal, or cancel
provoke:	*pro-* ("forth") = *vok*: to anger or irritate
invoke:	*in-* ("on") + *vok* = to call on for blessing or help
vocation:	*voc* + *ation* ("quality of") = the work or career toward which one believes oneself called

For each of the following sentences, choose the word from the list above that best completes the meaning of the sentence.

_____ 1. Tom changed his mind about joining the army because he decided to pursue a different _?_.

_____ 2. The retiring school superintendent will speak to the graduating seniors at the _?_ this year.

_____ 3. The angry young man seemed all too eager to _?_ a fight.

_____ 4. The judge said that she would _?_ the driving privileges of anyone found guilty of a drunk driving charge.

_____ 5. At the opening of the play *Oedipus Rex,* the main character said he would _?_ the gods to help rid his community of the plague.

Number correct _____ (total 5)

The Latin Root *fin* The target word *infinite* and the related words *infinitesimal, infinity,* and *finite* contain the root *fin,* which comes from the Latin word *finis,* meaning "end." Some words with the *fin* root are listed below, along with their definitions.

finale: concluding part, especially of a musical piece
finite: having measurable units; not infinite
infinite: lacking limits or bounds
indefinite: having no exact limits; not clear; vague
infinitesimal: too small to be measured
infinity: endless or unlimited space, time, distance, amount, etc.

31

For each of the following sentences, write the word from the list that best completes the meaning of the sentence.

_____ 1. The scientist reported that the amount of radiation produced by her experiment was _?_ and should therefore be considered harmless.

_____ 2. Since property lines were often _?_ in the early days of our country, surveyors were sometimes brought in to determine exact boundaries and settle disputes.

_____ 3. Modern physicists rely on the concept of _?_ to explain the mysteries of our expanding universe.

_____ 4. Although oil and coal are still abundant, they are _?_ resources that cannot be renewed.

_____ 5. During the _?_ of the Olympic Games, athletes from all of the countries walked hand in hand into the stadium.

Number correct _____ (total 5)

Number correct in Unit _____ (total 70)

The Last Word

Writing

Winston Churchill was so confused by the actions of Russia in 1939 that he complained to the British: "I cannot forecast to you the action of Russia. It is a riddle wrapped in a mystery inside an *enigma*." Think of an enigma in your own life or in the world around you. Describe this engima and explain what makes it so mysterious.

Speaking

Alien creatures have always been a fascinating subject for movies and books. Imagine if the tables were turned: What would happen if you were transported to another world? How would other intelligent life forms describe your appearance? Try to describe yourself as a nonhuman creature might perceive you.

Group Discussion

The ability to *adapt* is one of the most remarkable human traits. Discuss how you might adapt—or fail to adapt—to one or more of the following challenges: (1) the loss of a limb, (2) an economic depression in which thirty percent of the adult population is unemployed, (3) the loss of sight, or (4) the loss of all your personal possessions. Discuss what character traits enable people to adapt to hardships.

UNIT 3

Part A *Target Words and Their Meanings*

1. agitate (aj′ ə tāt′) v.
2. alter ego (ôl′ tər ē′ gō, eg′ ō) n.
3. ambiguity (am′ bə gyōō′ ə tē) n.
4. authority (ə thôr′ ə tē, -thär′-) n.
5. code (kōd) n.
6. considerable (kən sid′ ər ə b′l) adj.
7. constituency (kən stich′ oo wən sē) n.
8. cynic (sin′ ik) n.
9. dilemma (di lem′ ə) n.
10. dimension (də men′ shən) n.
11. diverse (dī vurs′, də-; dī′ vurs) adj.
12. enterprise (en′ tər prīz′) n.
13. estrangement (ə strānj′ mənt) n.
14. formally (fôr′ məl ē) adv.
15. hostility (häs til′ ə tē) n.
16. mindless (mīnd′ lis) adj.
17. naive (nä ēv′) adj.
18. paradoxical (par′ ə däk′ si k′l) adj.
19. reflexive (ri flek′ siv) adj.
20. ultimately (ul′ tə mit lē) adv.

Inferring Meaning from Context

For each sentence write the letter of the word or phrase that is closest to the meaning of the word or words in italics. Use context clues to help you determine the correct answer.

_____ 1. The sprinter was so *agitated* after losing the race that she kicked her locker in frustration.

a. withdrawn b. pleased c. disturbed d. exhilarated

_____ 2. At the office, John works very hard, and he seldom has time for anything other than his job; on the baseball field, however, his *alter ego* takes over, and he shows his sociable, fun-loving side.

a. persistence b. bad side c. other self d. generosity

_____ 3. Because of *ambiguity* in the wording of the contract, the two parties interpreted it in two different ways.

a. fine print b. unclear meaning c. conformity d. precision

_____ 4. If, for any reason, the President cannot fulfill the requirements of office, the Vice-President assumes the *authority* of the presidency and takes over decision-making responsibilities.

a. power b. wisdom c. blame d. salary

_____ 5. In World War II, military intelligence operations specialized in breaking the enemy's secret *codes*; many lives were saved as a result of the successful efforts to unscramble enemy messages.

a. requirements b. tactics c. set of symbols for communicating messages d. alphabetized directories

33

_____ 6. Dorothy Sayers was one of the first women to graduate from Oxford University in England; she achieved *considerable* success by writing best-selling detective stories and a highly respected translation of Dante's *Divine Comedy*.

a. insignificant   b. great   c. controversial   d. tenuous

_____ 7. As she voted on each issue before Congress, the senator kept the needs of her *constituency* in mind; as a result, they reelected her.

a. company   b. business associates   c. foreign friends   d. state's voters

_____ 8. Because of his harsh and bitter life, Mr. Altira was a *cynic*; he always doubted the sincerity of the people who tried to help him.

a. politician   b. dreamer   c. skeptical person   d. religious fanatic

_____ 9. Many young people in nineteenth-century Europe faced a serious *dilemma*: tolerate a shortage of land and jobs in their home countries, or face a long ocean voyage and the difficulties of the North American frontier.

a. desire   b. failure   c. choice between difficult options   d. enigma

_____ 10. The soccer players complained that the *dimensions* of their practice field were not the same as those of the game field; they calculated that the practice field was ten feet shorter.

a. ticket sales   b. playing conditions   c. measurements   d. equipment requirements

_____ 11. Winnipeg is a city of *diverse* national backgrounds; many residents are the children of immigrants from Germany, France, and the Ukraine.

a. close-knit   b. varied   c. unknown   d. uniform

_____ 12. Starting your own store is a risky *enterprise*; statistics show that the majority of such businesses fail within one year.

a. business venture   b. stunt   c. form of entertainment   d. design problem

_____ 13. No one is able to say what caused the *estrangement* between Pete and Kathy; they had been good friends for a very long time, but now they don't even speak to one another.

a. separation   b. romance   c. agreement   d. wedding

_____ 14. Although the hiring committee had not *formally* announced its decision, most people were certain that Ms. Reynaldo would be named principal.

a. awkwardly   b. secretly   c. sincerely   d. officially

_____ 15. We felt the *hostility* of the crowd as soon as we entered the auditorium and saw their angry stares.

a. fear   b. unfriendliness   c. friendliness   d. indifference

_____ 16. When Luis told us that he would use astrology to choose his college, we immediately criticized his *mindless* plan; however, we breathed a sigh of relief when he said he was only joking.

a. senseless   b. ambitious   c. clever   d. rational

_____ 17. Only a *naive* person would believe the promises made in television commercials without doing some critical thinking and evaluation.

a. wealthy b. gullible c. native-born d. dishonest

_____ 18. It was *paradoxical* that a trusted and highly respected bank officer turned out to be the thief.

a. easily understandable b. typical c. fortunate d. seemingly contradictory

_____ 19. The Russian psychologist Pavlov became famous for his study of animals' *reflexive* responses to their environment; he showed that even involuntary bodily functions could be changed by conditioning.

a. aggressive b. verbal c. fearful d. instinctive

_____ 20. Whether or not we buy a new car next year will *ultimately* depend upon how much money we save; if we cannot save enough for a down payment, we will have to wait.

a. finally b. certainly not c. arbitrarily d. humorously

Number correct _____ (total 20)

Part B Target Words in Reading and Literature

You should now have a general idea of the meaning of each target word. Refine your understanding by examining the shades of meaning these words have in the following excerpt.

Don't Love the Press, But Understand It

Henry Grunwald

What is the function of the press in a democracy? That question has been debated since the founding of our country. Some have argued that the government needs to place limits on the press. Others, such as the author of this essay, argue that a press free from governmental regulation is a vital ingredient of democracy.

Americans have always had mixed feelings about their press. In folklore, the reporter is Superman's **alter ego**, but he is also the front page **cynic** who would trade in his grandmother for a scoop[1]. By way of a more elevated example, almost everybody (at least among journalists) remembers Jefferson's famous remark that if he had to choose between a government without newspapers and 5 newspapers without a government, he would pick the latter. But few recall that Jefferson also wrote on another occasion: "Nothing can now be believed which is seen in a newspaper."

Thus, attacks on the press are a good old American tradition, and the press should be able to take it. Journalists deserve much of the criticism directed at 10

_____

[1] scoop: advantage gained over a competitor by being first, specifically in reporting a news item

35

them and ought to examine themselves and their practices far more carefully rather than wrapping themselves in the First Amendment at any sign of **hostility**.

But in recent years, attacks on the press have taken on a new **dimension** and . . . they have become **mindless** and **reflexive** . . . The press should never expect to be loved or admired. But it has a right to be understood, and too many Americans do not seem to understand what the press is about and what part it must play in the American system. An **estrangement** between the press and large numbers of Americans is dangerous, not merely to the press but to the country.

True, the nature of the American press is confusing. It is a profitmaking **enterprise**, but it is not judged chiefly by commercial success. It performs a public service, but it is neither regulated nor licensed. Journalists have **considerable** power to help or hurt, but there is no **code**, no professional association to judge their performance. **Paradoxical** though all this may appear, it simply means that the American press is free—and would lose all its value to the country if it were otherwise.

That freedom raises many moral **ambiguities** about the source and limits of the **authority** of the press. One way in which these are frequently expressed is through the question hurled at reporters: Who elected you? The answer is nobody—and that's the way it should be. No one should want a society in which all positions of influence and power are filled through the political process alone.

A **diverse** society needs all kinds of people—business people, professionals, artists—who are not chosen by the ballot. But while not **formally** elected, they all have their **constituencies** upon whose approval they **ultimately** depend. If the approval is withheld, they can hardly continue to function—and this is true of the press.   35

   Not that the moral **dilemma** ends here. Newsmen constantly wrestle with the problem of how to find their way among the innumerable shadings of truth and the often agonizing choices about what to print and what not to print. Despite the public's frequently **naive** faith in "objective," just-the-facts reporting, every   40
newsman must interpret and judge; which things to put in among various indisputable facts and what to leave out often constitutes the most important form of judgment of all . . .

   The journalist cannot assert the right to print everything and anything; he must decide each case on its merits, while remaining accountable to his editor and,   45
ultimately, to his audience. The decision is usually a battle of conscience waged by journalists far more seriously than most outsiders realize. In general, the American press today is far more responsible, far less "yellow," than at any time in its **agitated** history.

Refining Your Understanding

   For each of the following items, consider how the target word is used in the passage. Write the letter of the word or phrase that best completes each sentence.

_____ 1. The phrase "Superman's *alter ego*" (line 2) suggests that people have sometimes viewed reporters   a. as heroes   b. as childish and silly   c. as if they were evil versions of Superman.

_____ 2. When the author uses the words "new *dimension*" (line 13) in referring to recent attacks on the press, he is probably referring to   a. new measurements for recording the attacks   b. a change in the nature or degree of the attacks   c. a decrease in the number of people who criticize the press.

_____ 3. The freedom of the press is *paradoxical* (line 24) because   a. a free press is essential for a democracy, even though it sometimes abuses its freedom   b. the press should be tightly restrained to avoid hurting people   c. the press never makes a mistake or misuses its power.

_____ 4. "Moral *ambiguities*" (line 27), suggests that   a. we should not trust the motives of the press   b. the press does not care about issues of right and wrong   c. the power and freedom of the press creates situations where right and wrong are not always clear.

_____ 5. The author uses the term *agitated* (line 49) to describe the history of the American press because   a. journalists are usually excited or mad when they write   b. the press is often a subject of controversy   c. people are tired of being attacked by the press.

Number correct _____ (total 5)

Part C Ways to Make New Words Your Own

This section presents a variety of reinforcement activities that will help you make these words part of your permanent vocabulary.

Using Language and Thinking Skills

Finding the Unrelated Word Write the letter of the word that is not related in meaning to the other words in the set.

_____ 1. a. finally   b. eventually   c. ultimately   d. clearly

_____ 2. a. indefiniteness   b. uncertainty   c. clarity   d. ambiguity

_____ 3. a. rule   b. code   c. anarchy   d. law

_____ 4. a. paradoxical   b. straightforward   c. puzzling   d. incongruous

_____ 5. a. solution   b. problem   c. dilemma   d. difficulty

_____ 6. a. mindless   b. thoughtful   c. unintelligent   d. stupid

_____ 7. a. personality   b. dimension   c. measurement   d. height

_____ 8. a. voters   b. citizens   c. representatives   d. constituency

_____ 9. a. disturb   b. excite   c. agitate   d. calm

_____ 10. a. ceremonially   b. formally   c. casually   d. officially

Number correct _____ (total 10)

Practicing for Standardized Tests

Analogies Each item below consists of a related pair of words followed by five pairs of words. Write the letter of the pair of words that best expresses a relationship similar to that of the original pair. For an explanation of analogies, see page 54.

_____ 1. AMBIGUITY : VAGUENESS ::   (A) essay : conclusion   (B) stream : ocean   (C) north : south   (D) expansion : enlargement   (E) wheat : flour

_____ 2. DILEMMA : SOLUTION ::   (A) conductor : train   (B) diversity : uniformity   (C) wheel : bicycle   (D) disease: cure   (E) question : inquiry

_____ 3. UNION : ESTRANGEMENT ::   (A) detective : investigation   (B) consent : approval   (C) idea : mind   (D) belief : disbelief   (E) basketball : game

_____ 4. ENEMY : HOSTILITY ::   (A) artist : creativity   (B) country : Chile   (C) foe : opponent   (D) musician : orchestra   (E) diffusion : fusion

_____ 5. AUTHORITY : BADGE ::   (A) story : conclusion   (B) marriage : wedding ring   (C) memory : experience   (D) wood : fuel   (E) rumor : lie

_____ 6. FOOL : MINDLESS ::   (A) kitten : Siamese   (B) ballerina : graceful   (C) nonconformist : uniform   (D) infinity : finite   (E) tragedy : comic

_____ 7. CYNIC : DISBELIEF ::   (A) optimist : hope   (B) idealist : despair   (C) coach : player   (D) dancer : costume   (E) flame : ashes

_____ 8. NAIVE : SOPHISTICATED ::   (A) rational : mental   (B) angered : annoyed   (C) cooperative : helpful   (D) accidental : arbitrary   (E) infinite : finite

_____ 9. BUSINESS : ENTERPRISE ::   (A) house : building   (B) departure : return   (C) pages : lines   (D) vacation : work   (E) tree : forest

_____ 10. ENIGMA : CONFUSION ::   (A) artist : brush   (B) exercise : fitness   (C) music : literature   (D) array : flowers   (E) harmony : opposition

Number correct _____ (total 10)

Spelling and Wordplay

Word Maze   Find and circle each target word in this maze.

C	O	N	S	I	D	E	R	A	B	L	E	C	R	A
W	O	A	U	L	T	I	M	A	T	E	L	Y	E	S
S	H	N	U	D	I	M	E	N	S	I	O	N	F	P
E	S	Y	S	Y	L	L	A	M	R	O	F	I	L	A
Y	S	X	L	T	E	V	I	A	N	S	B	C	E	R
T	E	X	A	M	I	N	E	J	R	B	A	L	X	A
I	L	Z	M	W	Y	T	T	V	E	L	A	C	I	D
U	D	A	M	E	H	Q	U	E	T	M	L	W	V	O
G	N	G	E	X	D	I	V	E	R	S	E	U	E	X
I	I	I	L	A	B	R	R	O	N	P	C	Q	L	I
B	M	T	I	F	O	E	N	Y	M	C	R	D	G	C
M	C	A	D	T	G	D	O	C	X	E	Y	I	B	A
A	U	T	H	O	R	I	T	Y	C	O	D	E	S	L
F	M	E	T	N	E	M	E	G	N	A	R	T	S	E
R	V	D	H	O	S	T	I	L	I	T	Y	A	B	D

agitate
alter ego
ambiguity
authority
code
considerable
constituency
cynic
dilemma
dimension
diverse
enterprise
estrangement
formally
hostility
mindless
naive
paradoxical
reflexive
ultimately

39

Part D   Related Words

A number of words are closely related to the target words you have studied. Use your knowledge of the target words and of word parts to determine the meanings of these words. If you are unsure of any definitions, use your dictionary.

1. agitation (ag′ ə tā′ shən) n.
2. ambiguous (am big′ yōō wəs) adj.
3. authoritarian (ə thôr′ ə ter′ ē ən, -thär′-) adj., n.
4. authoritative (ə thôr′ ə tāt′ iv, -thär′-) adj.
5. authorize (ô′ thə rīz′) v.
6. constituent (kən stich′ ōō wənt) adj., n.
7. cynical (sin′ i k'l) adj.
8. diversify (də vʉr′ sə fī′) v.
9. diversion (də vʉr′ zhən, dī-) n.
10. diversity (də vʉr′ sə tē, dī-) n.
11. divert (də vʉrt′) v.
12. enterprising (en′ tər prīz′ iŋ) adj.
13. estrange (ə strānj′) v.
14. formality (fôr mal′ ə tē) n.
15. hostile (häs′ t'l, -tīl) adj.
16. naiveté (nä ēv tā′) n.
17. paradox (par′ ə däks′) n.
18. ultimatum (ul′ tə māt′ əm) n.

Understanding Related Words

Sentence Completion   Write the word from the list that best completes the meaning of the sentence.

_____   1. Tamara believed that most people were phony; this ? attitude prevented her from making many friends.

_____   2. The President can ? a state of national emergency if a crisis arises.

_____   3. The Catholics and Protestants of Northern Ireland have been ? toward one another for centuries.

_____   4. The photograph of the homeless person sleeping outside the luxury hotel dramatically conveyed the ? of poverty amid great wealth.

_____   5. Many students enjoy the ? of proms because it gives them a chance to wear tuxedos or long dresses.

_____   6. Dictatorships are ? forms of government.

_____   7. As the opposing team scored the winning point, the coach's hoarse yells unmistakably revealed his ?.

_____   8. Through a monthly newsletter, the representative kept the ?(s) in his district well-informed on issues.

_____   9. This book is an ? resource; it provides up-to-date information about every college in the country.

_____   10. Some people view reading as a pleasant ?; others approach reading as a difficult chore.

40

_____ 11. Very young children believe that people are actually inside the television talking to them; such _?_ makes them particularly susceptible to advertising.

_____ 12. We turned down the wrong street because the directions our friend gave us were _?_.

_____ 13. Marla's single-mindedness vanished and her interests began to _?_ when she met people of different backgrounds.

_____ 14. We tried to _?_ the dog's attention away from the hamburgers on the picnic table.

_____ 15. Janelle revealed the _?_ of her talent by playing both classical music and jazz during her recital.

Number correct _____ (total 15)

Turn to **The Final Silent _e_** on page 210 of the **Spelling Handbook**. Read the rule and complete the exercises provided.

One-Word Ideas Write the word from the list below that most closely describes the idea expressed in the sentence.

ambiguous   cynical   diversity   enterprising   estranged
formality   hostile   naiveté   paradox   ultimatum

_____ 1. Fred often assumed that other people were trying to cheat him or deceive him, even when he had no evidence.

_____ 2. Because of a bitter argument, the two brothers had not spoken to each other for years.

_____ 3. When the football coach saw two of his players collide while they were learning a new play, he realized that his instructions were not as clear as they should have been.

_____ 4. A letter from the merchant directed us to pay the bill immediately or face prosecution.

_____ 5. Each of the President's cabinet officers must be sworn in by a judge before he can assume responsibility.

_____ 6. Cary talked about the importance of tolerance, but often showed surprising intolerance in her dealings with people.

_____ 7. The college student started a successful mail-order business.

_____ 8. The community took pride in its mixture of ethnic groups.

_____ 9. The young child flatly stated that he would put an end to all war when he became President.

_____ 10. When an animal bares its teeth, it is not being friendly.

Number correct _____ (total 10)

Analyzing Word Parts

Word Endings In each of the following sentences, there is a blank followed by a target word in parentheses. Change the ending of the target word to form one of the related words. Be sure the newly formed word fits the sentence.

1. Because the results of our first experiment were _____ (ambiguity), we decided to repeat the test.

2. According to the Constitution, only the Congress has the right to _____ (authority) a state of war.

3. Many of the senator's _____ (constituency) wrote letters praising his stand on the tax issue.

4. Only a _____ (cynic) person could doubt his good intentions.

5. To succeed, magicians must master the art of _____ (diverse).

Number correct _____ (total 5)

Number correct in Unit _____ (total 75)

Word's Worth: cynic

The word *cynic* comes from the Greek term *kynikos,* meaning "doglike." The original Cynics were the unconventional and unkempt followers of Antisthenes, a philosopher who scorned wealth, comfort, and social customs as obstacles to the life of virtue. Antisthenes' most famous pupil was Diogenes, an unlikable man who chose to live as a beggar, sleep in public buildings, drink out of his hands, and own only one garment (a blanket). The term *cynic* probably originated from public disapproval of such a way of life. The term also may have been the public's way of getting even with the man who mocked their wealth and insisted that people were only prisoners of their possessions. In fairness to the Greek public, however, it is important to note that Diogenes invited such abuse by his habit of showing his teeth and barking at those whom he did not like. Even though Diogenes was unlikable and unkempt, he was no doubt sincere in his pursuit of truth and virtue. Ironically, the term *cynic* now refers to someone who suspects that everyone is insincere. Modern-day cynics, unlike Diogenes, do not live their lives in pursuit of a higher truth.

The Last Word

Writing

Clichés are overused expressions. The English language is filled with them: *short and sweet, devil may care, footloose and fancy-free, go around in circles,* and *snake in the grass,* to name but a few. Once-clever expressions, clichés have been overused to the point of boredom. A good vocabulary helps weed out such expressions.

The following sentences contain clichés. Rewrite each sentence, replacing the cliché with one of the following target words: *dilemma, mindless, ultimately, agitated, naive.* You may add or delete words if necessary.

1. Sheila was between the devil and the deep blue sea: if she worked after school, she would have money but no free time; if she didn't work, she'd have time but no money.

   _____

   _____

2. The science teacher said that Jay's suggestion that we send scientists to explore the surface of the sun was one brick short of full load.

   _____

   _____

3. Coach Jones was madder than a hornet when the runner fumbled the ball.

   _____

4. Ky must have been born yesterday; he thinks going to the prom won't cost him anything.

   _____

5. When all is said and done, hard work is the most essential ingredient for success.

   _____

Speaking

One of the most famous stories about an *alter ego* is Robert Louis Stevenson's *Strange Case of Dr. Jekyll and Mr. Hyde.* In this story the respectable and handsome Dr. Jekyll is transformed into the evil and ugly Mr. Hyde, with terrifying results. Imagine what would happen if you could create another version of yourself. Perhaps this other self would be the ideal embodiment of your best qualities. Or perhaps your other self might be the dark side of you, the side you seldom show. Give a brief talk describing the alter ego you would create.

Group Discussion

A *cynical* person can be defined as someone who distrusts everyone's motives. In contrast, a *naive* person believes that everyone is sincere. Compare and contrast the consequences of these two very different approaches to human behavior. Of the two, which attitude do you think is preferable?

UNIT 4:   Review of Units 1–3

Part A   Review Word List

Unit 1 Target Words

1. arbitrary
2. circumstance
3. comprehend
4. concentration
5. conform
6. consent
7. constitute
8. despotism
9. diffuse
10. obligate
11. posterity
12. precede
13. proclaim
14. prone
15. subdivision
16. subsequent
17. susceptible
18. tyranny
19. unalterable
20. uniform

Unit 1 Related Words

1. antecedent
2. arbitrator
3. comprehensible
4. comprehensive
5. concede
6. conformity
7. constitution
8. despot
9. diffusion
10. fusion
11. infuse
12. nonconformist
13. obligation
14. obligatory
15. proceed
16. recede
17. transfusion
18. tyrannical
19. uniformity
20. unison

Unit 2 Target Words

1. adapt
2. alien
3. array
4. classify
5. diminutive
6. enigma
7. evoke
8. fragility
9. frigid
10. infinite
11. interior
12. merge
13. mingle
14. parasite
15. perennial
16. persistent
17. sprawl
18. stunted
19. tenuous
20. undulate

Unit 2 Related Words

1. adaptable
2. adaptation
3. adapter
4. alienate
5. classification
6. enigmatic
7. finite
8. frigidity
9. infinitesimal
10. infinity
11. persist
12. persistence
13. stunt

Unit 3 Target Words

1. agitate
2. alter ego
3. ambiguity
4. authority
5. code
6. considerable
7. constituency
8. cynic
9. dilemma
10. dimension
11. diverse
12. enterprise
13. estrangement
14. formally
15. hostility
16. mindless
17. naive
18. paradoxical
19. reflexive
20. ultimately

Unit 3 Related Words

1. agitation
2. ambiguous
3. authoritarian
4. authoritative
5. authorize
6. constituent
7. cynical
8. diversify
9. diversion
10. diversity
11. divert
12. enterprising
13. estrange
14. formality
15. hostile
16. naiveté
17. paradox
18. ultimatum

44

Inferring Meaning from Context

For each sentence write the letter of the word or phrase that is closest to the meaning of the word or words in italics.

_____ 1. Bill felt *obligated* to vote for that particular senator.
a. duty-bound b. pressured c. reluctant d. relieved

_____ 2. When Olivia felt the snake in her sleeping bag, she realized her *dilemma*: neither moving nor staying still could guarantee her safety.
a. enigma b. danger c. predicament d. fear

_____ 3. Phoebe said she would write her life story for the sake of *posterity*.
a. her contemporaries b. her grandparents c. future generations
d. past generations

_____ 4. The Constitution is our best defense against *tyranny*.
a. despotism b. aggression c. military power d. conformity

_____ 5. In June, when the two companies *merge,* their combined assets will total 100 million dollars.
a. split b. go bankrupt c. become one d. talk

_____ 6. The young children were *sprawled* on the floor, watching an exciting movie.
a. stretched out b. kneeling c. sitting in a row d. playing

_____ 7. All of Paul's friends agreed that his recent decision was *paradoxical*.
a. imaginative b. contradictory c. appropriate d. deceitful

_____ 8. The 100-mile canoe trip was quite *an enterprise* for the scout troop.
a. a bold undertaking b. an enigma c. a routine d. a disaster

_____ 9. Kate possesses many *diverse* talents.
a. athletic b. identical c. incredible d. varied

_____ 10. The customer had to choose from *an array* of expensive perfumes.
a. a limited quantity b. a cabinet c. a catalog d. a display

_____ 11. The decision to postpone the game was *arbitrary*; play could have continued for another inning.
a. made by an umpire b. made without reason c. reasonable
d. cynical

_____ 12. Next Saturday night a fireworks display will *precede* the baseball game.
a. come before b. follow c. cancel d. interrupt

_____ 13. A police officer has *authority* to preserve law and order within a particular region.
a. no legal right b. unofficial power c. training d. official power

_____ 14. A good salesperson must always be *adaptable*.
a. able to charm b. able to travel c. able to change d. able to sell

_____ 15. Henry was told to *classify* his English compositions according to when they were written.

a. store   b. group   c. mingle   d. publish

Number correct _____ (total 15)

Using Review Words in Context

Using context clues, determine which word from the list below best completes each sentence in the reading selection. Write the word in the blank.

adapted	alien	arbitrary	authority	circumstances
code	considerable	despot	diminutive	formally
posterity	proclaimed	subsequent	tyranny	ultimately

Napoleon Bonaparte

The complex figure of Napoleon Bonaparte has long fascinated students of world history. In Napoleon one finds an intriguing assortment of contradictions. He had romantic ideals but also relentless ambition; fierce discipline and childish behavior; keen rationalism and _____ whim.

As a leader Napoleon did not possess the qualities of a typical hero. He was short and stocky, with a weak chin and generally unimpressive appearance. More importantly, this native of Corsica was something of an _____ in France, a stranger from a poor Mediterranean island far removed from the centers of power. Even his Italian name, originally spelled *Buonaparte,* marked him as an outsider. His career had an undistinguished beginning, with a mediocre performance in military school, where he finished near the bottom of his class. All of these factors fueled his unquenchable ambition.

The _____ man who was known as the "Little Corporal" is generally acknowledged as the greatest military leader of the nineteenth century. He showed a boldly original grasp of military strategy, an uncanny ability to exploit the enemy's weakness, and decisive leadership on the battlefield. Rising quickly through the ranks, he became an enormously successful general who could turn his battlefield victories into political power. _____ , his military talent made him the strongest leader in Europe. His achievements created a new map of Europe, with France as its largest and most powerful country. Yet his ambition had enormous human costs, as evidenced by his failed invasion of Russia, which brought about the deaths of more than 500,000 French soldiers. After Napoleon's downfall at Waterloo, France was left smaller and weaker than it had been before Napoleon came to power.

As a political leader, Napoleon combined the humanitarian ideals of the Age of Enlightenment with ruthless _____ , which explains why both his critics and supporters referred to him as an enlightened _____ . As a young man he _____ the democratic virtues of the French Revolution and fought valiantly on its behalf. Later, Napoleon brilliantly _____ to the changing _____ of French politics; for him each crisis in the French government became another stepping stone to power. His meteoric rise reached its peak when he had himself _____ crowned as emperor for life. Though Napoleon loved power for its own sake, he also used his _____ to implement a number of far-reaching reforms. In law, banking, government, and education, Napoleon's _____ influence is felt even today. Indeed, the entire legal system of France is still based upon the _____ of laws that he devised.

Napoleon ended his life in defeat, a prisoner exiled to the remote island of St. Helena, off the west coast of Africa. Since his death, _____ generations have alternately praised him for his achievements or condemned him for his excesses. Though his reputation will always be subject to disagreement, we can be certain of this: _____ will never forget the exploits of Napoleon.

Number correct _____ (total 15)

Part B *Review Word Reinforcement*

Using Language and Thinking Skills

Finding Examples Write the letter of the situation that best demonstrates the meaning of the boldfaced word.

_____ 1. **arbitrary**

a. For no apparent reason, the custodian suddenly announced that we could no longer play baseball in the schoolyard.
b. The Chang family settles their disputes in a family court that they conduct in their kitchen.
c. Only the judges know the names of the winning contestants.

_____ 2. **enigma**

a. In ancient Greece the oracles at Delphi were famous for making prophecies in the form of riddles.
b. When he was digging for clams, Mr. Grinelli found the wedding ring that he had lost.
c. The nurse came into the room to administer the injection.

_____ 3. **dilemma**

    a. Sandy felt uncomfortable; she knew only a few of the guests.

    b. Scott did not know the answer, so he ventured a guess.

    c. When we discovered that we were lost, we had to choose between trying to find the trail and staying put.

_____ 4. **naive**

    a. Ms. Martinez gave the con artist her life savings to invest in the stock market, but the con artist put the money in his own bank account.

    b. Eileen felt disappointed when she learned that her younger sister made the team instead of her.

    c. Unable to find his wallet, Joe knew it was going to be a tough day.

_____ 5. **parasite**

    a. Deer could often be seen on the estate feeding off the land.

    b. Elvin says that his lazy cousin has mastered the art of living off of friends and relatives.

    c. This vaccine will help produce antibodies that will fight disease.

_____ 6. **prone**

    a. The neighbors supported the idea of building a new playground.

    b. The mountain water is so clean that we will be able to lie down and drink directly from the stream.

    c. The hunters stood in the marsh, waiting for the ducks to appear.

_____ 7. **ambiguity**

    a. A good basketball player can dribble with either hand.

    b. In this experiment, if the temperature is below thirty degrees, a chemical reaction will occur.

    c. When half of our guests got lost on the way to our house, we realized that our directions were probably confusing.

_____ 8. **authority**

    a. The class responded to the question with a deafening silence.

    b. The taxi driver loved to argue with his passengers about any topic.

    c. The historian summarized her extensive research on the role of women in the Civil War.

_____ 9. **cynical**

    a. He was one of the greatest Chinese emperors; unfortunately, he was assassinated at the height of his power.

    b. A 1960's slogan was "Never trust anyone over thirty."

    c. The scientists reported their findings after the evidence was analyzed.

_____ 10. **infinite**

    a. Raymond's dazzling speed impressed the coaches at the tryout.

    b. The concept of eternity is hard for the human mind to comprehend.

    c. The national debt has grown dramatically in the last two decades.

Number correct _____ (total 10)

Practicing for Standardized Tests

Antonyms Write the letter of the word that is most nearly *opposite* in meaning to the capitalized word.

_____ 1. ALIENATE: (A) befriend (B) estrange (C) classify (D) adapt (E) diffuse

_____ 2. CYNICAL: (A) suspicious (B) tyrannical (C) agitated (D) trusting (E) enterprising

_____ 3. ESTRANGEMENT: (A) ultimatum (B) diversion (C) union (D) division (E) dilemma

_____ 4. FORMAL: (A) obligatory (B) casual (C) solemn (D) hostile (E) alien

_____ 5. FRAGILITY: (A) frigidity (B) weakness (C) ambiguity (D) glassware (E) sturdiness

_____ 6. HOSTILE: (A) friendly (B) mindless (C) adaptable (D) healthy (E) argumentative

_____ 7. UNALTERABLE: (A) susceptible (B) fixed (C) changeable (D) contradictory (E) allied

Number correct _____ (total 7)

Synonyms Write the letter of the word whose meaning is closest to that of the capitalized word.

_____ 1. ALTER EGO: (A) despot (B) authority figure (C) tyrant (D) enemy (E) another self

_____ 2. AMBIGUOUS: (A) obvious (B) arbitrary (C) unclear (D) classified (E) sprawling

_____ 3. CIRCUMSTANCE: (A) situation (B) dilemma (C) method (D) dimension (E) obstacle

_____ 4. COMPREHEND: (A) precede (B) diversify (C) oblige (D) understand (E) seize

_____ 5. CONSTITUTE: (A) conform (B) mingle (C) finish (D) draw on (E) make up

_____ 6. DIFFUSE: (A) recede (B) concentrate (C) proclaim (D) adapt (E) spread out

_____ 7. DILEMMA: (A) diversion (B) predicament (C) ultimatum (D) hostility (E) pleasure

_____ 8. OBLIGATE: (A) bind (B) annoy (C) liberate (D) occupy (E) defend

Number correct _____ (total 8)

Spelling and Wordplay

Middle Message   In the blanks, spell the *related word* that matches the clue to the left. Read vertically, the letters in the boxes in the middle will reveal a basic right found in the First Amendment to our Constitution.

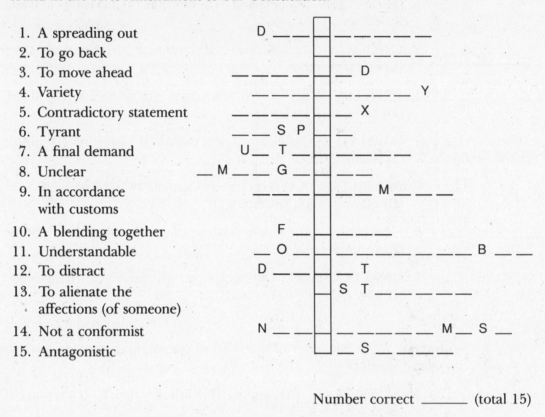

1. A spreading out   D __ __ ☐ __ __ __ __ __
2. To go back   ☐ __ __ __ __
3. To move ahead   __ __ __ __ ☐ D
4. Variety   __ __ __ ☐ __ __ __ Y
5. Contradictory statement __ __ __ __ ☐ X
6. Tyrant   __ __ S P ☐ __
7. A final demand   U __ T __ ☐ __ __
8. Unclear   __ M __ __ G __ ☐ __ __
9. In accordance   __ __ __ ☐ __ __ M __ __ __
   with customs
10. A blending together   F __ __ ☐ __ __ __
11. Understandable   __ O __ ☐ __ __ __ __ __ B __ __
12. To distract   D __ __ __ ☐ T
13. To alienate the   ☐ S T __ __ __ __ __
    affections (of someone)
14. Not a conformist   N __ __ ☐ __ __ __ __ M __ S __
15. Antagonistic   ☐ __ S __ __ __

Number correct _____ (total 15)

Part C   Related Words Reinforcement

Using Related Words

Write the related word from the list below that best completes each sentence.

adaptable	antecedent	arbitrator	classification	diverted
enterprising	infinity	paradox	persistence	stunt

_____ 1. In grammar, a pronoun usually refers to a noun, called the $\underline{?}$, that comes before the pronoun.

_____ 2. Commander Lewis covertly $\underline{?}$ government money to a special military operation of his own.

_____ 3. The $\underline{?}$ of U.S. naval ships is easy if you remember that battleships are named after states, submarines after fish, cruisers after cities, and destroyers after naval heroes.

_____ 4. Although it may seem to be an $\underline{?}$, the distance one can see through the telescope on Mount Palomar, California, is only 7,028,835,200,000,000,000,000 miles.

_____ 5. The author Joseph Conrad is considered a _?_ because he chose to write in his third language even though he knew Polish and French better than English.

_____ 6. Virginia Woolf scandalized England when she and her friends pulled an amazing _?_; they toured the battleship HMS *Dreadnought* after convincing the admiral that they were visiting from Ethiopia.

_____ 7. To help settle the dispute between the baseball players and the team owners, a professional _?_ was brought in.

Number correct _____ (total 7)

Reviewing Word Structures

The Latin Roots *cede, con, fin, fus,* **and** *uni* Complete each of the following sentences with a word from the Review Word List (page 44). Follow the directions in parentheses, using a word with the designated root.

1. Quality-control workers are trained to inspect the _____ of products. (Use a word with the root *uni.*)

2. The testing of the fruits and vegetables detected only an _____ amount of residue from the pesticides. (Use a word with the root *fin.*)

3. The Puritans valued _____ as a way of maintaining social order and religious discipline. (Use a word with the root *con.*)

4. The advertising director said that his latest plan represented a _____ of the two previous plans. (Use a word with the root *fus.*)

5. The choreographer hopes to _____ the dance company with new enthusiasm and new ideas. (Use a word with the root *fus.*)

6. The flood waters should _____ by the end of the week. (Use a word with the *cede* root.)

7. When the oil tanker ran aground, the crew took steps to limit _____ of the leaking oil. (Use a word with the *fus* root.)

8. The girls shouted in _____ , but their friend was too far away to hear them. (Use a word with the *uni* root.)

9. Oil and coal are _____ resources; once they are used up, they cannot be replaced. (Use a word with the *fin* root.)

10. The candidate held a press conference in order to _____ defeat. (Use a word with the *cede* root.)

Number correct _____ (total 10)

Number correct in Unit _____ (total 92)

Vocab Lab 1

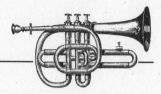

FOCUS ON: Music

The poet Henry Wadsworth Longfellow once stated that "music is the universal language of mankind." You may feel that the language of music is Greek to you, but even if you can't read a note and have a tin ear, you can still speak knowledgeably *about* music. To further enrich your increasing vocabulary, become familiar with the following musical terms.

a cappella (ä′ kə pel′ ə) adv., adj. without an instrumental accompaniment. • Although an organist usually performed with the choir, the group decided to sing their last song *a cappella.*

allegro (ä leg′ rō, -lä′ grō) adv., adj. fast and lively. • Most rock music is played *allegro.*

arpeggio (är pej′ ē ō) n. a series of notes played in succession rather than at the same time. • Musicians practice *arpeggios* to develop their technique.

cantata (kən tät′ ə) n. a musical composition for one or more vocal soloists that tells a story, like an opera, but is not acted. • Listening to the *cantata*, Allison became emotionally involved in the story.

chord (kôrd) n. three or more musical tones played in harmony at the same time. • Jason learned to play *chords* on the guitar before he learned to play melodies.

crescendo (krə shen′ dō) n. a gradual increase in loudness. • The march ended with a dramatic *crescendo* that grew from the sound of a single piccolo to a blending of all the instruments of the band playing as loudly as possible.

finale (fə nal′ ē) n. the last section of a musical composition. • Some people in the audience didn't realize that the concerto wasn't over, and they left before the *finale.*

flat (flat) n., adj. a note that is a half step lower in pitch than a given note. • On a piano, the note B-*flat* is the black key located between the white keys for the notes A and B.

fortissimo (fôr tis′ ə mō′) adv., adj. very loud. • When a brass band plays *fortissimo,* the sound can be heard a mile away.

measure (mezh′ ər) n. a division of musical time with a specific number of beats. • In a waltz, each *measure* has three beats.

mezzo (met′ sō) adj. medium; adv. moderately. • The range of a *mezzo-soprano's* voice is midway between that of a soprano and a contralto.

moderato (mäd ə rät′ ō) adv., adj. with a moderate tempo. • Since the tempo marking on the new symphony was *moderato,* the conductor kept the orchestra from playing it too fast or too slow.

octave (äk′ tiv) n. an interval of eight notes. • If you cannot reach the high notes in the music, sing the entire piece an *octave* lower.

piano (pē ä′ nō) adv., adj. soft. • A passage marked *piano* should be played softly.

staccato (stə kät′ ō) adj. characterized by short notes played distinctly, and sharply separated from one another. • The composer created the impression of gunfire by having the drums play *staccato* passages.

Writing Sentences Many of the musical terms you have just learned, and others, have gained widespread acceptance in our language and now are used in situations that have nothing to do with music. For example, most jazz solos are performed *ad libitum,* which means "in any way the musician wishes." This musical term has entered our everyday language in a shortened form, *ad lib.* This colloquial expression means "to do something without preparation," "to play it by ear." For each of the musical terms listed below, write a sentence that uses the word in a nonmusical context. Use your dictionary if necessary.

Example *ad lib:* Elisa was so confident that she decided to *ad lib* her address to the graduating seniors.

1. chord: _____

_____

2. crescendo: _____

_____

3. finale: _____

_____

4. measure: _____

_____

5. staccato: _____

_____

Number correct _____ (total 5)

FOCUS ON: *Analogies*

Various activities help build vocabulary skills, such as synonym, antonym, and sentence completion exercises. An analogy exercise is another way to enrich your understanding of words. An **analogy** shows a relationship between words. A typical analogy problem looks like this:

> Choose the lettered pair of words that best expresses a relationship similar to that expressed in the original pair.
>
> _____ SNOW : SKI ::   (A) ice : freeze   (B) rain : drench   (C) water : surf   (D) pool : swim   (E) mountain : climb

The analogy can be expressed this way: *"Snow* is to *ski* as ? is to ? ."

To answer an analogy problem, first determine the relationship between the original pair of words. State this relationship in a sentence:

"Snow is the surface that people *ski* on."

Then decide which word pair expresses a similar relationship. You can test your choice by substituting the pair for the original pair in the sentence. It becomes apparent that *(C)* is the best answer when you use the test:

"Water is the surface that people *surf* on."

Here are the most common types of relationships used in analogies:

Type of Analogy	Example
cause to effect	virus : cold :: carelessness : errors
part to whole	finger : hand :: spoke : wheel
object to purpose	car : transportation :: lamp : illumination
action to object	dribble : basketball :: fly : kite
item to category	salamander : amphibian :: corn : vegetable
age	kitten : cat :: cygnet: swan
type to characteristic	owl : nocturnal :: lion : carnivorous
word to synonym	nice : pleasant :: gratitude : thankfulness
synonym variants	pliant : flexibility :: unruly: disobedience
word to antonym	nice : unpleasant :: lazy : industrious
antonym variants	spotless : filth :: faultless : inaccuracy
object to its material	shoe : leather :: necklace : gold
product to source	apple : tree :: milk : cow
worker and creation	composer : symphony :: author : novel
worker and tool	carpenter : hammer :: surgeon : scalpel
worker and work place	mechanic : garage :: judge : courtroom
time sequence	sunrise : sunset :: winter : spring
spatial sequence	mountain top : valley :: engine : caboose
word and derived form	act : action :: image : imagine
degree of intensity	pleased : ecstatic :: drizzle : downpour
manner	shout : speak :: swagger : walk

Analogies Solve the following analogy problems, which use words from previous units. Write the letter of the word or word pair that best completes the analogy.

_____ 1. DESPOT : DICTATORSHIP :: (A) president : presidency (B) king : monarchy (C) rebel : anarchy (D) Pluto : plutocracy (E) Republican : republic

_____ 2. FRAGILITY : GLASS :: (A) hostility : host (B) fluidity : sand (C) rigidity : steel (D) altitude : airplane (E) individuality : student

_____ 3. CYNIC : BELIEF :: (A) despot : compassion (B) alien : strangeness (C) athlete : fitness (D) martyr : self-denial (E) optimist : hope

_____ 4. POSTERITY : ANCESTRY :: (A) father : son (B) grandmother : mother (C) relative : in-law (D) future : past (E) brother : sister

_____ 5. PROCLAIM : DECLARE :: (A) adore : abhor (B) understand : comprehend (C) punch : pat (D) lower : hoist (E) scowl : weep

_____ 6. INFINITE : FINITE :: (A) dark : dim (B) unnecessary : obligatory (C) intolerable : unbearable (D) mistaken : taken (E) everlasting : eternal

_____ 7. CODE : DECIPHER :: (A) stunt : perform (B) mystery : mystify (C) oven : bake (D) computer : compute (E) actor : rehearse

_____ 8. UNDULATE : WAVE :: (A) fracture : bone (B) spiral : tornado (C) explain : understanding (D) bore : lecture (E) flatter : insult

_____ 9. UNALTERABLE : CHANGEABLE :: (A) same : similar (B) uncomplicated : simple (C) persistent : stubborn (D) naive : sophisticated (E) diverse : varied

_____ 10. CLASSIFY : CLASSIFICATION :: (A) conform : confirmation (B) agitate : agitation (C) state : station (D) effect : affectation (E) nationalize : nation

_____ 11. FRIGID : HOT :: (A) primary : colorful (B) sweet : sugary (C) ear-splitting : quiet (D) overweight : fat (E) smoke : fiery

_____ 12. WIDTH : DIMENSION :: (A) hunger : meal (B) sight : sound (C) dehydration : thirst (D) sadness : emotion (E) love : hate

_____ 13. DIVIDE : SUBDIVISION :: (A) laugh : joke (B) think : idea (C) organize : disorder (D) purchase : cost (E) travel : geography

_____ 14. SPRAWL : UPRIGHT :: (A) diffuse : concentrated (B) alienate : separated (C) consent : agreeable (D) merge : united (E) comprehend : understood

_____ 15. ANALOGY : RELATIONSHIP :: (A) dime : nickel (B) geology : earth (C) salinity : ocean (D) clarinet : woodwind (E) painting : canvas

Number correct _____ (total 15)

Number correct in Vocab Lab _____ (total 20)

UNIT 5

Part A Target Words and Their Meanings

1. ascetic (ə set′ ik) adj., n.
2. benign (bi nīn′) adj.
3. brood (brood) v., n.
4. condense (kən dens′) v.
5. conviction (kən vik′ shən) n.
6. estuary (es′ choo wer′ ē) n.
7. exquisite (eks′ kwi zit, ik skwiz′ it) adj.
8. idol (ī′ d'l) n.
9. imperceptible (im′ pər sep′ tə b'l) adj.
10. interminable (in tur′ mi nə b'l) adj.
11. luminous (loo′ mə nəs) adj.
12. meditative (med′ ə tāt′ iv) adj.
13. nautical (nôt′ i k'l) adj.
14. pacific (pə sif′ ik) adj.
15. personify (pər sän′ ə fī′) v.
16. placid (plas′ id) adj.
17. serenity (sə ren′ ə tē) n.
18. somber (säm′ bər) adj.
19. tolerant (täl′ ər ənt) adj.
20. virtue (vur′ choo) n.

Inferring Meaning from Context

For each sentence write the letter of the word or phrase that is closest to the meaning of the word or words in italics. Use context clues to help you determine the correct answer.

_____ 1. The old man of the mountain was truly *ascetic*; he allowed himself none of the material comforts of life.
   a. authoritarian   b. self-denying   c. despotic   d. tyrannical

_____ 2. The vicious-looking dog was actually *benign* and had never hurt anyone.
   a. stern   b. cynical   c. sleeping   d. gentle

_____ 3. Upset by her poor performance, Angela *brooded* about her math score.
   a. bragged   b. forgot   c. talked   d. sulked

_____ 4. The paragraphs must be *condensed*. They are wordy.
   a. diffused   b. expanded   c. reorganized   d. trimmed

_____ 5. Vernon had strong *convictions* about the rights of animals and spent much time trying to interest others in his cause.
   a. beliefs   b. enigmas   c. suspicions   d. transfusions

_____ 6. The city of New Orleans is located on *an estuary,* off the Gulf of Mexico.
   a. a lake   b. an island   c. an inlet   d. a plateau

_____ 7. The wedding guests complimented the bride when they saw her *exquisite* dress with its delicate lace and hand-worked beading.
   a. mediocre   b. ostentatious   c. extremely beautiful   d. trendy

_____ 8. To their admirers, television stars are often *idols*— flawless and godlike individuals.

a. sources of wisdom   b. phony   c. lazy   d. objects of worship

_____ 9. Even small, *imperceptible* changes in the ozone layer can have serious negative effects on the earth's climate and crops.

a. unimportant   b. subtle   c. very strong   d. unexpected

_____ 10. After two hours, the restless audience began to feel that the commencement speaker's address was *interminable*.

a. interesting   b. illuminating   c. endless   d. mindless

_____ 11. The moon was *luminous*, glowing above us in the summer night sky.

a. eclipsed   b. shimmering   c. cold   d. clouded

_____ 12. Sitting before the fire, the scientist was in a *meditative* mood, quietly considering the theory he had formulated.

a. thoughtful   b. cheerful   c. troubled   d. hostile

_____ 13. Because covered wagons looked like ships crossing the prairie, they were given a *nautical* name —"prairie schooners."

a. naughty   b. modest   c. sea-related   d. prairie-related

_____ 14. Mood music and a quiet atmosphere made the *pacific* restaurant a haven for anyone looking for a relaxed evening.

a. peaceful   b. boring   c. outstanding   d. stimulating

_____ 15. Smokey the Bear *personifies* the law-abiding, safety-conscious attitude that is so important to the preservation of our forests.

a. condenses   b. discourages   c. classifies   d. represents

_____ 16. When Irene came home for dinner two hours late, her mother was anything but *placid*.

a. nervous   b. calm   c. troubled   d. emotional

_____ 17. The quiet *serenity* inside the little church contrasted sharply with the hustle and bustle of the city streets.

a. virtue   b. sermon   c. sadness   d. calmness

_____ 18. Losing the state tournament put the basketball team in *a somber* mood.

a. an alien   b. a cheerless   c. a generous   d. an enthusiastic

_____ 19. A wise person is *tolerant* of other people's ideas, listening carefully and considering them thoughtfully.

a. conscious   b. unconscious   c. respectful   d. neglectful

_____ 20. *Virtue* brings more happiness than does evil, its opposite.

a. Comfort   b. Power   c. Goodness   d. Wickedness

Number correct _____ (total 20)

Part B Target Words in Reading and Literature

You should now have a general idea of the meaning of each target word. Refine your understanding by examining the shades of meaning these words have in the following excerpt.

Heart of Darkness

Joseph Conrad

This excerpt from the novel Heart of Darkness *is typical of Conrad's style. What is more remarkable than Conrad's style, however, is the fact that English was Conrad's third language, a language he did not learn until he was twenty. Born in Poland, Conrad went to France to become a sailor at the age of sixteen. It was during those early voyages on French ships sailing to England that this Polish boy began to learn the English language. Note Conrad's use of description in this selection. Does his life on the sea color the way he writes?*

The Nellie, a cruising yawl,[1] swung to her anchor without a flutter of the sails, and was at rest.

The Thames stretched before us like the beginning of an **interminable** waterway. The sea and the sky were welded together without a joint, and in the **luminous** space the tanned sails of the barges drifting up with the tide seemed to stand still in red clusters of canvas sharply peaked. A haze rested on the low shores that ran out to sea in vanishing flatness. The air was dark above Gravesend, and farther back still seemed **condensed** into a mournful gloom, **brooding** motionless over the biggest, and the greatest, town on earth.[2]

The Director of Companies was our captain and our host. We four affectionately watched his back as he stood in the bows looking to seaward. On

5

10

---

[1] yawl: a type of sailing vessel with two masts
[2] biggest and greatest town on earth: Conrad refers here to London

the whole river there was nothing that looked half so **nautical.** He resembled a pilot, which to a seaman is trustworthiness **personified.** It was difficult to realize his work was not out there in the luminous **estuary,** but behind him, within the brooding gloom. 15

Between us there was the bond of the sea. Besides holding our hearts together through long periods of separation, it had the effect of making us **tolerant** of each other's yarns—and even **convictions.** The Lawyer—the best of old fellows—had, because of his many years and many **virtues,** the only cushion on deck, and was lying on the only rug. The Accountant had already 20 brought out a box of dominoes, and was architecturally toying with them. Marlow sat cross-legged. He had sunken cheeks, a yellow complexion, a straight back, an **ascetic** aspect, and, with his arms dropped, the palms of hands outwards, resembled an **idol.** The director, satisfied the anchor had good hold, made his way aft and sat down amongst us. We exchanged a few words 25 lazily. Afterwards there was silence on board the yacht. For some reason or other we did not begin that game of dominoes. We felt **meditative,** and fit for nothing but **placid** staring. The day was ending in a **serenity** of still and **exquisite** brilliance. The water shone **pacifically;** the sky, without a speck, was a **benign** immensity of unstained light. Only the gloom to the west, brooding 30 over the upper reaches, became more **somber** every minute, as if angered by the approach of the sun.

And at last, in its curved and **imperceptible** fall, the sun sank low, and from glowing white changed to a dull red without rays and without heat, as if about to go out suddenly, stricken to death by the touch of that gloom brooding over a 35 crowd of men.

Refining Your Understanding

For each of the following items, consider how the target word is used in the passage. Write the letter of the word or phrase that best completes each sentence.

_____ 1. Conrad uses the word *interminable* (line 3) to emphasize the river's
a. depth   b. history   c. length.

_____ 2. If the sailors were *"tolerant* of each other's . . . *convictions"* (line 18), they probably   a. overlooked each other's prison records   b. argued regularly   c. became accepting of opposing opinions.

_____ 3. Because Marlow has an *ascetic* aspect (line 23), he would probably *not* enjoy   a. a simple lunch   b. hard work   c. a luxurious party.

_____ 4. In this passage, words such as *meditative, placid, serenity, pacifically* and *benign* convey a feeling of   a. affection   b. calm   c. boredom.

_____ 5. In contrast, words such as *brooding, somber, mournful gloom,* and *stricken to death* seem to foreshadow   a. that the trip will be discontinued   b. an enjoyable journey   c. some trouble to come.

Number correct _____ (total 5)

Part C   *Ways to Make New Words Your Own*

By now you are familiar with the target words and their meanings. This section presents reinforcement activities that will help you make these words part of your permanent vocabulary.

Using Language and Thinking Skills

Understanding Multiple Meanings Each boldfaced word in this exercise has several definitions. Read the definitions and then the sentences that use the word. Write the letter of the definition that applies to each sentence.

> **brood**
> a. used for breeding (adj.)
> b. the offspring of a family, or a group of birds or other animals produced at one hatching or birth (n.)
> c. to sit on eggs to hatch them (v.)
> d. to think long and deeply (v.)

_____ 1. An insecure person will often *brood* about a problem rather than take effective action.

_____ 2. The father ushered his large *brood* into the department store.

_____ 3. The *brood* mare brought a handsome price at auction.

_____ 4. Only one of the *brood* of geese survived the frigid night.

_____ 5. Rather than *brood* all day, Greg decided to ask his friend for help.

_____ 6. During the tour, the farmer proudly showed his visitors how hens *brood*.

> **exchange**
> a. the act of trade or mutual substitution (n.)
> b. the rate at which one currency can be exchanged for another (n.)
> c. to give or receive one thing in place of another (v.)
> d. relating to the exchanging of places (adj.)

_____ 7. The *exchange* student quickly learned the customs of her host country.

_____ 8. Some think it rude to *exchange* a gift for cash.

_____ 9. Because of the favorable rate of *exchange*, the travelers were able to purchase more than they had anticipated.

_____ 10. In the *exchange*, the Yankees obtained two needed relief pitchers.

Number correct _____ (total 10)

Practicing for Standardized Tests

Analogies Write the letter of the pair of words that best expresses a relationship similar to that of the original pair.

_____ 1. BROOD : DUCKLING :: (A) litter : puppy (B) ancestor : father
(C) Pennsylvania : state (D) sketch : artist (E) alien : stranger

_____ 2. ESTUARY : SEA :: (A) valley : mountain (B) planet : sun
(C) observation : eye (D) peninsula : land (E) government : democracy

_____ 3. ANCHOR : NAUTICAL :: (A) skillet : culinary (B) wing : soaring
(C) jail : confined (D) course : coarse (E) tension : tense

_____ 4. SOMBER : GRAY :: (A) depressing : gloomy (B) refreshing : tiring
(C) artistic : musical (D) hostile : benign (E) colorful : yellow

_____ 5. IDOL : HERO :: (A) battery : flashlight (B) shadow : daylight
(C) proclamation : announcement (D) whole : part (E) son : grandson

_____ 6. ASCETIC : MONK :: (A) uncooked : dinner (B) prosaic : poet
(C) funny : comedian (D) cloudy : rain (E) irreparable : repair

_____ 7. VIRTUE : LOYALTY :: (A) courage : hero (B) nail : hammer
(C) wedding : marriage (D) piano : organ (E) vice : stealing

_____ 8. CONVICTION : BELIEF :: (A) religion : ceremony (B) crime : jail
(C) lawyer : court (D) endurance : stamina (E) guilty : innocent

_____ 9. PERSONIFY : SYMBOLIZE :: (A) capitalize : punctuate
(B) endanger : threaten (C) think : act (D) compare : contrast
(E) fizzle : explode

_____ 10. CONDENSE : EXPAND :: (A) lie : lay (B) fasten : disengage
(C) lengthen : extend (D) write : communicate (E) focus : concentrate

Number correct _____ (total 10)

Synonyms Write the letter of the word that is closest in meaning to the capitalized word in each set.

_____ 1. IMPERCEPTIBLE: (A) visual (B) aware (C) impressive
(D) unnoticeable (E) close-minded

_____ 2. MEDITATIVE: (A) medicinal (B) considerable (C) self-denying
(D) enigmatic (E) reflective

_____ 3. INTERMINABLE : (A) confident (B) deathly (C) occasional
(D) endless (E) calm

_____ 4. BENIGN: (A) naive (B) diseased (C) mean (D) kind (E) bleak

_____ 5. CONDENSE : (A) compress (B) evaporate (C) imitate
(D) consume (E) wrap

_____ 6. SERENITY: (A) tranquility (B) anxiety (C) thoughtfulness
(D) posterity (E) friendliness

_____ 7. ASCETIC: (A) sour (B) peaceful (C) artistic (D) refined (E) strict

_____ 8. VIRTUE: (A) depravity (B) calmness (C) faith (D) goodness
(E) ambiguity

_____ 9. PLACID: (A) recreational (B) distinct (C) emotional (D) calm
(E) inconspicuous

_____ 10. LUMINOUS: (A) secure (B) radiant (C) insane (D) agreeable (E) dull

Number correct _____ (total 10)

Spelling and Wordplay

Crossword Puzzle Read each clue to determine what word will fit in the corresponding squares. There are several target words in the puzzle.

ACROSS

1. One type of figure of speech
10. Suffix meaning "most"
11. Cautious
12. Adverb expressing degree
13. Abbr. Right
14. Israeli psychic _ _ _ Geller
15. To demand
17. Drinking vessel
18. Abbr. British Thermal Unit
19. Large woody plant
20. Abbr. Each
22. _ _ _ _ facto, Latin for "by that very fact"
23. Made an attempt
24. Chemical symbol for iridium
25. Abbr. Connecticut
26. Abbr. Iowa
27. Abbr. Very
28. To respond
29. Prep. Near; by
30. Objects of worship
31. A laugh
32. To disappear
36. Not harmful
40. To bend the head forward
41. Unnecessary bother
42. To get ready for publication
45. The look or appearance of something
46. Peaceful

DOWN

1. Became aware
2. Inlet
3. Abbr. Right
4. Exclamation of pain
5. Adj. meaning "of sailors, ships, or navigation"
6. To burst
7. Abbr. For Your Information
8. One who practices self-denial
9. Allows; permits
16. Contemplative
19. Permissive
21. To make more compact
29. Word of exclamation
33. Negative
34. Singular homonym of 30 Across
35. At this place
36. Large motor coach
37. Abbr. Extra Sensory Perception
38. To receive
39. Abbr. North Dakota
41. Fourth tone of the musical scale
43. Not out

62

Part D   Related Words

The words below are closely related to the target words. Use your knowledge of the target words and of word parts to determine the meanings of these words. (For information about word parts analysis, see pages 6–12.)

1. asceticism (ə set′ ə siz'm) n.	11. pacify (pas′ ə fī′) v.
2. brooding (brōōd′ iŋ) adj.	12. perceive (pər sēv′) v.
3. condensation (kän′ dən sā′ shən) n.	13. perception (pər sep′ shən) n.
4. idolatry (ī däl′ ə trē) n.	14. personification (pər sän′ ə fi kā′ shən) n.
5. idolize (ī′ d'l īz′) v.	15. serene (sə rēn′) adj.
6. illumination (ī lōō′ mə nā′ shən) n.	16. terminal (tʉr′ mə n'l) adj., n.
7. intolerant (in täl′ ər ənt) adj.	17. terminate (tʉr′ mə nāt′) v.
8. meditate (med′ ə tāt′) v.	18. tolerate (täl′ ə rāt′) v.
9. meditation (med′ ə tā′ shən) n.	19. virtuous (vʉr′ chōō wəs) adj.
10. pacification (pas′ ə·fi kā′ shən) n.	

Understanding Related Words

Matching Definitions   Match each word in the preceding list with its definition below. Write the word in the blank.

_____   1. the process of making something more dense or compact

_____   2. bigoted; prejudiced

_____   3. a way of life in which one practices self-denial

_____   4. deep reflection, especially of a mystical nature

_____   5. worship of idols

_____   6. either end of a transportation line

_____   7. the act of making calm or tranquil

_____   8. a way of describing a thing as if it were a person

_____   9. a supplying of light; clarification

_____   10. to calm or tranquilize

_____   11. to love or admire excessively

_____   12. to reflect or ponder

_____   13. to recognize or observe through the senses

_____   14. to allow, permit, or put up with

_____   15. calm; peaceful

Number correct _____ (total 15)

Turn to **Words with *ie* and *ei*** on page 215 of the **Spelling Handbook.** Read the rule and complete the exercises provided.

Finding the Unrelated Word   Write the letter of the word that is not related in meaning to the other words in the set.

_____ 1. a. perception   b. awareness   c. knowledge   d. ignorance

_____ 2. a. tolerant   b. understanding   c. forgiving   d. intolerant

_____ 3. a. upset   b. serene   c. quiet   d. undisturbed

_____ 4. a. concluding   b. beginning   c. terminal   d. final

_____ 5. a. virtuous   b. dishonest   c. righteous   d. moral

_____ 6. a. moping   b. brooding   c. despondent   d. cheerful

_____ 7. a. tolerate   b. allow   c. challenge   d. accept

_____ 8. a. despise   b. adore   c. worship   d. idolize

_____ 9. a. reflect   b. act   c. ponder   d. meditate

_____ 10. a. irritate   b. relieve   c. pacify   d. appease

Number correct _____ (total 10)

Analyzing Word Parts

Homonyms   Homonyms are words that are pronounced the same but have different meanings and spellings.   The target word *idol* and the words *idle* and *idyll* all sound alike, but their meanings have little in common.   *Idle,* when used as an adjective, means "useless or worthless."   Used as a verb, *idle* means "to waste." *Idyll* is a noun that refers to a poem that describes simple, peaceful, rural scenes. Use context clues and your knowledge of suffixes to complete the sentences with the correct homonym or related word from the list below.

idol   idle   idyll   idolize
idolatry   idleness   idylic

1. Once outside the city, we looked for an _____ spot to hold a picnic.

2. The worship of idols is called _____ .

3. The museum curator was excited by the excavation of a pre-Columbian

    stone _____ .

4. My grandmother says that _____ is the ruin of young people today; she wonders where the belief in hard work has gone.

5. Although an _____ usually celebrates the simple, country life, most of these poems were written by sophisticated city poets.

6. After Elvis Presley's death, many fans began to _____ the man who was often called the "king of rock and roll."

7. Rumors about the plant closing were _____ talk; in fact, the company increased its production schedule.

Number correct _____ (total 7)

The Latin Root *pac* The word *pacific* comes from the Latin word *pax* or *pacis,* meaning "peace." Using your knowledge of word suffixes, complete the following sentences with the *pac* words below.

pacify   pacification   pacifier

1. When the baby started fussing in the restaurant, I put a _____ in her mouth.

2. Both countries' leaders sought a _____ program that would be acceptable to all sides in the controversy.

3. To _____ our parents, we agreed to be home by midnight and to stay home the rest of the weekend.

Number correct _____ (total 3)

Number correct in Unit _____ (total 90)

Word's Worth: idol

You hear the word *idol* frequently, usually referring to an admired person. If you *idolize* someone, you literally worship that person. In fact, *idol* comes from the Greek word *eidos,* meaning "image" or "form." Ancient Greeks worshipped idols or images, usually stone carvings of Greek gods and goddesses. This was a custom that some other religions opposed. For example, the first of the biblical Ten Commandments strongly prohibits worship of idols.

In nonreligious contexts the word *idol* has taken on a broader meaning— referring to nearly anything that people worship. Cars, clothes, and movie stars can be idols in this modern sense of the word.

The Last Word

Writing

1. Imagine an inanimate object having life and personality. Write a *personification* of that object. For example, you might personify a car: What is its favorite trip? Does it groan when it sees the driver approaching, or is it happy to be going out? Other objects that lend themselves to personification include telephones, trees, textbooks, purses and wallets, and desks.

2. I cannot *tolerate* _____. Write a paragraph or an essay on your "pet peeve."

Speaking

Prepare a speech approximately three to five minutes in length on one of the following topics:

1. The process of *condensation* or *illumination*
2. A firmly held *conviction*
3. The use and/or abuse of *meditation* in modern society
4. A *nautical* adventure
5. What (or who) is a *virtuous* human being?

Organize your speech with an attention-grabbing introduction, a two-to-four point body, and a memorable conclusion.

Group Discussion

Read and discuss the two quotations that follow. To what extent do you agree with the quotes? Support your conclusions with specific examples.

1. "For the man sound in body and *serene* in mind there is no such thing as bad weather!" —George Gissing

2. "I have learned silence from the talkative, toleration from the *intolerant,* and kindness from the unkind; yet strange, I am ungrateful to those teachers."—Kahlil Gibran

UNIT 6

Part A Target Words and Their Meanings

1. capacity (kə pas′ ə tē) n.
2. compensate (käm′ pən sāt′) v.
3. convulsive (kən vul′ siv) adj.
4. derive (di rīv′) v.
5. enhance (in hans′) v.
6. ensure (in shoor′) v.
7. illusion (i lōō′ zhən) n.
8. initial (i nish′ əl) adj., n.
9. lax (laks) adj.
10. malformation (mal′ fôr mā′ shən) n.
11. masochist (mas′ ə kist, maz′-) n.
12. mettlesome (met′′l səm) adj.
13. prerequisite (pri rek′ wə zit) adj.
14. prolong (prə lôŋ′) v.
15. relentless (ri lent′ lis) adj.
16. resilient (ri zil′ yənt, -ē ənt) adj.
17. sustain (sə stān′) v.
18. swoon (swōōn) v.
19. taut (tôt) adj.
20. tendency (ten′ dən sē) n.

Inferring Meaning from Context

For each sentence write the letter of the word or phrase that is closest to the meaning of the word or words in italics. Use context clues to help you determine the correct answer. (For information about how context helps you understand vocabulary, see pages 1–5.)

_____ 1. Our school auditorium has a large *capacity*; the entire student body can be seated at one time.
   a. entrance   b. amount of space   c. advertisement   d. constituency

_____ 2. Thousands of people with disabilities prove this point every day: hard work and dedication can *compensate for* physical handicaps.
   a. prevent   b. cause   c. contribute to   d. make up for

_____ 3. Although she tried to stop, Maria's body shook with *convulsive* laughter.
   a. imperceptible   b. comprehensible   c. angry   d. uncontrollable

_____ 4. States that *derive* a great deal of income from tourism do not find it necessary to impose heavy taxes on their residents.
   a. gain   b. diffuse   c. concede   d. reject

_____ 5. A smile will *enhance* your chance of making friends.
   a. diminish   b. improve   c. alienate   d. guarantee

_____ 6. Loud alarms on smoke detectors *ensure* that sleepers will awaken if a room should fill with smoke.
   a. raise the possibility   b. make certain   c. destroy the hope
   d. authorize

_____ 7. As we came closer, the lake that we thought we saw in the desert proved to be *an illusion*, merely a mirage.

a. a misleading perception   b. a dilemma   c. a transfusion
d. our destination

_____ 8. The youngest person to make *an initial* solo flight was Cody Locke, who took off and landed a plane by himself for the first time when he was only nine years old.

a. an attempted   b. an accompanied   c. an unsuccessful   d. a first

_____ 9. Sometimes enforcement of drug laws is *lax*, encouraging illegal drug use.

a. strict   b. ideal   c. unlawful   d. weak

_____ 10. Many *malformations* that physicians see in the human body, such as cleft palate and harelip, can now be remedied with surgery.

a. emotional difficulties   b. diseases   c. abnormal formations
d. wondrous aspects

_____ 11. Because she often worked to the point of exhaustion, her friends called her a *masochist*.

a. person with high expectations   b. person who gets pleasure from pain or self-denial   c. tyrant   d. cynic

_____ 12. One of the most *mettlesome* people in Texas history was lifeguard Leroy Colombo, who saved 907 people from drowning in the Galveston Island area from 1917 through 1974!

a. courageous   b. troublesome   c. curious   d. mindless

_____ 13. Algebra is *a prerequisite for* trigonometry; you cannot enroll in "trig" until you have taken algebra.

a. a help for   b. an outcome of   c. something required before taking
d. a substitute for

_____ 14. Neither Iran nor Iraq had any desire to *prolong* their war; the countries thus were finally able to agree on a peace settlement.

a. end   b. limit   c. draw out   d. begin

_____ 15. "It never quits," pioneers said of the *relentless* wind that blows across the Dakota prairies all year long.

a. arbitrary   b. persistent   c. occasional   d. tenuous

_____ 16. Anna Smith is certainly *resilient*, her neighbors commented. On Monday she had an appendectomy, on Wednesday she was released from the hospital, and on Friday she was mowing her lawn.

a. authoritative   b. comprehensive   c. particular about her property
d. quick to recover

_____ 17. The Pilgrims who set sail for the New World on the *Mayflower* were *sustained by* their faith, courage, and vision for a better life.

a. rejecting   b. substituting   c. agitated by   d. supported by

_____ 18. The hunger striker, having refused food for ten days, *swooned* when the delicious dinner was set before him; he had to be revived with smelling salts.

a. ate ravenously   b. picked at his food   c. fainted   d. died

_____ 19. She crouched nervously on the starting block, her lean, *taut* body ready to explode into action.

a. pacific   b. tense   c. arbitrary   d. relaxed

_____ 20. Charles Blondin of France had *à tendency* to do dangerous stunts. For example, in 1859 he walked a tightrope stretched across Niagara Falls, carrying his 145-pound friend on his back!

a. a diversion   b. an inclination   c. an obligation   d. an ultimatum

Number correct _____ (total 20)

Part B   *Target Words in Reading and Literature*

You should now have a general idea of the meaning of each target word. Refine your understanding by examining the shades of meaning these words have in the following excerpt.

Dance to the Piper

Agnes De Mille

Born in 1909, dancer, choreographer, and director Agnes De Mille decided early in life that she wanted to dance. In this passage from her autobiography, she gives the reader an idea of the determination it took to overcome physical limitations and realize her ambitions.

Ballet technique is arbitrary and very difficult. It never becomes easy; it becomes possible. The effort involved in making a dancer's body is so long and **relentless,** in many instances so painful, the effort to maintain the technique is so grueling, that unless a certain satisfaction is **derived** from the disciplining and punishing, the pace could not be maintained. Most dancers are to an extent   5
masochists."What a good pain! What a profitable pain!" said Miss Fredova as she stretched her insteps in her two strong hands. "I have practiced for three hours. I am exhausted, and I feel wonderful."

Paradoxically enough, ballet dancing is designed to give the impression of lightness and ease. Nothing in classic dancing should be **convulsive** or   10
tormented.   Derived from the seventeenth- and eighteenth-century court dances, the style is kingly, a series of harmonious and balanced postures linked by serene movement. The style involves a total defiance of gravity, and because this must perforce[1] be an **illusion,** the effect is achieved first by an enormous strengthening of the legs and feet to produce great **resilient** jumps and second   15

---

[1] perforce: by necessity; necessarily

by a coordination of arms and head in a rhythm of the legs which have no choice but to take the weight of the body when the body falls. But the slow relaxed movement of head and arms gives the illusion of **sustained** flight, gives the sense of effortless ease.

The lungs may be bursting, the heart pounding in the throat, sweat springing [20] from every pore, but hands must float in response, the head stirs gently as though **swooning** in delight. The diaphragm must be lifted to expand the chest fully, proudly, the abdomen pulled in flat. The knees must be **taut** and flat to give the extended leg every inch of length. The leg must be turned outward forty-five degrees in the hip socket so that the side of the knee and the long unbroken line [25] of the leg are presented to view and never the **lax,** droopy line of a bent knee. The leg must look like a sword. The foot arches to **prolong** the line of extension. The supporting foot turns out forty-five degrees to **enhance** the line of the supporting leg, to keep the hips even, and to **ensure** the broadest possible base for the support and balancing of the body. [30]

The ideal ballet body is long limbed with a small compact torso. This makes for beauty of line; the longer the arms and legs, the more exciting the body line. The ideal ballet foot has a high taut instep and a wide stretch in the Achilles'

tendon.[2] This tendon is the spring on which a dancer pushes for his jump, the hinge on which he takes the shock of landing. If there is one tendon in a dancer's body more important than any other, it is this tendon. It is, I should say, the **prerequisite** for all great technique. When the heel does not stretch easily and softly like a cat's, as mine did not, almost to the point of **malformation**, the shock of running or jumping must be taken somewhere in the spine by sticking out behind, for instance, in a sitting posture after every jump. I seemed to be all rusty wire and safety pins. My torso was long with unusually broad hips, my legs and arms abnormally short, my hands and feet broad and short. I was fat besides. What I did not know was that I was constructed for endurance and that I developed through effort alone a **capacity** for outperforming far, far better technicians. Because I was built like a mustang, stocky, **mettlesome,** and sturdy, I became a good jumper, growing special **compensating** muscles up the front of my shins for the lack of a helpful heel. But the long, cool, serene classic line was forever denied me.

And at first, of course, the compensations and adjustments were neither present nor indicated. Every dancer makes his own body. He is born only with certain physical **tendencies.** This making of a ballet leg takes approximately ten years and the **initial** stages are almost entirely discouraging, for even the best look awkward and paralyzed at the beginning.

---

[2] Achilles' tendon: the tendon connecting the back of the heel with the muscles of the calf of the leg

Refining Your Understanding

For each of the following items consider how the target word is used in the passage. Write the letter of the word or phrase that best completes each sentence.

_____ 1. "Most dancers are to an extent *masochists*" (lines 5–6). Other professionals who might be considered masochists are   a. bankers   b. golfers   c. marathoners.

_____ 2. A word meaning the opposite of *convulsive* (line 10) is   a. smooth   b. jerky   c. unalterable.

_____ 3. By "*sustained* flight" (line 18) Ms. De Mille probably means   a. smooth flight   b. flapping movements with the arms   c. apparent flight that seems to last awhile.

_____ 4. If your knee is *taut* (line 23), it will be   a. relaxed   b. in a kicking position   c. stiff and straight.

_____ 5. De Mille states that potential dancers have only "certain physical *tendencies*" (line 51), to emphasize the fact that   a. dancers are born, not made   b. dancers must develop their potential through practice   c. possessing certain physical traits will guarantee success as a dancer.

Number correct _____ (total 5)

Part C *Ways to Make New Words Your Own*

By now you are familiar with the target words and their meanings. This section presents reinforcement activities that will help you make these words part of your permanent vocabulary.

Using Language and Thinking Skills

Finding Examples Write the letter of the situation that best demonstrates the meaning of each word.

_____ 1. **convulsive**

    a. spinning through space
    b. shifting gears
    c. having spasms along with a high fever

_____ 2. **swoon**

    a. fainting from a painful injury
    b. thanking someone for a compliment
    c. enjoying your favorite television show

_____ 3. **ensure**

    a. a fan predicting which baseball team will win the World Series
    b. an aerial artist stepping along a high wire above a circus tent
    c. a traveler arriving early to make sure he or she gets a good seat

_____ 4. **prerequisite**

    a. having to pass a chemistry test
    b. having to complete first-year before taking second-year Spanish
    c. being required to read *The Red Badge of Courage*

_____ 5. **capacity**

    a. a requirement that you achieve at least seventy percent on an exam
    b. the number of gallons of gasoline held by a car's gas tank
    c. a small number of spectators at a football game

_____ 6. **mettlesome**

    a. someone who has a tendency to mind others' business
    b. a person who gets along well with everyone
    c. a soldier who receives a Purple Heart for bravery in a war

_____ 7. **compensate**

    a. studying hard to make up for being poor in sports
    b. making a purchase from any business
    c. exaggerating a problem

_____ 8. **tendency**

    a. being hit by a meteorite
    b. regularly losing your temper
    c. rarely walking to school

_____ 9. **malformation**
   a. a cat with six claws on one paw
   b. a perfectly formed snowflake
   c. the timberline on a mountain

_____ 10. **illusion**
   a. a chance meeting
   b. a reference to Greek mythology
   c. a magician pulling live rabbits from a hat

Number correct _____ (total 10)

Practicing for Standardized Tests

Antonyms Write the letter of the word that is the antonym of the capitalized word in each set.

_____ 1. RELENTLESS: (A) yielding (B) persistent (C) fragile
   (D) diminutive (E) enthusiastic

_____ 2. METTLESOME: (A) intrepid (B) flexible (C) compact
   (D) cowardly (E) quarrelsome

_____ 3. ILLUSION: (A) dream (B) belief (C) disappointment (D) reality
   (E) reference

_____ 4. RESILIENT: (A) indecisive (B) well-maintained (C) inflexible
   (D) reflexive (E) expansive

_____ 5. SUSTAIN: (A) maintain (B) recover (C) overlook (D) call forth
   (E) break down

_____ 6. TAUT: (A) nautical (B) rigid (C) loose (D) ignorant (E) somber

_____ 7. PROLONG: (A) extend (B) merge (C) wave (D) shorten
   (E) discourage

_____ 8. LAX: (A) adaptable (B) indifferent (C) fragile (D) ambiguous
   (E) strict

_____ 9. INITIAL: (A) opening (B) closing (C) anonymous (D) unclaimed
   (E) susceptible

_____ 10. ENHANCE: (A) beautify (B) praise (C) detract (D) brood
   (E) collect

Number correct _____ (total 10)

Word's Worth: derive

Derive is a word with a watery past. The Latin root, *derivare*, comes from *de*, meaning "away" or "from," and *rivus*, meaning "stream." *Derive* is associated with one of the ancient Romans' most magnificent accomplishments—the moving of rivers out of their normal channels and into an elaborate system of aqueducts that brought fresh water to Roman cities. In Old French, *deriver* meant "to draw away from" as well as "to drain off." *Rival*, a relative of *derive*, comes from the Latin *rivalis*, "one who shares the same stream," and later, "a near neighbor." In English, the etymologies of many apparently dissimilar words reveal surprising relatives.

Spelling and Wordplay

Word Maze Find and circle each target word in this maze.

```
M A L F O R M A T I O N
P D G C A P A C I T Y A
R R E L E N T L E S S E
O E E N S U R E N I C M
L S N R T C I I I H O E
O I H E E J L N A C M T
N L A V N Q L I T O P T
G I N I D S U T S S E L
H E C R E W S I U A N E
R N E E N O I A S M S S
V T P D C O O L P I A O
K L A X Y N N T U A T M
B C O N V U L S I V E E
```

capacity
compensate
convulsive
derive
enhance
ensure
illusion
initial
lax
malformation
masochist
mettlesome
prerequisite
prolong
relentless
resilient
sustain
swoon
taut
tendency

Turn to **The Prefix** *com* on page 205 of the **Spelling Handbook**. Read the rule and complete the exercises provided.

Part D   Related Words

A number of words are closely related to the target words you have studied. Use your knowledge of the target words and of word parts to determine the meanings of these words. (For information about word parts analysis, see pages 6–12.)

1. compensation (käm′ pən sā′ shən) n.
2. convulse (kən vuls′) v.
3. convulsion (kən vul′ shən) n.
4. derivation (der′ ə vā′ shən) n.
5. enhancement (in hans′ mənt) n.
6. illusory (i lōō′ sər ē) adj.
7. initiate (i nish′ ē āt′) v.
8. initiation (i nish′ ē ā′ shən) n.
9. laxity (lak′ sə tē) n.
10. mettle (met′ ′l) n.
11. prolongation (prō lôŋ gā′ shən) n.
12. relent (ri lent′) v.
13. requisite (rek′ wə zit) adj.
14. resilience (ri zil′ yəns, -e əns) n.
15. sustenance (sus′ ti nəns) n.
16. tend (tend) v.
17. unrelenting (un ri len′ tiŋ) adj.

Understanding Related Words

Sentence Completion Write the word from the preceding list that best completes the meaning of the sentence.

1. An infant with a high fever may experience a (an) _____ .

2. Many people say that a _____ in discipline contributes to problems in our schools.

3. The priest showed his _____ by driving through a severe snowstorm to reach a dying man.

4. The vegetables and fruits grown on their farm provided all the _____ they needed.

5. Our insurance paid us twelve hundred dollars in _____ for damage the windstorm did to our roof.

6. The first meeting for the new members of the Kiwanis Club was a

   (an) _____ .

7. He thought he saw a water hole in the desert, but as he got nearer and saw

   only sand, he realized the first image had been merely _____ .

8. People from Norway, Sweden, and Finland _____ to be light-haired and light-skinned.

9. The world's most _____ drought occurred in Chile and lasted for four hundred years.

10. Uncle Zeke showed great _____ by recovering from his stroke.

Number correct _____ (total 10)

Analyzing Word Parts

The Latin Root *initia* The target word *initial*, the related words *initiate* and *initiation*, as well as words such as *initially* and *initiative*, all derive from the Latin word *initium*, meaning "beginning." Using this knowledge and your knowledge of suffixes, write the word from the list below that best completes the meaning of each sentence.

initial   initially   initiates   initiation   initiative

_____ 1. As part of the new members' ceremony, the _?_ (s) were required to memorize a pledge.

_____ 2. By taking the _?_ to create a new accounting system for the company, Jameson earned a promotion.

_____ 3. The _?_ votes had been counted, and Lorenzo had taken a slim lead over Tomkins in the election.

_____ 4. During the _?_ , the fraternity required each new member to eat a live goldfish.

_____ 5. _?_ Ralph wanted to go sky diving, but later he decided not to.

Number correct _____ (total 5)

Number correct in Unit _____ (total 60)

The Last Word

Writing

Choose one of the following topics and develop a composition. Back up each statement with ample detail and real-life examples.

1. The Most *Mettlesome* Person I've Met
2. *Illusions* That Can Lead to Problems
3. Some Problem *Tendencies* I Have
4. A *Prerequisite* for a Happy Life
5. What or Who *Sustains* Me in Times of Crisis

Group Discussion

Agnes De Mille describes how she achieved success as a dancer. What character traits helped her? What character traits are necessary for success in any field? List three traits that you think are most important for achieving success. Then discuss the most frequently cited choices with the class.

Speaking

From the list of character traits generated by the class, choose a trait that you feel is most likely to lead to success. Develop a brief talk about one person who exhibits that trait—a relative, a friend, a neighbor, or perhaps someone you've only read about.

UNIT 7

Part A   Target Words and Their Meanings

1. apprehension (ap rə hen′ shən) n.
2. bleak (blēk) adj.
3. confrontation (kän′ frən tā′ shən) n.
4. conversion (kən vʉr′ zhən) n.
5. dispose (dis pōz′) v.
6. disquieting (dis kwī′ ət iŋ) adj.
7. fleeting (flēt′ iŋ) adj.
8. grotesque (grō tesk′) adj.
9. impregnable (im preg′ nə b'l) adj.
10. instinctively (in stiŋk′ tiv lē) adv.
11. memorable (mem′ ər ə b'l) adj.
12. ostentatious (äs′ tən tā′ shəs) adj.
13. regard (ri gärd′) v., n.
14. rejection (ri jek′ shən) n.
15. relic (rel′ ik) n.
16. resentment (ri zent′ mənt) n.
17. spurious (spyo͞or′ ē əs) adj.
18. transient (tran′ shənt) adj., n.
19. turmoil (tʉr′ moil) n.
20. unpretentious (un pri ten′ shəs) adj.

Inferring Meaning from Context

For each sentence write the letter of the word or phrase that is closest to the meaning of the word or words in italics. Use context clues to help you determine the correct answer. (For information about how context helps you understand vocabulary, see pages 1–5.)

_____ 1. It was with considerable *apprehension* that Mother went to the door. Who could be knocking at midnight?

   a. enthusiasm   b. swooning   c. anxiety   d. boredom

_____ 2. They were stranded on the highway with no gasoline, fifty miles from a gas station, in subzero weather. The situation looked *bleak* for the Hopkinson family.

   a. exciting   b. grim   c. incredible   d. like justice

_____ 3. In the *confrontation* between General Custer's regiment and the Sioux tribe along the Little Bighorn Creek, Custer's troops were massacred.

   a. initiation   b. showdown   c. deliberations   d. contrast

_____ 4. A religious *conversion* from one faith to another is something most people undertake solemnly.

   a. contract   b. revival   c. experience   d. changeover

_____ 5. To *dispose of* its garbage, New York City is building a pyramid of trash two hundred feet higher than the Statue of Liberty.

   a. terminate   b. get rid of   c. enhance   d. classify

_____ 6. The scientists arrived at *a disquieting* conclusion: various forms of pollution are changing the earth's climate.

   a. a comforting   b. an illusory   c. an unnecessary   d. a disturbing

_____ 7. The prophet explained that our lives are brief and *fleeting*; we are born and soon die, like the grass in the fields.
a. comfortable   b. difficult to understand   c. quickly passing
d. unnecessary

_____ 8. The masquerade bordered on frightening because of the *grotesque* masks some party-goers were wearing.
a. original   b. bizarre   c. beautiful   d. expensive

_____ 9. Medieval castles were so well built that they were *impregnable*—until the advent of gunpowder and cannons.
a. captured   b. vulnerable   c. unconquerable   d. architecturally sound

_____ 10. In the fall, bears *instinctively* seek out a cave to hibernate for the winter.
a. instantly   b. unnaturally   c. intuitively   d. deliberately

_____ 11. Abraham Lincoln's Gettysburg Address is as *memorable* today as it was when he first delivered it more than a century ago.
a. remembered   b. relentless   c. mediocre   d. ambiguous

_____ 12. A European designer produced what must have been the world's most *ostentatious* dress, enhanced with hundreds of diamonds, rubies, and emeralds, and worth over a million dollars!
a. carefully sewn   b. comprehensive   c. imperceptible
d. conspicuously expensive

_____ 13. Imagine how the other guests at a party would *regard* a woman who arrived in a million-dollar dress covered with jewels.
a. reform   b. alienate   c. look upon   d. authorize

_____ 14. Judge Manthei's *rejection* of Kevin's plea meant that Kevin's conviction for driving under the influence of alcohol was upheld.
a. acceptance   b. knowledge   c. refusal   d. illumination

_____ 15. One valuable *relic* in New York's Metropolitan Museum of Art is a Greek vase dating back to the sixth century A.D.
a. ancient artifact   b. realistic painting   c. mechanism   d. illusion

_____ 16. Be quick to forgive; *resentment* destroys friendship and health.
a. understanding   b. bitterness   c. idolatry   d. counseling

_____ 17. Miners attracted to Gilt Edge by rumors of gold, discovered that these rumors were *spurious,* and they left for more promising areas.
a. genuine   b. false   c. unalterable   d. reflexive

_____ 18. The physical pain from my fall was *transient,* but my embarrassment lasted for days.
a. permanent   b. infinite   c. short-lived   d. on my right side

_____ 19. The soldiers created *turmoil* in the town, causing hundreds of confused villagers to flee in all directions.
a. rebellion   b. bitterness   c. paralysis   d. an uproar

_____ 20. Although Mr. Sokalowski is the wealthiest person in town, he is
unpretentious, preferring to dress and act like everyone else.
a. humble   b. hard-working   c. ostentatious   d. honest

Number correct _____ (total 20)

Part B   Target Words in Reading and Literature

You should now have a general idea of the meaning of each target word. Refine your understanding by examining the shades of meaning these words have in the following excerpt.

Innocent Blood

P. D. James

In the following passage from the mystery novel Innocent Blood, *Philippa, an adopted child, finally meets her real mother, who is in prison for committing a murder. Notice how the author's description creates an emotionally charged and suspenseful atmosphere that mirrors Philippa's anticipation and fear.*

Philippa opened the door slowly. The room was empty. She shut the door and leaned against it for a moment, glad of the comforting strength of wood against her back. Like Miss Henderson's office, this room had a **spurious** comfort. It was a place of transit but without the **ostentatious** vulgarity of an airport departure lounge; **unpretentious,** stuffy, overcrowded with furniture   5 which looked as if it had been rejected from a dozen different homes. Nothing it contained was **memorable.** It was designed to be used and then mercifully forgotten. No **transient** would look back on this room with regret or be tempted to leave a humming chord of her misery or hope on the **bleak** air. There were too many chairs, assorted in size or shape, **disposed** around half a dozen small,   10

highly polished tables. The walls were plain and smudged in places, as if someone had cleansed them of graffiti. Over the fireplace was a print of Constable's *Hay Wain*[1] and below it on the mantelshelf a glass vase of artificial flowers. In the middle of the room was set a small octagonal table with two facing chairs. In contrast to the informality of the room, they looked as if they had been specially arranged. Perhaps a helpful inmate, instructed to see that the room was tidy, had placed them there, seeing every visit as a formal **confrontation** across an invisible but **impregnable** grille.

The waiting minutes seemed to stretch for hours. Occasionally footsteps passed the door. It was as cheerfully noisy as school at mid-morning break. Philippa's mind was a **turmoil** of emotions: excitement, **apprehension, resentment,** and finally anger. What was she doing abandoned here in this dreary room where the furniture was too clean, the walls too grubby, the flowers artificial? They had a large enough garden, surely they could at least provide fresh flowers. A cell would have been less **disquieting** to wait in. At least it didn't pretend to be anything but what it was. And why wasn't her mother here, waiting for her? She knew that she was coming, she must have known the time of the bus. What was she finding to do that was more important than being here? Her mind spun with **grotesque** images. Hair that had once been golden but was now dry as straw, dancing with threaded beads, her mother's face sagging under the weight of make-up, hands with painted talons stretched out to her throat. She thought: "Suppose I don't like her. Suppose she can't stand me . . ." She walked over to the window and looked out across the cobbled courtyard at the second set of stables. She would make herself think about the architecture . . . This stable block was later than the house; it might even be neo-Georgian.[2] But the clock turret[3] with its swinging golden cock looked older. Perhaps they had reerected it when the original stables were demolished. They had made a good job of the **conversion.** But where was her mother? Why didn't she come?

The door opened. She turned around. Her first impression, but so **fleeting** that the thought and its **rejection** were almost simultaneous, was that her mother had sent a friend to break the news that she had changed her mind, that she didn't want to meet her after all. It was stupid to have expected so much older a woman. And, at first, she looked so ordinary; a slight, attractive figure in a gray, pleated skirt with a paler cotton shirt blouse and a green scarf knotted at the neck. All her grotesque imaginings fled like shrieking demons before a **relic.** It was like recognizing oneself. It was the beginning of identity. Surely if she had met this woman anywhere in the world she would have known herself to be flesh of her flesh. **Instinctively** they each slowly took a chair and **regarded** each other across the table. Her mother said, "I'm sorry I've kept you waiting. The bus was early. I didn't want to watch out for it in case you didn't come."

---

[1] Constable's *Hay Wain*: John Constable, 1776–1837, an English painter, famous for his landscape paintings, such as *The Hay Wain*

[2] neo-Georgian: in the style popular during the reigns of King George I, II, III, and IV of Great Britain (1714–1830)

[3] turret: a small tower, usually on the corner, on a building

Refining Your Understanding

For each of the following items, consider how the target word is used in the passage. Write the letter of the word or phrase that best completes each sentence.

_____ 1. "A *spurious* comfort" (line 3) indicates that the room was
a. homey   b. somewhat comfortable   c. not genuinely comfortable.

_____ 2. Assorted sizes and shapes of chairs "*disposed* around half a dozen small, highly polished tables" (lines 10–11) suggests that around the tables the chairs were   a. thrown.   b. arranged.   c. missing.

_____ 3. Which of the following meanings of *turmoil* (line 21) does the author intend?
a. mess   b. convulsion   c. confusion.

_____ 4. The author's use of the word *relic* (line 46) suggests
a. an object that has survived from the past   b. an object that has magical powers   c. something that has been wrecked.

_____ 5. The verb *regarded* (line 49) suggests that mother and daughter
a. were curious about each other   b. became close friends immediately   c. initially felt hostile toward each other.

Number correct _____ (total 5)

Part C   Ways to Make New Words Your Own

This section presents a variety of reinforcement activities that will help you make these words part of your permanent vocabulary.

Using Language and Thinking Skills

Finding the Unrelated Word Write the letter of the word that is not related in meaning to the other words in each set.

_____ 1. a. counterfeit   b. spurious   c. illegitimate   d. genuine

_____ 2. a. serenity   b. dread   c. apprehension   d. worry

_____ 3. a. grotesque   b. placid   c. tranquil   d. peaceful

_____ 4. a. conversion   b. alteration   c. modification   d. persistence

_____ 5. a. permanent   b. transient   c. fleeting   d. momentary

_____ 6. a. opposition   b. argument   c. cooperation   d. confrontation

_____ 7. a. view   b. survey   c. ignore   d. regard

_____ 8. a. modest   b. humble   c. unpretentious   d. ostentatious

_____ 9. a. bleak   b. exquisite   c. somber   d. dismal

_____ 10. a. impregnable   b. defenseless   c. sturdy   d. invincible

Number correct _____ (total 10)

Practicing for Standardized Tests

Synonyms Write the letter of the word that is closest in meaning to the capitalized word.

_____ 1. INSTINCTIVELY: (A) naturally (B) carefully (C) intensely (D) studiously (E) hopefully

_____ 2. TRANSIENT: (A) portable (B) cross-country (C) cynical (D) unalterable (E) fleeting

_____ 3. DISQUIETING: (A) placid (B) noisy (C) unnecessary (D) inconsiderate (E) agitating

_____ 4. MEMORABLE: (A) spurious (B) wise (C) honorable (D) old (E) notable

_____ 5. RELIC: (A) keepsake (B) mold (C) machine (D) prolongation (E) jewel

_____ 6. DISPOSE: (A) question (B) wrangle (C) arrange (D) challenge (E) contradict

_____ 7. RESENTMENT: (A) obligation (B) crime (C) unfairness (D) bitterness (E) tyranny

_____ 8. REJECTION: (A) refusal (B) enigma (C) conviction (D) dishonesty (E) persistence

_____ 9. IMPREGNABLE: (A) sterile (B) confident (C) arbitrary (D) invincible (E) illusory

_____ 10. APPREHENSION: (A) derivation (B) opposition (C) uneasiness (D) tranquility (E) laxity

Number correct _____ (total 10)

Spelling and Wordplay

Crossword Puzzle Read each clue to determine what word will fit in the corresponding squares. There are several target words in the puzzle.

ACROSS

1. Defiant opposition
11. Egg-shaped
12. Line between countries
14. Titles
16. Past tense of *to be*
17. Skilled
20. An age in time
23. Slang: On the — — —; escaping punishment for a crime
24. Abbr. Elevated Railway
26. To rid oneself of
29. Keepsake of historic value
31. — — — — nam, a S.E. Asian country
32. What we breathe
33. To make the sign of the cross
34. To retain
35. Abbr. Tank
36. Abbr. Ireland
37. Slang: Sticky substance
38. 3.14159265
39. Abbr. Tuberculosis
40. Not off
41. State of commotion
43. Former time
47. To observe
48. Artificial or false
52. Slang: Hello
54. Fears
57. Prefix: Two or twice
58. Modest

DOWN

1. Transformations
2. Plural of *ovum*
3. Viet — — —
4. Passing swiftly
5. Abbr. Obstetrics
6. At this moment
7. Temporary
8. Advertisements
9. Abbr. Tellurium
10. Abbr. Individual Retirement Account
13. Worth remembering
15. Abbr. Senior
18. Gloomy
19. Abbr. Los Angeles
21. Singular of 8 Down
22. — — — s and pans
25. To gain knowledge
27. Contraction of: *I have*
28. Slang: Energy
30. Abbr. Long Island
34. Slang: Knockout
35. What the clock keeps
38. The newspaper business
39. 7th tone of the scale
42. Objective case of *we*
43. Baby dog
44. Abbr. Air-Raid Precautions
45. Knight's title
46. Foot digit
49. Hurting sensation
50. Interj.: Like *huh*
51. Abbr.: Southeast
52. Santa's laugh
53. Not out
55. A cashew is one
56. Spanish for *yes*
57. Abbr. Duke

Part D   Related Words

A number of words are closely related to the target words you have studied. Use your knowledge of the target words and of word parts to determine the meanings of these words. (For information about analyzing word parts, see pages 6–12.)

1. apprehend (ap′ rə hend′) v.
2. apprehensive (ap′ rə hen′ siv) adj.
3. confront (kən frunt′) v.
4. convert (kən vurt′) v. (kän′ vərt) n.
5. disposition (dis′ pə zish′ ən) n.
6. fleet (flēt) adj., n.
7. inject (in jekt′) v.
8. instinct (in′ stiŋkt) n.
9. pretentious (pri ten′ shəs) adj.
10. project (präj′ ekt, -ikt) n. (prə jekt′) v.
11. reject (ri jekt′) v. (rē′ jekt) n.
12. resent (ri zent′) v.
13. transitory (tran′ sə tôr′ ē, -zə-) adj.

Understanding Related Words

Sentence Completion   Write the related word from the preceding list that best completes the sentence.

1. After a lengthy chase, Sheriff Boggs managed to _____ the two bank robbers ten miles west of town.

2. I couldn't dodge my enemy forever; I had to _____ him sooner or later.

3. A successful reporter must have an _____′ for newsworthy stories.

4. We generally prefer honest, down-to-earth people to those who are

   _____ .

5. We will _____ our old furnace from a coal-burner to an oil-fueled unit.

6. People were surprised when Anna became depressed; she had always had such

   a sunny _____ .

7. The operating-room nurse told the patients that feeling _____ was normal before undergoing surgery.

8. For our course _____ , three of us chose to study the United States women's suffrage movement of the nineteenth century.

9. The people waiting in line at the post-office counter will _____ your cutting in front of them.

10. Green Flag Transport began with only two tractor-trailers but soon expanded

    its _____ to more than thirty rigs.

Number correct _____ (total 10)

Turn to **The Suffix *-ion*** on page 214 of the **Spelling Handbook**. Read the rule and complete the exercises provided.

Analyzing Word Parts

The Latin Root *ject* *Reject* and *rejection,* words studied in this unit, are descendants of the Latin word *jacere,* "to throw." Words containing forms of *jacere,* which appear in English as *jac* and *ject,* usually have something to do with throwing. Thus, to *reject* something literally means "to throw it back." The noun *conjecture* means "to predict from incomplete information"; literally, the word means "to throw together." Choose the *ject* word below that best completes each sentence and write the word in the blank.

  dejected   eject   inject   project   reject

1. The speech professor told Ricardo to _____ his voice so that he could be heard in the back of the room.

2. In case of emergency, a special seat will _____ the pilot, who can then parachute to the ground below.

3. In his speech at the opening of the school year, the student-body president urged everyone to _____ drugs and alcohol.

4. Some diabetic patients must _____ insulin into their bodies every day.

5. The lost dog we took in looked sad and _____ until its owner showed up to claim it.

Number correct _____ (total 5)

Number correct in Unit _____ (total 60)

Word's Worth: relic and derelict

The words *relic* and *derelict* started from the same place but took different paths in life. Both are formed from the Latin word *relinquere,* "to leave from." *Relic* suggests "something left over," the "remains." The word is usually applied to objects, and the connotation is usually positive—an antique, a keepsake, or an object of religious devotion. *Derelict,* however, refers to people, and the word has a negative connotation. With the prefix *de-* ("entirely") added, the adjective came to describe someone who has negligently abandoned something. The noun refers to a person who is poor, friendless, and abandoned.

The Last Word

Writing

The following sentences contain clichés and unnecessary words. Rewrite each sentence, replacing clichés and unnecessary words with one of the target words from the list below. You may add or delete words if necessary.

apprehensive   instinctive   ostentatious   spurious   transient

1. News that Big George was coming made the men gathered around the card table shiver and shake with fear.

   _____

   _____

2. In came Sheila, dressed to the nines, overly eager to impress.

   _____

3. Grandfather described the new people moving into our town as here today, gone tomorrow.

   _____

4. Rick's claim that he caught a record-size walleye in Pelican Lake was as phony as a three-dollar bill.

   _____

   _____

5. I can't explain how I knew the storm was coming; it was just a gut-level feeling.

   _____

Speaking

The excerpt from *Innocent Blood* describes a person who feels a mixture of expectation and *apprehension*. Try to recall apprehensive experiences from your own life that were mixed with happiness, expectation, or opportunity. In a five-to-ten-minute talk, briefly describe the experience and tell what it taught you.

Group Discussion

The target word *transient* has taken on new meaning in recent years. As the ranks of *transient* or homeless people in our country increase, so does the realization that new policies must be developed to house people. Use the following list to discuss the problem of homelessness in America.

1. There are a number of possible reasons why people are homeless. List four that you think are the most important.
2. What are some things that are being done to help transients? Consider the activities of various agencies, such as churches and government.
3. What new attitudes and policies would be most effective?

UNIT 8:   Review of Units 5–7

Part A   Review Word List

Unit 5 Target Words

1. ascetic
2. benign
3. brood
4. condense
5. conviction
6. estuary
7. exquisite
8. idol
9. imperceptible
10. interminable
11. luminous
12. meditative
13. nautical
14. pacific
15. personify
16. placid
17. serenity
18. somber
19. tolerant
20. virtue

Unit 5 Related Words

1. asceticism
2. brooding
3. condensation
4. idolatry
5. idolize
6. illumination
7. intolerant
8. meditate
9. meditation
10. pacification
11. pacify
12. perceive
13. perception
14. personification
15. serene
16. terminal
17. terminate
18. tolerate
19. virtuous

Unit 6 Target Words

1. capacity
2. compensate
3. convulsive
4. derive
5. enhance
6. ensure
7. illusion
8. initial
9. lax
10. malformation
11. masochist
12. mettlesome
13. prerequisite
14. prolong
15. relentless
16. resilient
17. sustain
18. swoon
19. taut
20. tendency

Unit 6 Related Words

1. compensation
2. convulse
3. convulsion
4. derivation
5. enhancement
6. illusory
7. initiate
8. initiation
9. laxity
10. mettle
11. prolongation
12. relent
13. requisite
14. resilience
15. sustenance
16. tend
17. unrelenting

Unit 7 Target Words

1. apprehension
2. bleak
3. confrontation
4. conversion
5. dispose
6. disquieting
7. fleeting
8. grotesque
9. impregnable
10. instinctively
11. memorable
12. ostentatious
13. regard
14. rejection
15. relic
16. resentment
17. spurious
18. transient
19. turmoil
20. unpretentious

Unit 7 Related Words

1. apprehend
2. apprehensive
3. confront
4. convert
5. disposition
6. fleet
7. inject
8. instinct
9. pretentious
10. project
11. reject
12. resent
13. transitory

Inferring Meaning from Context

For each sentence write the letter of the word or phrase that is closest to the meaning of the word or words in italics.

_____ 1. Monks live *ascetic* lives, putting aside worldly things for spiritual concerns.
a. arbitrary b. transient c. self-denying d. grotesque

_____ 2. The surgeon was pleased to discover that the tumor was *benign*.
a. prolonged b. harmless c. malformed d. harmful

_____ 3. Refusing to attend the tournament as a spectator, the tennis player stayed home and *brooded* about his broken arm.
a. read b. sulked c. argued d. meditated

_____ 4. Although everyone was staring at him, George was unable to stop his *convulsive* fit of laughter.
a. violent b. taut c. humorous d. fleeting

_____ 5. Salvador Dali's paintings are sometimes described as having *a grotesque* or nightmarish quality about them.
a. an ostentatious b. a serene c. a bizarre d. a memorable

_____ 6. The Great Wall of China was built in the third century B.C. to keep China *impregnable* from her enemies.
a. vulnerable b. protected c. diffused d. imperceptible

_____ 7. The *initial* flight plan was thrown out in favor of the second one.
a. rejected b. first c. successive d. condensed

_____ 8. The governor's hour-long speech on the budget seemed *interminable*.
a. memorable b. endless c. instinctive d. short

_____ 9. The Hunchback of Notre Dame had an obvious *malformation*.
a. torso b. flourish c. virtue d. deformity

_____ 10. Although her family was wealthy and influential, Heather was down-to-earth and *unpretentious*.
a. not boastful b. ostentatious c. fun-loving d. enigmatic

_____ 11. Sergeant Alvin C. York received the Congressional Medal of Honor for his *mettlesome* actions during World War I.
a. reflexive b. courageous c. relentless d. reverent

_____ 12. To many, the owl has come to *personify* wisdom.
a. preserve b. illuminate c. symbolize d. idolize

_____ 13. Taking the SAT is *a prerequisite* for application to many colleges.
a. an option b. a hindrance c. a requirement d. a compensation

_____ 14. A slow-motion film of how a golf ball changes after being struck is proof of its *resilient* quality.
a. elastic b. taut c. rigid d. imperceptible

_____ 15. There was *a spurious* ring to the politician's speech as he claimed never to have said a disrespectful word about his opponent.

    a. an authentic b. a false c. an apprehensive d. a tyrannical

Number correct _____ (total 15)

Using Review Words in Context

Using context clues, determine which word from the list best completes each sentence in the story. Write the word in the blank. Each word may be used only once.

apprehensive	conversion	interminable	resentment
bleak	conviction	lax	resilient
brood	disquieting	placid	serenity
capacity	imperceptible	pretentious	tolerate
confrontation	instinctively	rejection	turmoil

Mother Knows Best

Jorge had recently moved from the quiet and _____ plains of Texas to the bustling and noisy _____ of Chicago. At first Jorge tried to think positively; he was _____ ; he could rebound from any setback. Then _____ thoughts began to nag him about whether he would fit in. What Jorge feared most was _____ by his peers. He began to sit in his room alone and _____ about being an outsider. He started to feel a bitter hurt that developed into _____ against his parents for leaving Texas. To Jorge the future that stretched ahead seemed as _____ , barren, and colorless as the winter landscape outside his window.

After three weeks of watching her son slip from a slight, almost _____ sadness into a deep depression, Mrs. Diez took action.

"Jorge, I'm sick and tired of your _____ self-pity. I've been _____ in letting the situation go on this long, and I'm not going to _____ it any longer. Get out of bed and go do something!"

This sudden, face-to-face _____ with his mother jarred Jorge loose. He recognized the _____ in her voice, a determination that was underscored by the broom she was using to point toward the door. The peaceful _____ was gone, as was her _____ for patience. He knew she meant business.

As he burst into the cold outside air, a sudden change came over him. Hopelessness was replaced at first by a hint of optimism, and then as the fresh air took effect, the _____ became complete and he felt good.

89

That evening at the supper table, Jorge excitedly poured out the events of the day. He told of how he had followed his nose, how it had _____ led him to the YMCA. Although he was _____ as he opened the door, his concern vanished as he stepped into the lobby.

"Jorge! Jorge! Over here!" It was a classmate, who told Jorge that her group needed him to round out their basketball team. Of course Jorge accepted. Because he could brag to his family without sounding _____ , he described how he had been the high scorer for the afternoon.

Number correct _____ (total 20)

Part B   Review Word Reinforcement

Using Language and Thinking Skills

Words and Idioms   An idiom is a phrase that cannot be translated by literally defining each word. Match the target word with the idiomatic phrase that comes closest to it in meaning.

_____ 1. compensate   a. at first glance

_____ 2. confront   b. face up to

_____ 3. initial   c. to make up for

_____ 4. exquisite   d. to snap back

_____ 5. transient   e. tight as a drum

_____ 6. ostentatious   f. putting on the dog

_____ 7. placid   g. pretty as a picture

_____ 8. regard   h. passing fancy

_____ 9. resilient   i. smooth as glass

_____ 10. taut   j. size up

Number correct _____ (total 10)

Practicing for Standardized Tests

Analogies   Write the letter of the word pair that best expresses a relationship similar to that expressed in the original pair.

_____ 1. RELIC : HISTORY ::   (A) religion : idol   (B) keepsake : memory (C) mercury : liquid   (D) author : book   (E) military : uniform

_____ 2. FLEETING : ENDURING ::   (A) serene : tranquil   (B) bleak : barren (C) annoyed : agitated   (D) alien : native   (E) brooding : sulking

_____ 3. METTLESOME : HERO ::   (A) uncourageous : coward   (B) postal : parcel (C) vain : monk   (D) wealthy : money   (E) spontaneous : thought

_____ 4. MAGICIAN : ILLUSION ::   (A) perimeter : rectangle   (B) musician : orchestra   (C) sculptor : clay   (D) artist : painting   (E) soldier : furlough

_____ 5. ESTUARY : SEA ::   (A) chaos : order   (B) acrobat : somersault (C) foothill : mountain   (D) idol : stone   (E) harbor : safety

_____ 6. ASCETIC : SELF-INDULGENT ::   (A) wolf : carnivorous (B) machine : mechanical   (C) tyrant : benevolent   (D) perfume : fragrant   (E) heart : coronary

_____ 7. SPURIOUS : COUNTERFEIT ::   (A) genuine : legitimate (B) virtuous : dishonest   (C) hostile : amiable   (D) transient : permanent   (E) tolerant : prejudiced

_____ 8. PREREQUISITE : REQUIREMENT ::   (A) authority : dictator (B) apprehension : certainty   (C) ambiguity : clarity   (D) time : schedule   (E) ancestor : forebear

_____ 9. INITIAL : TERMINAL ::   (A) imported : foreign   (B) instinctive : unborn   (C) bleak : bright   (D) relentless : prolonged   (E) sad : pitiful

_____ 10. UPSETTING : DISQUIETING ::   (A) perturbed : hostile   (B) lax : taut   (C) dreary : elated   (D) candid : open   (E) resilient : rigid

Number correct _____ (total 10)

Synonyms Write the letter of the word whose meaning is closest to that of the capitalized word.

_____ 1. APPREHENSIVE :   (A) anxious   (B) placid   (C) confident (D) somber   (E) sprawled

_____ 2. BROOD :   (A) worry   (B) conform   (C) ignore   (D) regard   (E) swoon

_____ 3. CONVULSIVE :   (A) naive   (B) serene   (C) agitated   (D) social   (E) harsh

_____ 4. DERIVE :   (A) regress   (B) trace   (C) estimate   (D) initiate   (E) evolve

_____ 5. ENSURE :   (A) merge   (B) pacify   (C) prolong   (D) guarantee   (E) dispose

Number correct _____ (total 5)

Antonyms Write the letter of the word that is most nearly _opposite_ in meaning to the capitalized word.

_____ 1. ASCETIC :   (A) self-indulging   (B) pretentious   (C) idolizing (D) cynical   (E) severe

_____ 2. BLEAK : (A) diverse   (B) mettlesome   (C) bright   (D) somber   (E) grim

_____ 3. RELENTLESS :   (A) resilient   (B) arrayed   (C) persistent   (D) lenient (E) meditative

_____ 4. ENHANCE :   (A) illuminate   (B) intensify   (C) prolong   (D) detract (E) preserve

_____ 5. FLEETING : (A) initial   (B) alien   (C) adaptive   (D) brief   (E) sustained

_____ 6. GROTESQUE :   (A) normal   (B) uniform   (C) strange
(D) diminutive   (E) paradoxical

_____ 7. LUMINOUS :   (A) well known   (B) insignificant   (C) dark
(D) expensive   (E) bright

_____ 8. IMPERCEPTIBLE :   (A) unapparent   (B) distinct   (C) diverse
(D) impregnable   (E) unpretentious

_____ 9. INTERMINABLE :   (A) initiated   (B) agitated   (C) memorable
(D) desperate   (E) fleeting

_____ 10. TURMOIL :   (A) estrangement   (B) serenity   (C) rejection
(D) apprehension   (E) relentlessness

Number correct _____ (total 10)

Spelling and Wordplay

Fill-Ins Spell the target word correctly in the blanks to the right of its definition.

1. inlet: __ __ __ __ a r y

2. endless: i n __ __ __ __ __ __ __ __ __ __ __ __

3. elaborate: e x __ __ __ __ __ __ __

4. bizarre: __ __ __ __ __ __ q u __

5. unbeatable: i m __ __ __ __ __ __ __ __ l e

6. loose: __ __ x

7. requirement: p __ __ __ __ __ __ __ __ __ __ __ __

8. showy: o __ __ __ n t __ __ __ __ __ __ __

9. modest: u n __ __ __ __ t __ __ t __ __ __ __

10. elastic: __ __ __ __ __ l __ __ __ __ t __

Number correct _____ (total 10)

Part C   Related Words Reinforcement

Using Related Words

True-False Decide whether each statement is true or false. Write **T** for True and **F** for False.

_____ 1. The beautiful colors of fall are _transitory_.

_____ 2. A _pacification_ treaty gives one country the right to declare war on another.

_____ 3. A fabric that has _resilience_ will not wrinkle easily.

_____ 4. Seniors listen to *initiation* addresses at graduation ceremonies.

_____ 5. Spreading gossip is considered a *virtuous* trait.

_____ 6. Good athletes *tend* to take good care of their bodies.

_____ 7. An animal that is *fleet* of foot is easy to catch.

_____ 8. Santa Claus is the *personification* of Christmas good will.

_____ 9. One way to provide *compensation* for city services is to tax the residents.

_____ 10. The amount of foreign currency you receive when you *convert* U.S. dollars depends on the exchange rate.

_____ 11. A religion based on *idolatry* would discourage the worship of images.

_____ 12. A person who *convulses* with laughter remains perfectly still.

_____ 13. If you wish to *confront* someone, you should hide when the person approaches.

_____ 14. Someone who is easily *pacified* is hard to please.

_____ 15. A high-school diploma is usually a *requisite* to college admission.

Number correct _____ (total 15)

Reviewing Word Structures

Word Parts   Complete the exercise below by changing each verb to its noun form, using *-ion*.

Example recreate : recreation

1. apprehend _____

2. compensate _____

3. convert _____

4. convict _____

5. convulse _____

6. derive _____

7. initiate _____

8. pacify _____

9. personify _____

10. reject _____

Number correct _____ (total 10)

Number correct in Unit _____ (total 105)

Vocab Lab 2

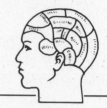

FOCUS ON: Psychology

Psychology is the scientific study of mental processes and behavior. It explores questions about thoughts, feelings, and actions—and can help us understand why people behave as they do. Broaden your vocabulary by learning the following words commonly used in the field of psychology.

claustrophobia (klôs′ trə fō′ bē ə) n. an abnormal fear of enclosed places. ● Because Otis suffered from *claustrophobia,* he would not ride in elevators.

ego (ē′ gō) n. the self; in psychology, the conscious part of the mind that balances conflicts between personal desires and the demands of society. ● A person must have a healthy *ego* to be a happy, contributing member of society.

euphoria (yoo fôr′ ē ə) n. an exaggerated feeling of well-being. ● Although Jacob had an overwhelming feeling of *euphoria* as he completed the marathon, he collapsed a few minutes later.

hypochondria (hī′ pə kän′ drē ə) n. an abnormal concern with one's health so that one becomes depressed or imagines oneself to have some illness. ● Stacy worried about her health so much that people wondered if she suffered from *hypochondria.*

id (id) n. in psychology, the part of the mind that consists of instincts and unconscious desires. ● The psychologist had an explanation for my recurring dream about my fifth birthday; he explained that my *id* was longing for a happier time.

kleptomania (klep′ tə mā′ nē ə) n. an irresistible impulse to steal. ● Although Michelle could afford to buy whatever she needed, she suffered from *kleptomania* and was arrested several times for shoplifting.

manic-depressive (man′ ik di pres′ iv) adj. characterized by alternating periods of extreme confidence (mania) and utter hopelessness (depression); n. a person exhibiting that behavior. ● Jack's moods were so unpredictable and changed so quickly that his mother thought he might be *manic-depressive.*

neurosis (noo rō′ sis, nyoo-) n. a mild personality disorder usually involving excessive anxiety, fear, or uncontrollable behavior. ● Vernon's abnormal neatness was a symptom of an underlying *neurosis.*

paranoia (par′ ə noi′ ə) n. unrealistic feelings of importance or suspicions that other people intend to harm you. ● Art's mother insisted that nothing was hiding in the closet and that his fear was *paranoia.*

phobia (fō′ bē ə) n. a strong, unreasonable fear of a particular thing or situation. ● Although Susan had been traveling on airplanes for years, she suddenly developed a *phobia* about flying.

psychosis (sī kō′ sis) n. a severe personality disorder involving loss of contact with reality. ● People suffering from *psychosis* should receive medical attention, because they can be dangerous to themselves or to others.

sadist (sad′ ist, sā′ dist) n. a person who gets pleasure from hurting others. ● The coach gave his athletes such brutal, unreasonable workouts that some considered him a *sadist*.

schizophrenia (skit′ sə frē′ nē ə, skiz′ ə-) n. a serious mental illness characterized by disordered thinking and emotions and a confused sense of reality. ● People with *schizophrenia* often suffer from hallucinations.

superego (soo′ pər ē′ gō) n. in psychological theory, the part of the mind that includes moral attitudes and judgment; the conscience. ● The psychiatrist told the jury that the criminal had a weak *superego*.

trauma (trou′ mə, trô′-) n. a physical or emotional injury or shock. ● Edward never fully recovered from the *trauma* of the accident.

Sentence Completion   On the line, write the word or phrase in parentheses that best completes the sentence.

_____ 1. A kleptomaniac would usually be considered a (thief, liar, coward).

_____ 2. A sadist would probably rather (be kind to, harm, talk to) another person.

_____ 3. Your superego is what makes you feel (hungry, unloved, guilty).

_____ 4. An impulse from your id might lead you to (eat a large bowl of ice cream, work all night long, feel guilty about something you said).

_____ 5. Someone with extreme paranoia would be constantly (exercising, looking over his or her shoulder, daydreaming).

Number correct _____ (total 5)

Matching Definitions   Write the letter of the correct definition in the blank preceding each word in the list below.

_____ 1. ego   a. the compulsion to steal

_____ 2. euphoria   b. the self

_____ 3. hypochondria   c. an unreasonable fear

_____ 4. kleptomania   d. a severe personality disorder

_____ 5. manic-depressive   e. a preoccupation with illness

_____ 6. neurosis   f. exaggerated good feeling

_____ 7. paranoia   g. a mild personality disorder

_____ 8. phobia   h. characterized by emotional highs and lows

_____ 9. psychosis   i. a serious mental illness marked by hallucinations

_____ 10. schizophrenia   j. a feeling that people are "out to get you"

Number correct _____ (total 10)

FOCUS ON: Dialects

What do you call a paper container—a *sack,* a *bag,* or a *poke?* What is the past tense of *dive*—*dove* or *dived?* When you pronounce *pa,* do you mean a baked dessert or a male parent?

There are no wrong answers to these questions. Your answers depend largely on what region of the country you come from. Variations in pronunciation, vocabulary, and grammar are the elements of dialect—a distinct form of language spoken in a certain geographic area or by a certain social or ethnic group. Everyone speaks at least one dialect, and most of us speak several—different ones for different situations.

How Did You Say That?

Pronunciation is probably the most easily recognized aspect of a dialect. This is what people commonly call "accent," and includes the Southern drawl, the Midwestern nasal twang, and the clipped speech patterns of New England. If you pronounce the word *pie* as *pa,* people will know that you either grew up in the South or spent a lot of time there. If you told someone you were going to "pahk the cah," that person might assume you were from Boston. You can't help it—your accent gives you away.

You Want a What?

Not only does the way people pronounce words differ from place to place, but the words themselves may differ too. For example, if you are in Gary, Indiana, and want a large sandwich of meat and cheese on a long roll for lunch, do you ask for a *hero,* a *submarine,* a *poor-boy,* a *hoagy,* or a *grinder?* Would you expect the waiter to bring you a *soda,* a *tonic,* a *pop,* or a *soft drink* to wash it down? Knowing about such regional differences in vocabulary will give you a taste of the richness and variety of our language. Further proof of this variety is found in the following list of synonyms for *earthworm* used in differing sections of the United States:

angle dog	bait worm	fish bait	fish worm	rain worm
angleworm	dew worm	fishing worm	mud worm	red worm

Grammatically Speaking

Natives of Kentucky say *dived* for the past tense of *dive;* Wisconsin residents prefer *dove.* In other areas people might use both forms. Variations in grammar—such as which preposition is preferred in an expression or what verb form is used—are also included in dialects. Do you say, "I got awake," or "I woke up"? Do you stand "in line" or "on line"? Do you get sick "to your stomach," "at your stomach," or "on your stomach"? Each of these grammatical variations is appropriate in a particular setting.

Your dialect adds personality to your speaking. But keep in mind that you are expected to use correct, standard English in public, in formal settings, and when writing. Part of being an effective communicator is knowing when you "might could" use a particular dialect and when you shouldn't.

Comparing Dialect For each item below, write the word or phrase you use most commonly from the group in parentheses.

_____ 1. sink fixture (faucet, hydrant, spicket, spigot, tap)

_____ 2. food eaten between meals (bite, lunch, piece meal, snack)

_____ 3. time (quarter of, quarter till, quarter to)

_____ 4. past tense of _see_ (saw, seed, seen)

_____ 5. heavy rainfall (cloudburst, downpour, frog strangler)

_____ 6. finished sleeping (got awake, waked up, woke up)

_____ 7. didn't in the past (didn't used to, used to didn't)

_____ 8. past tense of _climb_ (climbed, clime, clome, clum)

_____ 9. cooking utensil (frying pan, skillet, spider)

_____ 10. insect that glows at night (candle bug, firefly, glowworm, lightning bug)

_____ 11. become ill with a virus (catch cold, come down with a cold, get a cold, take cold)

_____ 12. grass strip between the sidewalk and street (berm, boulevard, parkway, sidewalk plot, tree lawn)

_____ 13. amusement-park ride (coaster, roller coaster, rolly-coaster, shoot-the-chutes)

_____ 14. vehicle for an infant (baby buggy, baby cab, baby carriage)

_____ 15. willfully (for purpose, on purpose)

Number correct _____ (total 15)

Number correct in Vocab Lab _____ (total 30)

During the next few years you will be taking many standardized tests that contain vocabulary questions. Employment tests, placement tests, and college entrance examinations—such as the Preliminary Scholastic Aptitude Test (PSAT), the Scholastic Aptitude Test (SAT), and the American College Testing Program Assessment Test (ACT)—include such questions in order to measure your basic skills, or aptitude, in language. Some people believe that your scores on these standardized tests reflect the success you will have in future endeavors, such as college and your career. Therefore, it is to your advantage to prepare yourself for these tests in order to do as well as you possibly can.

Because standardized aptitude tests cover skills or learning gained over a long period of time, cramming is ineffective as a method of preparation. The best preparation for these tests is to concentrate on improving your language skills by working hard in your English classes. Another effective method of preparation is to study the different types of test questions you are likely to encounter on standardized tests. In the area of vocabulary, these include **antonyms, analogies,** and **sentence completion.**

This book provides you with extensive practice in these areas of vocabulary study. In addition, the following special unit contains important information that will help you prepare for standardized test-taking.

Part A   Antonyms

As you know, **antonyms** are words that are opposite in meaning. Standardized test questions covering antonyms are answered by selecting the choice most opposite in meaning to the given word. A typical problem looks like this:

Example

E	HAZARDOUS: (A) calm (B) dangerous (C) haphazard (D) inviting (E) safe

---

To answer an antonym question, use the following strategies:

1. Remember that you must find a word that is opposite in meaning. Do not be thrown off by *synonyms* (words that are similar in meaning) that are included among the possible answers.
2. Decide whether the given word is positive or negative, and then eliminate all possible choices that are in the same category as the given word.
3. Remember that many words have more than one meaning. If no word seems to fit your sense of the opposite meaning, think about other meanings for the given word.
4. If you do not know the meaning of a given word, try to analyze the word's prefix, suffix, or base word in order to define the word.

Exercise Using the strategies listed above, complete the following practice exercise.

_____ 1. ANTICIPATE: (A) foresee (B) argue (C) wish (D) participate (E) recollect

_____ 2. CURIOUS: (A) uninterested (B) inquisitive (C) careful (D) cursed (E) courageous

_____ 3. APPREHENSION: (A) condensation (B) misgiving (C) confidence (D) impression (E) dismay

_____ 4. ENTHUSIASM: (A) elation (B) adventure (C) trust (D) zeal (E) indifference

_____ 5. DIMINISH: (A) expand (B) engage (C) dwindle (D) dim (E) reduce

_____ 6. COMMON: (A) nonsensical (B) ordinary (C) logical (D) unusual (E) popular

_____ 7. EXTERNAL: (A) superficial (B) outer (C) peripheral (D) inclusive (E) internal

_____ 8. IDEAL: (A) optimal (B) conceptual (C) identical (D) flawless (E) imperfect

_____ 9. ACQUIRE: (A) obtain (B) procure (C) forfeit (D) inquire (E) secure

_____ 10. CONFRONT: (A) evade (B) confirm (C) encounter (D) confuse (E) meet

Number correct _____ (total 10)

Part B   Analogies

Analogies, as you will recall, are pairs of words that are related to each other. (For more detailed information about analogies, see pages 54-55.) In analogy questions, you are first given two words that are related to each other. Your job is to determine how the two words are related and then to find two other words that are related to each other in the same way. A typical analogy problem on a standardized test looks like this:

Example

> _B_   CHAIR : FURNITURE :: (A) cup : saucer (B) fork : utensil
> (C) table : desk (D) home : house (E) shoe : sock

To answer analogy questions, use the following strategies:

1. First, recall the many types of relationships expressed in analogies. Refer to the chart on page 54 for a listing of the most common of these relationships.
2. Second, determine the relationship between the first pair of words given. Then, create a sentence that contains both words and that shows the relationship between them. The first pair of words in the above example can be expressed as follows:

A *chair* is a kind of *furniture*.

3. Third, find the pair of words from among the answers that can replace the first pair in your sentence.

A *fork* is a kind of *utensil*.

Exercise Using the strategies listed above, complete the following analogies.

_____ 1. YESTERDAY : TODAY :: (A) decade : century (B) calendar : schedule (C) day : month (D) past : present (E) Sunday : Saturday

_____ 2. WRITER : PENCIL :: (A) reader : knowledge (B) painter : brush (C) milliner : hat (D) gardener : flower (E) mechanic : garage

_____ 3. DISTURB : BOTHER :: (A) like : dislike (B) weep : laugh (C) entertain : amuse (D) disapprove : command (E) soothe : hurt

_____ 4. MAGNIFY : BELITTLE :: (A) glorify : adore (B) manage : supervise (C) ebb : recede (D) shatter : crumble (E) grow : shrink

_____ 5. WOOD : BENCH :: (A) receptacle : container (B) paper : clip (C) lock : door (D) decoy : bait (E) cloth : suit

_____ 6. TULIP : FLOWER :: (A) tooth : mouth (B) milk : cow (C) maple : tree (D) daffodil : daisy (E) grass : yard

_____ 7. SCISSORS : CUT :: (A) locomotion : walk (B) bouquet : wilt (C) water : drink (D) ruler : measure (E) problem : solve

_____ 8. INSOMNIA : EXHAUSTION :: (A) sprain : swelling (B) cowardice : courage (C) magic : magician (D) food : hunger (E) integrity : virtue

_____ 9. BAKER : BREAD :: (A) strings : puppet (B) legume : bean (C) jockey : horse (D) secretary : office (E) sculptor : sculpture

_____ 10. ROOM : BUILDING :: (A) island : peninsula (B) silk : velvet (C) word : sentence (D) treaty : war (E) road : asphalt

Number correct _____ (total 10)

Part C   *Sentence Completion*

Sentence completion problems test your ability to use words and to recognize relationships among the parts of a sentence. You are given a sentence in which one or two words are missing.

You must then choose the word or words that best complete the sentence. A typical sentence completion problem looks like this:

Example

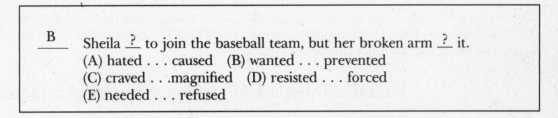

___B___ Sheila _?_ to join the baseball team, but her broken arm _?_ it.
(A) hated . . . caused   (B) wanted . . . prevented
(C) craved . . .magnified   (D) resisted . . . forced
(E) needed . . . refused

To solve sentence completion problems, use the following strategies:

1. Read the entire sentence carefully, noting key words. Pay particular attention to words that indicate contrast (*but, however*) or similarity (*and, another*). For example, the word *but* in the sample problem above gives you a clue that the correct word pair will contain words that are opposite in meaning.
2. Try each of the choices in the sentence. Eliminate those choices that make no sense, those that are grammatically incorrect, or those that contradict some other part of the statement. Make sure that *both* of the given words work in the sentence.
3. Look for grammatical clues within the sentence. Does the space call for a verb, an adjective, a noun? If the answer is a verb, in what tense must the verb be written to correspond with the rest of the sentence? Asking such questions may help you eliminate some incorrect answers.

Exercise   Using the strategies listed above, complete the following sentences.

_____ 1. During the graduation ceremony, Jonathan _?_ where he would be in five years.
(A) knows   (B) inquired   (C) wondered   (D) forgot   (E) hid

_____ 2. Several doctors gave their medical _?_, explaining that surgery was not necessary.
(A) advice   (B) degrees   (C) situations   (D) advantage   (E) possibilities

_____ 3. The composer _?_ a fast tempo to _?_ an energetic and upbeat mood.
(A) measured . . . temper   (B) employed . . . create   (C) wanted . . . ruin   (D) improved . . . delay   (E) showed . . . play

_____ 4. We _?_ the state border and _?_ north to our destination.
(A) increased . . . followed   (B) missed . . . sped   (C) misplaced . . . circled   (D) crossed . . . traveled   (E) magnified . . . vanished

_____ 5. Laurie's _?_ decision to study hard for the final examination _?_ her to receive the highest mark.
(A) wise . . . enabled   (B) impartial . . . convinced   (C) arbitrary . . . reminded   (D) unfortunate . . . allowed   (E) reckless . . . helped

Number correct _____ (total 5)

Number correct in Special Unit _____ (total 25)

Part D   *General Strategies*

No matter what type of problem you are solving, certain strategies can be applied to any part of a standardized test. Keep the following guidelines in mind. They can help you increase your chances of success. Remember, too, that a good mental attitude, plenty of sleep the night before a test, and the ability to relax can be important factors.

Basic Strategies for Taking Standardized Tests

1. **Read and listen to directions carefully.** This advice may seem obvious, but many students do poorly on tests because they misunderstand the directions. Read all the answer choices for a question before deciding on an answer.

2. **Budget your time carefully.** Most standardized tests are timed. It is important that you not spend too much time on any single item.

3. **Complete the test items you know first.** Go back and tackle the more difficult items later.

4. **Mark the answer sheet carefully and correctly.** Most standardized tests make use of computerized answer sheets. Students are required to fill in a circle corresponding to the correct answer in the test booklet, as follows:

    23. Ⓐ Ⓑ Ⓒ ● Ⓔ

    When using such computerized answer sheets, follow these guidelines:

    a. Always completely fill in the circle for the correct answer.
    b. Periodically check your numbering on the answer sheet, particularly if you skip an item. Make sure the number of the question you are answering matches the number on the answer sheet.
    c. Never make notes or stray marks on the answer sheet. These could be misread as wrong answers by the scoring machine. Instead, write on the test booklet itself or on scratch paper, as indicated in the directions.

5. **Be aware of distractors.** Distractors are answer choices that may seem correct at first glance but are actually wrong. For example:

    ____ HOT : COLD   (A) water : ice   (B) good : bad   (C) fat : obsese
    (D) first : second   (E) tepid : lukewarm

    Two choices, *(A) water : ice* and *(E) tepid : lukewarm* are distractors. Both choices relate to temperature, as does *hot : cold.* You may be tempted to choose one of these as the correct answer. However, neither of these choices presents the same relationship as *hot : cold.* The correct answer *(B) good : bad* shows the relationship of opposites *:* shown by *hot : cold.*

6. **Do not make random guesses.** Guessing is unlikely to improve your score. In fact, in some standardized tests, points are deducted for incorrect answers. On such a test, you should guess only if you are almost certain of an answer. If no points are deducted for a wrong answer, guess if you can eliminate one or more of the choices.

UNIT 9

Part A Target Words and Their Meanings

1. abstract (ab′ strakt) n. (ab strakt′) adj., v.
2. allegedly (ə lej′ id lē) adv.
3. assumption (ə sump′ shən) n.
4. attainment (ə tān′ mənt) n.
5. classic (klas′ ik) adj., n.
6. commitment (kə mit′ mənt) n.
7. conspicuous (kən spik′ yoo wəs) adj.
8. contemporary (kən tem′ pə rer′ ē) adj., n.
9. dominate (däm′ ə nāt′) v.
10. dynamic (dī nam′ ik) adj.
11. esoteric (es′ ə ter′ ik) adj.
12. estate (ə stāt′) n.
13. mythological (mith ə läj′ i k′l) adj.
14. oppression (ə presh′ ən) n.
15. paternalism (pə tʉr′ n′l iz′m) n.
16. predominantly (pri däm′ ə nənt lē) adv.
17. primitive (prim′ ə tiv) adj.
18. sector (sek′ tər) n.
19. theory (thē′ ə rē, thir′ ē) n.
20. thesis (thē′ sis) n.

Inferring Meaning from Context

For each sentence write the letter of the word or phrase that is closest to the meaning of the word or words in italics. Use context clues to help you determine the correct answer.

_____ 1. When Mr. Hernandez sensed that the students' discussion of the pros and cons of nuclear energy was becoming too *abstract*, he suggested that they focus on actual facts and figures.

a. theoretical   b. statistical   c. noisy   d. boring

_____ 2. *Allegedly*, Jean's jewels were taken by a burglar, but the police found no sign of unlawful entry, and none of her other belongings had been disturbed.

a. Incredibly   b. Supposedly   c. Unmistakably   d. Unexpectedly

_____ 3. Our *assumption* that Ruth would run for office proved to be wrong, although we knew she was the right person for the job and thought she was interested in it.

a. belief   b. concern   c. opposition to the suggestion   d. resolution

_____ 4. After working very hard to lose twenty pounds, Alice celebrated the *attainment* of her goal by treating herself to a chocolate soda.

a. regulation   b. alteration   c. reaching   d. discovery

_____ 5. The Hoover Dam on the Colorado River is often studied by engineers because it is *a classic* example of modern dam construction.

a. an incomprehensible   b. a flawed   c. an ancient   d. a model

103

_____ 6. The leaders of the fund drive were pleased when Joe made *a commitment* to participate, and they immediately put him to work.

a. a pretense   b. an estimate   c. a promise   d. a refusal

_____ 7. Marie felt very *conspicuous* at the music concert because she was the only band member who was not wearing a uniform.

a. serene   b. virtuous   c. mettlesome   d. noticeable

_____ 8. Because the population explosion is a relatively recent problem, zero population growth can be considered a *contemporary* issue.

a. modern   b. cosmic   c. insignificant   d. historical

_____ 9. Suzy's teammates were amazed at the way she *dominated* the action during the second half of the basketball game, scoring twenty of the team's twenty-four points.

a. adapted to   b. predicted   c. controlled   d. eluded

_____ 10. Ms. Moore is such *a dynamic* teacher that even students who never liked math respond to her enthusiasm and do well in her classes.

a. a somber   b. a vigorous   c. a visible   d. an arbitrary

_____ 11. Although the subject matter of his lecture was *esoteric,* the neurosurgeon tried to make it comprehensible to everyone in the audience.

a. invisible   b. susceptible   c. hard to use   d. understood by only a few

_____ 12. The value of the Micawbers' *estate* diminished drastically when a fire destroyed their house and most of their possessions.

a. marriage   b. friendship   c. property owned   d. insurance

_____ 13. Narcissus is *a mythological* figure from ancient Greek literature who falls in love with his reflection in a pool, pines away with longing, and when he dies, turns into the flower we call the narcissus.

a. an imaginary   b. an insensitive   c. a historical   d. an unrelenting

_____ 14. The *oppression* of blacks in many parts of Africa has prevented them from becoming independent and self-governing.

a. deceit   b. unhappiness   c. enhancement   d. persecution

_____ 15. In leaving home to escape parental authority, many young people find a similar *paternalism* at work in the business world.

a. homelike atmosphere   b. sibling rivalry   c. fatherlike system of control   d. brotherly love

_____ 16. Although many native American tribes settled in the Plains states, it was *predominantly* the Sioux who occupied the region of the Dakotas.

a. understandably   b. imperceptibly   c. primarily   d. gloriously

_____ 17. Many of the natural medicines used by *primitive* people are as effective as the sophisticated cures created by modern medical science.

a. advanced   b. uncivilized   c. sick   d. nineteenth-century

_____ 18. If the recession continues, small businesses will be the *sector* of the economy that is the most seriously hurt.

a. part   b. dilemma   c. opponent   d. compensation

_____ 19. Einstein's *theory* that mass could be converted into energy was the concept that led to successfully splitting the atom.

a. development   b. fear   c. idea   d. arbitration

_____ 20. Professor Snyder supported his *thesis* that the Midwest is returning to another period of drought by supplying statistics on Midwestern rainfall covering the past fifty years.

a. misconception   b. hope   c. plan   d. statement of idea

Number correct _____ (total 20)

Part B   *Target Words in Reading and Literature*

You should now have a general idea of the meaning of each target word. Refine your understanding by examining the shades of meaning these words have in the following excerpt.

Custer Died for Your Sins

Vine Deloria, Jr.

Relations between whites and native Americans have long been marked by mutual mistrust and misunderstanding. In this excerpt from Custer Died for Your Sins, *Vine Deloria, Jr., discusses the "invisibility" of the native American and points out some of the beliefs and policies that contribute to this situation.*

The deep impression made upon American minds by the Indian struggle against the white man in the last century has made the **contemporary** Indians somewhat invisible compared with their ancestors. Today Indians are not **conspicuous** by their absence from view. Yet they should be.

In *The Other America,* the **classic** study of poverty by Michael Harrington, the **thesis** is developed that the poor are conspicuous by their invisibility. There is no mention of Indians in the book. A century ago, Indians would have **dominated** such a work.

Indians are probably invisible because of the tremendous amount of misinformation about them. Most books about Indians cover some **abstract** and **esoteric** topic of the last century. Contemporary books are **predominantly** by whites trying to solve the "Indian problem." Between the two extremes lives a **dynamic** people in a social structure of their own, asking only to be freed from cultural **oppression.** The future does not look bright for the **attainment** of such freedom because the white does not understand the Indian and the Indian does not wish to understand the white.

Understanding Indians means understanding so-called Indian Affairs. Indian Affairs, like Gaul,[1] are divided into three parts: the government, the private

---

[1] Gaul: ancient division of the Roman Empire consisting of what is now mainly modern France, Belgium, Western Germany, and northern Italy

105

organizations, and the tribes themselves. **Mythological theories** about the three **sectors** are as follows: **paternalism** exists in the governmental area, assistance is always available in the private sector, and the tribes dwell in **primitive** splendor. All three myths are false. 20

The government has responsibility for the Indian **estate** because of treaty **commitments** and voluntary **assumption** of such responsibility. It **allegedly** cares for Indian lands and resources. Education, health services, and technical assistance are provided to the major tribes by the Bureau of Indian Affairs, which is in the Department of the Interior. 25

But the smaller tribes get little or nothing from the Interior Department. Since there are some 315 distinct tribal communities and only about thirty get any kind of federal services, there is always a crisis in Indian Affairs. 30

Refining Your Understanding

For each of the following items, consider how the target word is used in the passage. Write the letter of the word or phrase that best completes each sentence.

_____ 1. When talking about Michael Harrington's *classic* study of poverty (line 5), Deloria implies that the book is   a. a model of its kind   b. from the ancient Greeks and Romans   c. old-fashioned.

_____ 2. What information would you *not* expect to find in writings about native Americans that cover "some *abstract* and *esoteric*" topics (lines 10-11)?   a. scholarly histories   b. philosophical ideas about the culture   c. practical suggestions on how the people might improve their lives.

_____ 3. By describing the *theories* of Indian affairs as *mythological* (line 19), Deloria implies that these theories are   a. outdated   b. valid   c. inaccurate.

_____ 4. The government's voluntary *assumption* of responsibility for the Indian estate (line 24) suggests that   a. the government delegated these responsibilities to private individuals   b. the government has taken on responsibilities not specifically assigned to anyone   c. the Indians wanted the government to take on these responsibilities.

_____ 5. Deloria's use of the word *allegedly* (line 24) suggests that the government   a. takes good care of Indian lands and resources   b. is not sure if it should care for Indian lands and resources   c. may not take good care of Indian lands and resources.

Number correct _____ (total 5)

Part C   Ways to Make New Words Your Own

By now you are familiar with the target words and their meanings. This section presents reinforcement activities that will help you make these words part of your permanent vocabulary.

Using Language and Thinking Skills

Understanding Multiple Meanings   Each box in this exercise contains a boldfaced word and its various definitions. Read the definitions and then the sentences that follow. In the blank, write the letter of the definition that applies to each sentence.

commitment
a. the official delivery of a person to a prison or a mental institution by court order (n.)
b. a pledge or promise (n.)

_____ 1. The United States has a *commitment* to defend the countries of Western Europe.

_____ 2. Ms. Riemers has a *commitment* to excellence in her teaching.

_____ 3. The court ordered Bob's *commitment* to the state penitentiary after convicting him of his third criminal offense.

---

contemporary
a. living or happening in the same period (adj.)
b. of or in the style of the present or recent times; modern (adj.)
c. a person or thing about the same age or of the same period as another (n.)

_____ 4. Maud's choice of furnishings gave her home a *contemporary* look.

_____ 5. Environmental pollution is a serious *contemporary* problem.

_____ 6. Thomas Carlyle was a *contemporary* of John Stuart Mill; both wrote in the latter half of the nineteenth century.

_____ 7. Art *contemporary* with the work of Gauguin did not contain the rich color or abstract quality that sets his work apart.

---

classic
a. of the highest class; being a model of its kind; standard (adj.)
b. of the art, literature, and culture of the ancient Greeks or Romans; derived from these civilizations' literary and artistic standards (adj.)
c. a literary or artistic person or work generally recognized as excellent (n.)

_____ 8. *Tyrano v. Epwirth* is a *classic* case of antitrust action in the uranium industry.

_____ 9. Our coach said that Greg Louganis's style is a *classic* example of diving technique.

_____ 10. After our trip to Greece, we became very interested in *classic* culture.

_____ 11. Even before Georgia O'Keeffe's death, her paintings, such as *Summer Days* and *White Barn, No. 1,* were considered *classics.*

---

estate
a. a condition or state; stage of life (n.)
b. property; possessions (n.)
c. landed property; individually owned piece of land containing a large, expensive residence (n.)

_____ 12. Every year, thousands of people visit Monticello, Thomas Jefferson's lavish _estate_ in Virginia.

_____ 13. In her will, Mrs. Van Kemp left her _estate_ to several charities.

_____ 14. Their dream was to get rich and live on a large, elegant _estate_.

_____ 15. After graduating from high school, the seniors held a party to celebrate their new _estate_.

Number correct _____ (total 15)

Words on a Continuum   In each of the five sets of words below, number **1** is placed beside a target word; find the word's antonym and place a **4** beside it. Then number the two remaining words. Put a **2** beside the word that is closer in meaning to word **1**. Put a **3** next to the word that is closer in meaning to word **4**.

Example

1 excellent
2 good
3 fair
4 poor

1.

1 oppressive
_____ indulgent
_____ overbearing
_____ tolerant

2.

_____ likelihood
1 assumption
_____ estimate
_____ certainty

3.

_____ contemporary
_____ recent
_____ historic
1 primitive

4.

_____ dynamic
_____ active
_____ passive
1 unconscious

5.

_____ clear
_____ conspicuous
_____ indistinct
1 invisible

Number correct _____ (total 15)

One-Word Ideas   Choose the word from the list below that most clearly describes the idea in each sentence and write that word in the blank.

abstract	assumption	conspicuous	esoteric	paternalism
allegedly	commitment	contemporary	sector	predominantly

_____ 1. According to Bill Barnes, the Hilltown city officials are overprotective and treat the citizens like children.

_____ 2. What is worse, the current mayor does not address everyday issues in his speeches, but instead he makes political issues seem complicated, obscure, and mysterious.

_____ 3. The mayor's belief that everyone in town is satisfied and that no one would run against him in an election is unfounded, since he has done so little for the town.

_____ 4. Bill Barnes decides to run for mayor and vows to be the best city leader Hilltown has ever had.

_____ 5. Barnes is making a point of campaigning in every neighborhood in the city.

_____ 6. A new library and an updated airport are some of the things Bill thinks would help modernize the city.

_____ 7. Before checking his facts, the old mayor claims that Barnes' home does not lie within the city limits and that Bill therefore cannot hold public office in Hilltown.

_____ 8. During his campaign, Barnes is seen frequently in public, shaking hands, kissing babies, and participating in community activities.

_____ 9. An editorial in the local newspaper endorses Barnes, saying that the current mayor talks about hypothetical solutions to problems but never has any concrete plans for improving the city.

_____ 10. The largest voter turnout in the town's history elected Bill Barnes mayor.

Number correct _____ (total 10)

Practicing for Standardized Tests

Analogies Write the letter of the word pair that best expresses a relationship similar to that expressed in the original pair.

_____ 1. ALLEGEDLY : ACTUALLY ::   (A) partially : totally   (B) conspicuously : obviously   (C) carelessly : carefully   (D) apprehensively : fearfully   (E) dynamically : energetically

_____ 2. OPPRESSOR : OPPRESSION ::   (A) president : presidency   (B) kingdom : king   (C) slave : slavery   (D) inventor : invention   (E) ruler : realm

_____ 3. ATTAINMENT : GOAL ::   (A) achievement : failure   (B) exploration : discovery   (C) education : knowledge   (D) solution : problem   (E) resentment : bitterness

_____ 4. PATERNALISM : FATHER ::   (A) realism : dreamer   (B) maternalism : mother   (C) confusion : religion   (D) socialism : society   (E) journalism : reporter

_____ 5. CONFORMIST : CONSPICUOUS ::   (A) comedian : comical   (B) criminal : law-abiding   (C) politician : political   (D) teacher : educated   (E) physician : healthy

_____ 6. BULLY : DOMINATE :: (A) meal : dine (B) book : publish
(C) conductor : direct (D) garden : fertilize (E) telephone : communicate

_____ 7. CONTEMPORARY : FASHION :: (A) primitive : computer
(B) current : news (C) publicized : secret (D) mythological : history
(E) futuristic : present

_____ 8. SOCIETY : SECTOR :: (A) pie : piece (B) egg : chicken
(C) skyscraper : city (D) orchestra : music (E) brain : skull

_____ 9. CLASSIC : IDEAL :: (A) primitive : advanced (B) initial : primary
(C) mysterious : obvious (D) chaotic : orderly (E) esoteric : simple

_____ 10. ASSUMPTION : PROOF :: (A) life : death (B) guess : fact
(C) uneasiness : dread (D) love : hate (E) invention : creativity

Number correct _____ (total 10)

Spelling and Wordplay

Word Maze Find and circle each target word in this maze.

```
E  S  O  T  E  R  I  C  T  P  E  R  T  Y  B  A
A  C  O  N  S  P  I  C  U  O  U  S  L  H  O  S
F  O  O  F  E  D  O  M  I  N  A  T  E  P  W  S
M  M  C  N  C  G  N  V  D  G  N  A  L  A  I  U
T  M  I  T  T  U  E  Y  A  A  E  B  B  T  N  M
Y  I  S  H  O  E  N  T  N  D  S  S  I  E  O  P
L  T  S  E  R  A  M  I  A  I  T  T  S  R  I  T
D  M  A  S  M  L  M  P  Q  X  A  R  I  N  S  I
E  E  L  I  V  O  R  W  O  C  T  A  V  A  S  O
G  N  C  S  D  L  V  J  R  R  E  C  N  L  E  N
E  T  H  E  O  R  Y  S  B  U  A  T  I  I  R  D
L  P  R  I  M  I  T  I  V  E  Z  R  K  S  P  J
L  P  L  A  C  I  G  O  L  O  H  T  Y  M  P  P
A  T  T  A  I  N  M  E  N  T  Q  Y  K  E  O  X
```

abstract	classic	dominate	mythological	primitive
allegedly	commitment	dynamic	oppression	sector
assumption	conspicuous	esoteric	paternalism	theory
attainment	contemporary	estate	predominately	thesis

111

Part D Related Words

A number of words are closely related to the target words you have studied. Use your knowledge of the target words and of word parts to determine the meanings of these words. (For information about word parts analysis, see pages 6–12.) If you are unsure of any definitions, use your dictionary. Learning these related words expands your vocabulary.

1. abstraction (ab strak′ shən) n.
2. allegation (al′ ə gā′ shən) n.
3. allege (ə lej′) v.
4. assume (ə sōōm′, -syōō′) v.
5. commit (kə mit′) v.
6. committee (kə mit′ ē) n.
7. domination (däm ə na′ shən) n.
8. dynamo (dī′ nə mō′) n.
9. myth (mith) n.
10. mythology (mith äl′ ə jē) n.
11. oppressive (ə pres′ iv) adj.
12. paternal (pə tʉr′ n'l) adj.
13. predominate (pri dam′ ə nit) adj. (-nāt′) v.
14. primary (prī′ mer′ ē, -mər ē) adj.
15. prime (prīm) adj., n., v.
16. primeval (prī mē′ v'l) adj.
17. temporary (tem′ pə rer′ ē) adj.
18. theorem (thē′ ə rəm, thir′ əm) n.

Understanding Related Words

Sentence Completion In the blank, write the related word from the list that best completes each sentence.

allegation   domination   myth   primary   temporary
committee   dynamo   oppressive   primeval   theorem

1. The Student Council selected one member from each class to serve on the

   Homecoming Activities _____ .

2. Each culture has a unique _____ about the creation of the world.

3. The heat was so _____ that no one felt like moving.

4. The charge against the defendant would remain an _____ until the court determined his guilt or innocence.

5. Julie was a real _____ : she accomplished more in a day than most people did in a week.

6. Mark was under the complete _____ of his older brother, running errands for him and doing whatever he asked.

7. A painter can create every color of the spectrum by using various proportions

   of just the three _____ colors—red, blue, and yellow.

8. An idea that not only is assumed to be true but can also be proven is called

   a _____ .

9. The _____ earth was a seething mass of hot gases.

10. Janet was appalled at the shriveled appearance of her leg after the cast was removed, but the doctor assured her that the loss of muscle was only

_____ and the leg would return to normal after a few weeks.

Number correct _____ (total 10)

Turn to **Doubling the Final Consonant** on page 212 of the **Spelling Handbook.** Read the rule and complete the exercise provided.

Analyzing Word Parts

The Latin Root *prime* The target word *primitive* and the related words *primary, prime,* and *primeval* are based on the Latin root *prime,* which comes from the Latin word *primus,* meaning "first." *Primus* also suggests "beginning," "main," and "best." Other words that include the root *prime* and reflect the various meanings of "first" include *prima donna, primate, primer,* and *primogenitor.*

Using this knowledge, choose the word listed below that best describes each sentence, and write the word in the blank. Use your dictionary if necessary. Each word will be used only once.

prima donna   primate   primer   primeval   ·   primogenitor

_____ 1. The biologist was an expert on the order of mammals that includes human beings, monkeys, and apes.

_____ 2. My great-great-grandmother has more than one hundred descendants.

_____ 3. The painters applied a first coat of white paint to the walls before applying the final color.

_____ 4. The star of the show threw a tantrum and stalked off the stage during rehearsal.

_____ 5. The forest was so thick that it appeared to have existed since time began.

The Latin Root *temp* This root comes from two different Latin words—the oldest, *tempus,* meaning "time" or "season," and a derived word, *temperare,* meaning "to regulate or mix properly." Words based on this root include the target word, *contemporary,* the related word *temporary,* and others such as *temper, temperament, temperature,* and *tempo.*

Using your knowledge of this root, write the word from the list below that best completes each sentence. Use your dictionary if necessary.

temper   temperament   temperature   tempo   temporary

6. The pianist played the music at a faster _____ than the composer had indicated.

7. Alison had a naturally optimistic outlook and a pleasing _____ .

8. Two factors that determine the climate of a region are _____ and rainfall.

9. During their summer vacation, Angela and Paul had _____ jobs in their mother's office.

10. The young child was asked to leave the room until he could control his _____ .

Number correct _____ (total 10)

Number correct in Unit _____ (total 95)

Word's Worth: oppression

Oppression, meaning "a cruel exercise of power" or "a sense of being weighed down," comes from the Latin prefix *ob-*, meaning "against" and the verb *premere,* "to press." This Latin verb is the patriarch of a large family of words that can tell a whole story by themselves. For example, experiencing *oppression* can make you feel *depressed,* although you can *suppress* the feeling and refuse to buckle under the *pressure.* If you really feel bad, you can't put a *compress* on your psychic wound, but you can go off by yourself for awhile. It also might help to *express* your hurt to a sympathetic friend. You'll probably find that if you just *press* on, things will begin to look up. If nothing else, you'll be able to *impress* people with your *expressive* new vocabulary.

The Last Word

Writing

Sometimes it's good to be *conspicuous*, for example if you're trying to get a salesperson in a store to notice you. But what about the time at the choral concert when you kept on singing after everyone else had stopped, or when you wore a monster costume to the gathering that wasn't a masquerade party after all? Most people have experienced times like these when they wished they could disappear from the face of the earth. Write a short composition describing such a time when you wished you hadn't been so *conspicuous*.

Speaking

What makes a *dynamic* speaker? Is it the topic? the organization? the delivery? all of the above? Prepare a short speech in which you answer this question. Try to practice what you preach so that you won't just be describing a *dynamic* speaker, you'll be one.

Group Discussion

"*Abstract* Art: A product of the untalented, sold by the unprincipled to the utterly bewildered."—Al Capp

Discuss with your classmates whether you agree with Al Capp's opinion of abstract art or not. You may find it helpful to answer some of the following questions:

1. What is abstract art? How does it differ from realistic, or representational art?

2. Which type of art are people more likely to interpret in a variety of ways? Do you think a work of art has only one "right" meaning? Explain your answer.

UNIT 10

Part A   Target Words and Their Meanings

1. adjacent (ə jā′ sənt) adj.
2. associate (ə sō′ shē it, -sē-) v.(ə sō′ shē āt′, -sē-) adj., n.
3. component (kəm pō′ nənt) n., adj.
4. cycle (sī′ k'l) n.
5. effect (ə fekt′, i-) n., v.
6. export (eks′ pôrt) n., adj. (ik spôrt′) v.
7. hydrological (hī′ drə läj′ ik'l) adj.
8. incessant (in ses′ ənt) adj.
9. integral (in′ tə grəl, in teg′ rəl) adj.
10. nutrient (nōō′ trē ənt, nyōō′-) n., adj.
11. recurrence (ri kʉr′ əns) n.
12. restoration (res′ tə rā′ shən) n.
13. retain (ri tān′) v.
14. sediment (sed′ ə mənt) n.
15. simultaneous (sī′ m'l tā′ nē əs,-tān′ yəs) adj.
16. stimulate (stim′ yə lāt′) v.
17. subtle (sut′ 'l) adj.
18. tributary (trib′ yōō ter′ ē) n., adj.
19. velocity (və läs′ ə tē) n.
20. watershed (wôt′ ər shed′, wät′-) n.

Inferring Meaning from Context

For each sentence write the letter of the word or phrase that is closest to the meaning of the word or words in italics. Use context clues to help you.

_____ 1. Minnesota is *adjacent to* Wisconsin and shares part of its border with Wisconsin along the Mississippi River.

a. next to   b. under   c. east of   d. beyond

_____ 2. The mother advised her young son to spend time with other friends and not to *associate with* the boy who called him names.

a. make assumptions about   b. talk badly about   c. walk away from
d. get involved with

_____ 3. Good stereo speakers are an important *component* of a home audio system.

a. assumption   b. part   c. thesis   d. result

_____ 4. The *cycle* of changes in the butterfly's life represents perhaps the most interesting metamorphosis in nature.

a. whim   b. series   c. phenomenon   d. movement

_____ 5. The governor's announcement of an increase in taxes had an expected *effect*—massive protest marches in the state capital.

a. interest   b. success   c. consequence   d. expense

_____ 6. Iceland *exports* canned and smoked fish to many other countries.

a. compares   b. buys   c. excludes   d. sells abroad

_____ 7. Dams on large rivers are a major source of *hydrological* power.
  a. related to beavers b. inexpensive c. related to water d. hydrogen

_____ 8. There is *incessant* activity at a major airport, such as Chicago's O'Hare Field.
  a. constant b. illegal c. tired d. infrequent

_____ 9. Proper diet and exercise are *integral* parts of a healthy life style.
  a. essential b. invisible c. primitive d. conspicuous

_____ 10. The sea is a rich source of *nutrients*; farming of the sea could provide much of the food for the world's growing population.
  a. salt b. meat, fruit, and poultry c. nourishment d. liquids

_____ 11. There is a *recurrence* of Halley's Comet every seventy-six to seventy-nine years; it appeared in 1986, so it should appear next in the 2060's.
  a. creation b. destruction c. disappearance d. return

_____ 12. The old building is currently run-down, but the planned *restoration* will bring back its former elegance and charm.
  a. news report b. relocation c. reconstruction d. demolition

_____ 13. Immigrants to other countries often *retain* their native language and customs.
  a. shun b. forget c. keep d. absorb

_____ 14. The geologists examined *sediment* dredged from the bottom of the lake.
  a. dust b. liquid c. matter that settles to the bottom of a liquid d. plant and animal life

_____ 15. The ice skaters did *simultaneous* triple jumps, landing in perfect unison.
  a. dangerous b. occurring at the same time c. mediocre d. interminable

_____ 16. The fuel shortage *stimulated* the development of coal mining in Colorado, Utah, and Montana.
  a. spurred on b. had no effect on c. interfered with d. followed

_____ 17. Although the painting appeared to be only a jumble of geometric shapes, a closer examination revealed the *subtle* image of a face.
  a. loud b. not obvious c. bright d. noticeable

_____ 18. The Ohio River is *a tributary of* the Mississippi, entering the larger river near Cairo, Illinois.
  a. a diversion of b. a diminutive of c. an estuary of d. a stream that flows into

_____ 19. The *velocity* of the wind reached more than seventy miles per hour.
  a. speed b. sound c. direction d. elevation

_____ 20. The Mississippi River drains one-eighth of our continent; this area, or *watershed,* comprises 1,244,000 square miles.
  a. area drained by a river b. water tower c. pumping station d. drainage ditch

Number correct _____ (total 20)

Part B Target Words in Reading and Literature

You should now have a general idea of the meaning of each target word. Refine your understanding by examining the shades of meaning these words have in the following excerpt.

H_2O

Howard Peet

Water is the most plentiful substance on earth. Although it is a liquid, it is made up of the two most common atmospheric gases—hydrogen and oxygen. It covers seventy percent of the surface of our planet and makes up two-thirds of our own body mass. The following passage presents some interesting facts about the characteristics and power of water, and stresses the importance of preserving and conserving it.

Water is not only **integral** to life; it is integral to our life style. We may **associate** water with the obvious things like drinking, bathing, and washing clothes, as well as with the more **subtle** uses in the irrigation of crops and the operation of factories. Water **stimulates** the poet as well as the athlete. Each makes **simultaneous** use of the same body of water. The poet praises its calm beauty; the athlete shatters that calmness by skimming over its surface on slick water skis.

Water is power. A **watershed** drains an area into a small **tributary** that, in turn, discharges into the main river. At the conjunction of each tributary, the

5

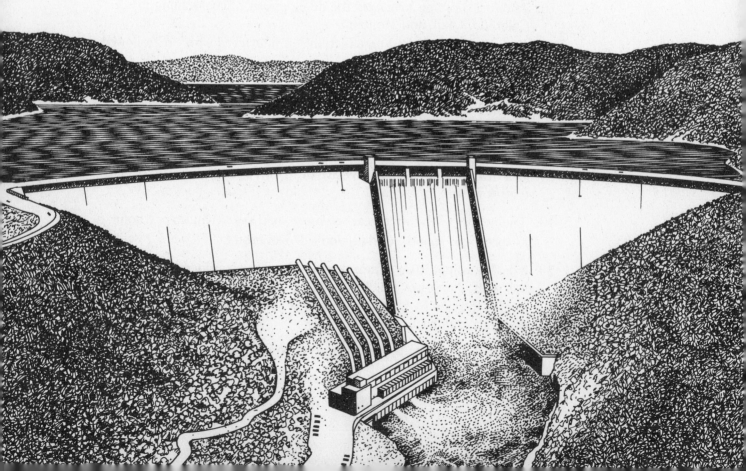

velocity of the main stream increases. The **effect** of this onrush is a power 10
that can turn huge turbines to create electricity for the world. This
world-wide waterpower has been estimated to be about 660,000,000
horsepower. That would produce about four times the power now produced
from every other source.

No wonder the cities of the world lie **adjacent** to bodies of water. Not only 15
does the water serve as a source of physical power; it is also a major
component of economic power. Water carries the bulk of our **exports.**
Passenger travel adds to this flow of dollars as well. In 1976 over one million
passengers from North America took pleasure cruises aboard luxury ships.

On our earth, water is what we might call a closed system. In an 20
incessant cycle, water evaporates upward, only to drop back to earth as
rain. Thus you might think of the raindrops pelting down in yesterday's
shower as a **recurrence** of rainstorms from many centuries ago, with the
same water used again and again. The earth will never lose any of this
water, but it will never gain any water, either, even though we may think we 25
need more.

Now, as water needs increase, **hydrological** studies become more
important. These studies investigate many areas, including the particles that
make up the **sediment** found at a river's mouth and the **nutrient** discharges
that bring about excess weed growth in lakes and streams. Hydrological 30
studies help us to understand the never-ending water **cycle.** They also help
us learn about the methods of **restoration** for our polluted waters, a
necessity if we are to **retain** the use of our waterpower for future
generations.

Refining Your Understanding

For each of the following items, consider how the target word is used in the
passage. Write the letter of the word or phrase that best completes each sentence.

_____ 1. The reason the author considers the use of water in farming and
manufacturing to be *subtle* (line 3) is probably that   a. not much water
is used in these two ways   b. these kinds of water use are not very
important   c. most people have not experienced these uses of water.

_____ 2. An example of a *tributary* (line 8) is   a. a creek   b. an ocean   c. a bank.

_____ 3. An aspect of nature that, like rain, follows "an *incessant* cycle" (line 21)
is   a. the seasons   b. thunderstorms   c. earthquakes.

_____ 4. *Nutrient* (line 29) discharges bring about weed growth by providing
a. wave action   b. substances needed for plant growth   c. good
drainage.

_____ 5. *Sediment* (line 29) is   a. heavier than water   b. lighter than water
c. about the same weight as water.

Number correct _____ (total 5)

Part C *Ways to Make New Words Your Own*

This section will help you make these words part of your permanent vocabulary.

Using Language and Thinking Skills

True-False Decide whether each statement is true or false. Write **T** for True and **F** for False.

_____ 1. The study of wind currents in mountains is called *hydrological* research.

_____ 2. A *subtle* football play is obvious to everyone.

_____ 3. If both trains leave at exactly 10:00 A.M, they leave *simultaneously*.

_____ 4. A farmer builds a *watershed* to house his cattle.

_____ 5. If a part is not *integral* to a machine's operation, it can be left out.

_____ 6. Canada is *adjacent* to Mexico.

_____ 7. *Velocity* is often measured in liters.

_____ 8. The *nutrients* in fertilizers help plants grow better.

_____ 9. Coffee beans are a major *export* of Brazil.

_____ 10. A *restoration* of an old car makes it look much better.

Number correct _____ (total 10)

Practicing for Standardized Tests

Synonyms Write the letter of the word that is closest in meaning to the capitalized word.

_____ 1. ADJACENT: (A) remote (B) neighboring (C) esoteric (D) uniform (E) finite

_____ 2. ASSOCIATE: (A) mingle (B) assume (C) agitate (D) assist (E) separate

_____ 3. COMPONENT: (A) example (B) machine (C) element (D) tributary (E) composition

_____ 4. INCESSANT: (A) continual (B) intermittent (C) mingled (D) enigmatic (E) irritating

_____ 5. INTEGRAL: (A) dimunitive (B) essential (C) fragile (D) abstract (E) unnecessary

_____ 6. RETAIN: (A) repress (B) detain (C) relieve (D) keep (E) reject

_____ 7. SIMULTANEOUS: (A) separate (B) ultimate (C) persistent (D) tenacious (E) concurrent

_____ 8. SUBTLE: (A) raw (B) understated (C) crude (D) cynical (E) stunted

Spelling and Wordplay

Crossword Puzzle

ACROSS

1. Renewal
10. Opponent
13. To consume
14. Unspecified amount
15. Half of Santa's laugh
16. In case that
17. Secondary stream
20. Baby cow
22. Pa's mate
23. Myself
24. To pull behind
25. Abbr. Utah
26. Examination
27. Abbr. Morning hours
28. Abbr. Alternating Current
29. To send to another country
31. A fragment
36. To choose
37. Nourishing food
38. Single unit
40. Abbr. Tellurium
41. Opposite of 28 Across
43. The letter *n*
45. Indefinite article
46. That man
48. Longing
50. Neuter pronoun
51. Second-hand
54. Speed
56. Person in charge; leader
57. Hen's product
59. To overturn
60. Next to
65. Word of choice
66. Abbr. Lines
67. Abbr. Sodium
68. Curved path
70. Plural suffix
71. Relating to the study of water

DOWN

1. To keep
2. Organ of hearing
3. To spur on
4. Abbr. Oregon State University
5. To decay
6. Abbr. American Medical Association
7. School year divisions
8. Word of surprise
9. Negative word
11. Lubricant
12. Result
18. Baseball stick
19. Until now
20. Element or part
21. __ __ shucks!
24. Payment made to help support the government
26. Attempted
28. Creative work
30. Not shut
31. To place
32. Abbr. Railroad
33. 7th tone of the scale
34. Abbr. Cable Network
35. Abbr. Lieutenant
39. Essential
42. Recurring pattern
44. Hard to detect
45. Advertisements
46. Abbr. Helium
47. Fairy tale character Cinder__ __ __ __
49. Abbr. East Indies
52. Makes dirty
53. Abbr. Extra Sensory Perception
55. Biblical *you*
58. The meaning of a green light
60. One of several
61. Father
62. Nickname of President Coolidge
63. To pester
64. Prefix: Three
69. Abbr. Cubic Centimeter

Part D   Related Words

The words below are closely related to the target words you have studied. Use your knowledge of the target words and of word parts to determine the meanings of these words. (For information about word parts analysis, see pages 6–12.) Learning these related words expands your vocabulary.

1. affect (ə fekt′) v., (af′ ekt) n.
2. association (ə sō′ sē ā′ shən, -shē-) n.
3. dehydrate (dē hī′ drāt) v.
4. deport (dē pôrt′) v.
5. detain (dē tān′) v.
6. detention (di ten′ shən) n.
7. hydrology (hī dräl′ ə jē) n.
8. hydrometer (hī dräm′ ə tər) n.
9. integrate (in′ tə grāt′) v.
10. integrity (in teg′ rə tē) n.
11. nutrition (noo trish′ ən, nyoo-) n.
12. nutritious (noo trish′ əs, nyoo-) adj.
13. portable (pôr′ tə b'l) adj., n.
14. portage (pôr′ tij) n., v.
15. porter (por′ tər) n.
16. recycle (rē sī′ k'l) v.
17. restore (ri stôr′) v.
18. simile (sim′ ə lē) n.
19. tenacious (tə nā′ shəs) adj.
20. tenure (ten′ yər, -yoor) n.

Understanding Related Words

Sentence Completion Write the word from the preceding list that best completes each sentence.

1. The study of water is called _____ .

2. A _____ is a figure of speech, a comparison containing the word *like* or *as*.

3. Upon completing three years of acceptable service in our school, a teacher is offered _____ , a permanent faculty position.

4. George Washington was honest and forthright; he was considered to be a man of _____ .

5. An instrument used to measure the specific gravity of liquids is called a _____ .

6. The civil rights movement of the 1960's paved the way for America to _____ its schools.

7. A balanced diet is needed to provide the proper _____ for a healthy body.

8. To help solve the world's growing problem of waste disposal, efforts are being made to _____ many products made of paper, glass, and metal.

9. Too much exercise in hot weather can _____ a person very quickly unless the water lost by perspiration is replaced.

10. The officer said he would have to _____ us at the border until our passports were checked.

Number correct _____ (total 10)

Turn to **The Addition of Prefixes** on page 204 of the **Spelling Handbook**. Read the rule and complete the exercise provided.

Analyzing Word Parts

Words Often Confused The words *affect* and *effect* are easily confused. However, paying attention to the way the word functions in a sentence—its part of speech—will help you determine which one to use.

Affect functions mainly as a verb and means "to influence" or "to pretend to feel or like." (The jury was strongly *affected* by the witness's testimony.) As a noun, *affect* (pronounced af′ ekt) means "emotional response." It is usually used within the context of clinical psychology. (Mark's *affect* was abnormally subdued after the car accident.)

Effect can function as either a verb or a noun. As a verb, *effect* means "to cause" or "to bring about." (Good study habits will *effect* an increase in your grades.) As a noun, *effect* means "result." (One *effect* of not studying is low grades.)

Complete each sentence below by writing either *affect* or *effect* in the blank. Also indicate whether the word is used as a verb or a noun by writing either *V* or *N* in the parentheses.

1. The _____ (n.) of the fire was devastating.

2. I hope the cold will not _____ (v.) you.

3. Only you can _____ (v.) a change in your personality.

4. The medication had an adverse _____ (n.) on George.

5. One symptom of mental illness is inappropriate _____ (n.).

6. We tried to _____ (v.) a loan to finance our new house.

7. Sheila's lack of sleep had an adverse _____ (n.) on her test performance.

8. "This book will _____ (v.) your entire outlook on life," the dust jacket claimed.

9. Sentimental movies seem to _____ (v.) me now more than they did when I was younger.

10. The tornado had no _____ (n.) on our house, although it destroyed the house across the street.

Number correct _____ (total 10)

The Latin Root *port* The target word *export* and the related words *portable, portage,* and *porter* come from the Latin word *portage,* meaning "to carry." Using your knowledge of this root and of prefixes and suffixes, answer the questions below. Refer to a dictionary if necessary.

1. What does a *porter* do?

_____

2. What are the advantages of a *portable* television set?

_____

3. What does a canoeist do on a *portage*?

_____

4. How does an *import* differ from an *export*?

_____

5. Why might a person be *deported* from a country?

_____

_____

Number correct _____ (total 5)

The Latin Root *ten* The target word *retain* and the related words *detain, detention, tenacious,* and *tenure* come from the Latin root *tenere,* meaning "to hold." The most common English spellings of this root are *ten* and *tain*. These five words and five others based on this root are listed below, along with ten definitions. Write each word in the blank next to its definition.

attention   detain   entertain   tenable   tenant
contain   detention   retain   tenacious   tenure

_____ 1. a person who pays rent to use land or a building

_____ 2. holding firmly; stubborn; tough

_____ 3. a close focusing of the mind

_____ 4. to keep in custody; to confine

_____ 5. to have within; to hold, enclose, or include

_____ 6. a keeping in custody; confinement

_____ 7. to keep in one's possession

_____ 8. able to be held, defended, or believed

_____ 9. the holding of a position in teaching on a permanent basis after meeting specified requirements

_____ 10. to hold the interest of and give pleasure to; divert; amuse

Number correct _____ (total 10)

Number correct in Unit _____ (total 80)

The Last Word

Writing

Many processes in nature and in human life occur in *cycles.* Think of a cyclic experience you have had, for example, a recurring dream, returning to school each fall, or making a new friend. Write a short composition describing this *recurrent* experience, explaining which aspects of it remain the same and which change each time it occurs.

Speaking

Present a short talk on a product that is an American *export.* Consider the following questions:
a. What countries import this product?
b. How is the product used?
c. What *effect* does the export of this product have on its domestic use?
d. How *integral* is this export to America's balance of trade?
e. Who benefits from the export of this product?

Group Discussion

Imagine that the water supply to your city or town were suddenly cut off. Discuss the activities that would be affected by this disaster and how you would cope with it.

UNIT 11

Part A   Target Words and Their Meanings

1. appallingly (ə pôl′ iŋ lē) adv.
2. bulbous (bul′ bəs) adj.
3. communal (käm′ yoon ′l, kə myōōn′l) adj.
4. defiance (di fī′ əns) n.
5. deft (deft) adj.
6. despondent (di spän′ dənt) adj.
7. disconsolately (dis kän′ sə lit lē) adv.
8. disdainful (dis dān′ fəl) adj.
9. distinguished (dis tiŋ′ gwisht) adj.
10. embrace (im brās′) n., v.
11. embryo (em′ brē ō′) n.
12. formidable (fôr′ mə də b'l) adj.
13. gloat (glōt) v.
14. nonchalant (nän′ shə länt′, nän′ shə lənt) adj.
15. paragon (par′ ə gän′, -gən) n.
16. refined (ri fīnd′) adj.
17. score (skôr) n., v.
18. superciliously (soo′ pər sil′ ē əs lē) adv.
19. timorously (tim′ ər əs lē) adv.
20. voluptuous (və lup′ choo wəs) adj.

Inferring Meaning from Context

For each sentence write the letter of the word or phrase that is closest to the meaning of the word or words in italics. Use context clues to help you determine the correct answer. (For information about how context helps you understand vocabulary, see pages 1–5.)

_____ 1. The monster in the movie was *appallingly* ugly, more grotesque than anything we had ever seen.

a. apparently   b. imperceptibly   c. horribly   d. sorrowfully

_____ 2. The clown had a *bulbous* nose that looked just like an oversized Ping-Pong ball.

a. beautiful   b. bulb-shaped   c. multicolored   d. turned up

_____ 3. The forest preserve is *communal* property, so anyone is allowed to use it.

a. public   b. private   c. crowded   d. esoteric

_____ 4. Cy was punished for his *defiance* when he refused to be home at 11:00 P.M., as his parents required.

a. resistance   b. timidity   c. forgetfulness   d. laxity

_____ 5. Dr. Sorgen is a *deft* surgeon, famous for performing delicate eye operations.

a. skillful   b. fearful   c. spurious   d. left-handed

_____ 6. After studying so hard for the exam, Len was *despondent* when he failed.

a. understanding   b. resigned   c. despairing   d. distinguished

_____ 7. Fred moped around the house and stared *disconsolately* at the picture of his deceased dog.

  a. unhappily   b. disdainfully   c. conspicuously   d. dominantly

_____ 8. Resentful that she lost the race, Julie gave the winner a *disdainful* look.

  a. scornful   b. affectionate   c. disguised   d. indifferent

_____ 9. The well-known author Samuel Clemens, who called himself Mark Twain, is the most *distinguished* person to have been born in our town.

  a. inconspicuous   b. famous   c. confused   d. tenuous

_____ 10. When Alan gave his kitten a loving *embrace,* she snuggled into his arms.

  a. tug   b. kick   c. hug   d. look

_____ 11. Ultrasonic photographs confirmed that there was more than one *embryo;* the mother-to-be was going to have twins.

  a. prototype   b. ancestor   c. descendant   d. life in its earliest stage

_____ 12. The wide river was a *formidable* barrier for the wagon train to cross.

  a. subtle   b. effortless   c. primitive   d. difficult

_____ 13. Alex *gloated* as he pulled into the parking space just ahead of the other car, but his pleasure dissipated when he saw the fire hydrant by the curb.

  a. cowered   b. broke the law   c. felt triumphant satisfaction   d. got angry

_____ 14. Tony was so *nonchalant* about giving the graduation address that no one would have guessed that he had never given a speech before.

  a. ill-prepared   b. ill-at-ease   c. appalled   d. casually indifferent

_____ 15. He was a *paragon* of thoughtfulness and consideration, an example other parents held up to their children.

  a. challenger   b. model   c. hater   d. poor example

_____ 16. The foreign dignitary's manners were so *refined* that guests felt clumsy in his presence and afraid they might do or say something inappropriate.

  a. whimsical   b. absent-minded   c. crude   d. elegant

_____ 17. In the Gettysburg Address, Abraham Lincoln measured the time between 1776 and 1863 as "four *score* and seven years."

  a. decades   b. period of twenty years   c. weeks   d. centuries

_____ 18. The uppity people at the party behaved so *superciliously* that Gene felt unwelcome and went home early.

  a. haughtily   b. sentimentally   c. violently   d. subtly

_____ 19. The inexperienced climber gazed *timorously* at the sheer cliff and cringed at the thought of climbing it.

  a. fearfully   b. hopefully   c. dynamically   d. splendidly

_____ 20. The soft, *voluptuous* cushions on the sofa looked very comfortable.

  a. symmetrical   b. dark-colored   c. luxurious   d. plastic-covered

Number correct _____ (total 20)

Part B   Target Words in Reading and Literature

You should now have a general idea of the meaning of each target word. Refine your understanding by examining the shades of meaning these words have in the following excerpt.

Arrowsmith

Sinclair Lewis

In this excerpt from Sinclair Lewis's novel, we meet Martin Arrowsmith—a medical student. Not accustomed to social situations, he is ill at ease as he takes his new sweetheart, Leora Tozer, to the medical fraternity ball.

For the Digamma Ball, the University Armory was extremely decorated. The brick walls were dizzy with bunting, spotty with paper chrysanthemums and plaster skulls and wooden scalpels[1] ten feet long.

In six years at Mohalis, Martin had gone to less than a **score** of dances, though the **refined** titillations[2] of **communal embracing** were the chief delight of   5
the coeducational university. When he arrived at the Armory, with Leora **timorously** brave in a blue crepe de chine[3] made in no recognized style, he did not care whether he had a single two-step, though he did achingly desire to have the men crowd in and ask Leora, admire her, and make her welcome. Yet he was too proud to introduce her about, lest he seem to be begging his friends to   10
dance with her. They stood alone, under the balcony, **disconsolately** facing the vastness of the floor, while beyond them flashed the current of dancers, beautiful, **formidable,** desirable.

Leora and he had assured each other that, for a student affair, dinner jacket and black waistcoat would be the thing, as stated in the Benson, Hanley, and   15

---

[1] scalpel: a small, light, straight knife with a very sharp blade, used by surgeons
[2] titillations: pleasant excitements
[3] crepe de chine: a soft, crinkled silk cloth

Koch Chart of Correct Gents' Wearing Apparel, but he grew miserable at the sight of **voluptuous** white waistcoats, and when that **embryo** famous surgeon, Angus Duer, came by, **disdainful** as a greyhound and pushing on white gloves (which are the whitest, the most **superciliously** white objects on earth), then Martin felt himself a hobbledehoy.[4]

"Come on, we'll dance," he said, as though it were a **defiance** to all Angus Duers.

He very much wanted to go home.

He did not enjoy the dance, though she waltzed easily and himself not too badly. He did not even enjoy having her in his arms. He could not believe that she was in his arms. As they revolved he saw Duer join a brilliance of pretty girls and **distinguished**-looking women about the great Dr. Silva, dean of the medical school. Angus seemed **appallingly** at home, and he waltzed off with the prettiest girl, sliding, swinging, **deft.** Martin tried to hate him as a fool, but he remembered that yesterday Angus had been elected to the honorary society of Sigma Xi.

Leora and he crept back to the exact spot beneath the balcony where they had stood before, to their den, their one safe refuge. While he tried to be **nonchalant** and talk up to his new clothes, he was cursing the men he saw go by laughing with girls, ignoring his Leora.

"Not many here yet," he fussed. "Pretty soon they'll all be coming, and then you'll have lots of dances."

"Oh, I don't mind."

("Won't somebody come ask the poor kid?")

He fretted over his lack of popularity among the dancing-men of the medical school. He wished Cliff Clawson were present—Cliff liked any sort of assembly, but he could not afford dress-clothes. Then, rejoicing as at sight of the best-loved, he saw Irving Watters, that **paragon** of professional normality, wandering toward them, but Watters passed by, merely nodding. Thrice Martin hoped and **desponded,** and now all his pride was gone. If Leora could be happy—

"I wouldn't care a hoot if she fell for the gabbiest fusser in the whole U. and gave me the go-by all evening. Anything to let her have a good time! If I could coax Duer over—No, that's one thing I couldn't stand: crawling to that dirty snob!"

Up ambled Fatty Pfaff, just arrived. Martin pounced on him lovingly. "H'lo, old Fat! You a stag tonight? Meet my friend Miss Tozer."

Fatty's **bulbous** eyes showed approval of Leora's cheeks and amber hair. He heaved, "Pleasedmeetch—dance starting—have the honor?" in so flattering a manner that Martin could have kissed him.

That he himself stood alone through the dance did not occur to him. He leaned against a pillar and **gloated.** He felt gorgeously unselfish. . . . That various girl wallflowers were sitting near him, waiting to be asked, did not occur to him either.

---

[4] hobbledehoy: a gawky adolescent boy

Refining Your Understanding

For each of the following items, consider how the target word is used in the passage. Write the letter of the word or phrase that best completes each sentence.

_____ 1. Lewis's use of *refined* (line 5) suggests that the party was
a. spontaneous   b. vulgar   c. dignified.

_____ 2. Angus Duer is described as an "*embryo* famous surgeon" (line 17) because he   a. operates on babies   b. has not yet completed his medical training   c. is really not famous.

_____ 3. By describing men's gloves as "*superciliously* white objects" (line 19), Lewis is associating them with   a. snobbery   b. masculinity   c. friendliness.

_____ 4. Angus seemed "*appallingly* at home" (line 28) because Martin himself felt so   a. tired   b. far from home   c. uncomfortable.

_____ 5. Martin *gloated* (line 57) because Leora was   a. clearly the most attractive woman at the dance   b. a wallflower   c. asked to dance by someone else.

Number correct _____ (total 5)

Part C   Ways to Make New Words Your Own

By now you are familiar with the target words and their meanings. This section presents a variety of reinforcement activities that will help you make these words part of your permanent vocabulary.

Using Language and Thinking Skills

Sentence Completion In the blank write the word from the list below that best completes each sentence.

| appallingly | defiance | distinguished | nonchalant | refined |
| communal | deft | formidable | paragon | timorously |

_____ 1. David's <u>?</u> of authority always gets him into trouble.

_____ 2. A <u>?</u> manner can often cover a lack of self-confidence.

_____ 3. Harry is an extraordinarily <u>?</u> juggler, often keeping ten balls in the air at one time.

_____ 4. Lily spoke so <u>?</u> that people often couldn't hear what she said.

_____ 5. Pam was a <u>?</u> of diligence and efficiency who was held up as a model by her teacher.

_____ 6. The politician thought the campaign would be easy, but he found his rival to be a _?_ opponent.

_____ 7. Mary was nearly satisfied with her painting, but thought it should be _?_ further before she displayed it.

_____ 8. As the most _?_ person at the banquet, the diplomat was seated at the head of the table.

_____ 9. Jones Beach is one of several _?_ recreational areas used by residents of New York City.

_____ 10. The tornado left a (an) _?_ large swath of destruction in its wake.

Number correct _____ (total 10)

Understanding Multiple Meanings Listed below are ten definitions for the word *score*. Read the definitions and the sentences that follow. Write the letter of the definition that applies to each sentence.

---

score
a. a mark, notch, or line (n.); to make such a mark (v.)
b. an amount due, as a debt (n.)
c. grudge (n.)
d. reason or cause (n.)
e. points in a contest (n.)
f. rating or grade on a test (n.); to rate or grade (v.)
g. twenty people or objects (n.)
h. a written copy of a musical composition (n.); to orchestrate (v.)
i. the way things really are (Colloq.) (n.)
j. to achieve or earn (v.)

_____ 1. When it comes to getting her own way with Dad, Mary knows the *score*.

_____ 2. What was the *score* of the game?

_____ 3. The music stand light went out, so the conductor could not read the *score*.

_____ 4. The glass cutter had to *score* the windowpane before cutting it.

_____ 5. I realized that I would have to confront Hank to settle my *score* with him.

_____ 6. A *score* of people came to the party.

_____ 7. Ms. Farmer said she would *score* our tests this afternoon.

_____ 8. Eighteen dollars will settle our *score*.

_____ 9. What did you *score* on the exam?

_____ 10. She had broken her ankle and was excused from gym class on that *score*.

Number correct _____ (total 10)

Practicing for Standardized Tests

Antonyms Write the letter of the word that is most nearly *opposite* in meaning to the capitalized word in each set.

_____ 1. DEFT: (A) dynamic (B) conspicuous (C) skillful (D) clumsy (E) agile

_____ 2. COMMUNAL: (A) political (B) shared (C) singular (D) religious (E) integral

_____ 3. BULBOUS: (A) bulb-shaped (B) rectangular (C) slender (D) committed (E) portable

_____ 4. FORMIDABLE: (A) easy (B) appalling (C) dreadful (D) adjacent (E) predominant

_____ 5. TIMOROUSLY: (A) tenaciously (B) timidly (C) integrally (D) convulsively (E) boldly

_____ 6. NONCHALANT: (A) unruffled (B) anxious (C) associated (D) incessant (E) esoteric

_____ 7. DISTINGUISHED: (A) separated (B) retained (C) stimulated (D) unknown (E) discerned

_____ 8. SUPERCILIOUSLY: (A) disdainfully (B) effectively (C) humbly (D) subconsciously (E) ambiguously

_____ 9. REFINED: (A) pure (B) crude (C) elegant (D) well-bred (E) deft

_____ 10. EMBRACE: (A) accept (B) contain (C) adopt (D) include (E) reject

Number correct _____ (total 10)

Word's Worth: supercilious

To the ancient Romans a raised eyebrow meant disdain or disapproval. The Romans passed on to us not only the meaning of that gesture but the word we use to describe it, *supercilious.* The Latin word for haughty disapproval, *supercilious,* comes from the word *supercilium,* meaning "eyebrow," or literally, "above the eyelid."

Humans are not the only creatures that attach meaning to raised eyebrows. In fact, as a supercilious person raises his or her eyebrows and looks down his or her nose to express scorn, that person is behaving like a baboon. By showing the pale skin of his or her eyelid, a supercilious person is engaging in a mild threat or warning such as that used by baboons.

Spelling and Wordplay

Word Maze Find and circle each target word in this maze.

```
S  U  P  E  R  C  I  L  I  O  U  S  L  Y  S        appallingly
Y  R  E  F  T  N  E  D  N  O  P  S  E  D  U        bulbous
L  E  M  B  R  A  C  E  S  C  O  R  E  E  O        communal
E  T  X  L  Y  R  E  F  U  R  E  H  S  F  U        defiance
T  A  T  Z  W  L  I  T  E  C  S  S  O  I  T        deft
A  B  P  A  U  G  S  F  O  I  R  G  A  P           despondent
L  U  A  P  Y  O  I  U  U  R  M  L  L  N  U        disconsolately
O  L  R  H  A  N  E  G  O  I  R  A  O  C  L        disdainful
S  B  A  J  E  L  N  M  D  R  M  N  A  E  O        distinguished
N  O  G  D  S  I  L  A  B  D  O  U  T  Z  V        embrace
O  U  O  G  T  A  B  I  S  R  S  M  L  J  D        embryo
C  S  N  S  N  L  N  K  N  R  Y  M  I  P  F        formidable
S  I  I  T  E  R  O  S  S  G  O  O  T  T  H        gloat
I  D  I  S  D  A  I  N  F  U  L  C  M  R  Q        nonchalant
D  N  O  N  C  H  A  L  A  N  T  Y  T  K  E        paragon
                                                   refined
                                                   score
                                                   superciliously
                                                   timorously
                                                   voluptuous
```

Part D   Related Words

A number of words are closely related to the target words you have studied. Use your knowledge of the target words and of word parts to determine the meanings of these words. (For information about word parts analysis, see pages 6–12.) If you are unsure of any definitions, use your dictionary. Learning these related words expands your vocabulary and helps you learn the target words more thoroughly.

1. appall (ə pôl′) v.
2. common (käm′ ən) adj.
3. commune (käm′ yōōn) n., (kə myōōn′) v.
4. communicate (kə myōō′ ni kāt′) v.
5. communism (käm′ yə niz′m) n.
6. community (kə myōō′ nə tē) n.
7. consolation (kän sə lā′ shən) n.
8. console (kən sōl′) v. (kän′ sōl) n.
9. defy (di fī′) v.
10. despond (di spänd′) v.
11. disdain (dis dān′) n., v.
12. distinguish (dis tiŋ′ gwish) v.
13. embryonic (em′ brē än′ ik) adj.
14. nonchalantly (nän shə länt′ lē) adv.
15. refine (ri fīn′) v.
16. timid (tim′ id) adj.

Understanding Related Words in Context

Matching Synonyms Match each related word on the left with its synonym.
Write the letter of the matching synonym in the blank.

_____ 1. appall   a. undeveloped

_____ 2. community   b. scorn

_____ 3. console   c. horrify

_____ 4. defy   d. society

_____ 5. despond   e. indifferently

_____ 6. disdain   f. shy

_____ 7. embryonic   g. comfort

_____ 8. nonchalantly   h. despair

_____ 9. refine   i. challenge

_____ 10. timid   j. improve

Number correct _____ (total 10)

Turn to **The Prefix _ad-_** on pages 204–205 of the **Spelling Handbook.**
Read the rules and complete the exercises provided.

Finding Examples In the blank, write the word from the list that best describes
the idea in each sentence.

appall	communicate	defy	disdain	embryonic
commune	consolation	despond	distinquish	nonchalantly

_____ 1. The student nurses at Community Hospital refuse to wear nursing uniforms.

_____ 2. Unruffled by the robber's demands, the teller calmly placed the packets of money into the canvas bag and then pressed the secret alarm button.

_____ 3. Although it is almost impossible to tell the two paintings apart, one is an original Warhol, and one is a copy.

_____ 4. Intending to shock her grandparents, Alison wore a punk-rock outfit and blue-streaked hair to the family reunion.

_____ 5. After their dog died, the heartbroken Daniels family went to the pet shop to choose a new puppy.

_____ 6. The idea for a perpetual-motion machine came to Erica in a moment of inspiration, but many years of work would be needed to actually create the machine.

_____ 7. On an Israeli kibbutz all the members work for the good of the community and receive services such as housing, food, child care and medical care instead of wages.

_____ 8. Marion talks on the telephone two hours each night.

_____ 9. The well-to-do Green family look down on their less wealthy neighbors.

_____ 10. After the accident, Jeremy seemed to lose interest in all of the people and activities that he used to enjoy.

Number correct _____ (total 10)

Analyzing Word Parts

The Latin Prefix _dis-_ _Dis-_ is a negative prefix meaning "not," "opposite," "apart," or "away." In addition to the target words _disconsolately, disdainful,_ and _distinguished_ and the related words _distinguish_ and _disdain,_ many other words are formed using this prefix. Using your knowledge of this prefix and of word roots, define the five words listed below. Use your dictionary if necessary.

1. disadvantage: _____

2. disconsolate: _____

3. disendow: _____

4. disorient: _____

5. dissect: _____

Number correct _____ (total 5)

The Latin Root _commun_ The target word _communal_ and its related words come from the Latin root _commun,_ meaning "common" or "shared." Complete each sentence below, using the appropriate word. Use your dictionary if necessary.

common   commonplace   communicable   communicate   communism

_____ 1. You'll have to ? your ideas more clearly if you want people to understand you.

_____ 2. Joan and Leslie have been friends for years, but recently they have less in ? and seem to be growing apart.

_____ 3. Because the doctor thought Martin's disease might be ?, she quarantined him from the rest of the family.

_____ 4. Theoretically, no property is privately owned under ? .

_____ 5. Everyone expected the fashion designer to create some radically new clothes, but the styles were rather ? .

Number correct _____ (total 5)

Number correct in Unit _____ (total 85)

The Last Word

Writing

Imagine that you are facing the most *formidable* opponent possible. Your battleground can be anything from a running track to a chessboard or a debate forum. Write two scenarios—one in which you face your opponent *timorously* and one in which you face him or her with *defiance*. Try to make both scenarios believable.

Group Discussion

How does a group of people achieve a feeling of *community?* Divide into groups of four members each to discuss the following questions. Then share your group's findings and views with the class.

1. What constitutes a community?

2. What kinds of communities are you a part of? (your class? your school? your neighborhood?)

3. What are some obstacles to achieving a feeling of community?

4. What are some ways of encouraging and nurturing community feeling?

UNIT 12: Review of Units 9–11

Part A   Review Word List

Unit 9 Target Words

1. abstract
2. allegedly
3. assumption
4. attainment
5. classic
6. commitment
7. conspicuous
8. contemporary
9. dominate
10. dynamic
11. esoteric
12. estate
13. mythological
14. oppression
15. paternalism
16. predominantly
17. primitive
18. sector
19. theory
20. thesis

Unit 9 Related Words

1. abstraction
2. allegation
3. allege
4. assume
5. commit
6. committee
7. domination
8. dynamo
9. myth
10. mythology
11. oppressive
12. paternal
13. predominate
14. primary
15. prime
16. primeval
17. temporary
18. theorem

Unit 10 Target Words

1. adjacent
2. associate
3. component
4. cycle
5. effect
6. export
7. hydrological
8. incessant
9. integral
10. nutrient
11. recurrence
12. restoration
13. retain
14. sediment
15. simultaneous
16. stimulate
17. subtle
18. tributary
19. velocity
20. watershed

Unit 10 Related Words

1. affect
2. association
3. dehydrate
4. deport
5. detain
6. detention
7. hydrology
8. hydrometer
9. integrate
10. integrity
11. nutrition
12. nutritious
13. portable
14. portage
15. porter
16. recycle
17. restore
18. simile
19. tenacious
20. tenure

Unit 11 Target Words

1. appallingly
2. bulbous
3. communal
4. defiance
5. deft
6. despondent
7. disconsolately
8. disdainful
9. distinguished
10. embrace
11. embryo
12. formidable
13. gloat
14. nonchalant
15. paragon
16. refined
17. score
18. superciliously
19. timorously
20. voluptuous

Unit 11 Related Words

1. appall
2. common
3. commune
4. communicate
5. communism
6. community
7. consolation
8. console
9. defy
10. despond
11. disdain
12. distinguish
13. embryonic
14. nonchalantly
15. refine
16. timid

Inferring Meaning from Context

For each sentence write the letter of the word or phrase that is closest to the meaning of the word or words in italics.

_____ 1. The government grant was used to finance the *hydrological* project.
a. mountain study   b. air study   c. water study   d. land study

_____ 2. The food at the banquet was not only well-prepared and beautifully presented, but it was *nutritious,* too.
a. contemporary   b. splendid   c. nourishing   d. tasty

_____ 3. The mathematician presented her calculus *theorem* at the convention.
a. principle   b. assumption   c. abstraction   d. sector

_____ 4. Among his classmates, John was considered a *paragon* of integrity.
a. myth   b. contradiction   c. reminder   d. model

_____ 5. In *defiance of* her parents, Joann refused to clean up her room.
a. agreement with   b. embarrassment for   c. awe of   d. resistance to

_____ 6. Shirley is too *timid* to be a cheerleader.
a. shy   b. tenacious   c. clumsy   d. despondent

_____ 7. We were *appalled* when we saw all the damage done by the vandals.
a. dismayed   b. distinguished   c. defiant   d. oppressed

_____ 8. The *incessant* ringing of the telephone was maddening.
a. intermittent   b. continual   c. dynamic   d. disconsolate

_____ 9. *A score of* invitations should be enough for the surprise party.
a. A bunch of   b. A hundred   c. Twenty   d. Ten

_____ 10. Batman and Robin, the *dynamic* duo, live in Gotham City.
a. conspicuous   b. energetic   c. dangerous   d. mythological

_____ 11. The professor's ideas were too *abstract* for the class to understand.
a. appalling   b. oppressive   c. theoretical   d. formidable

_____ 12. The baseball team glanced *disconsolately* at the scoreboard.
a. dejectedly   b. excitedly   c. disdainfully   d. nervously

_____ 13. Mrs. Jenkins played *an integral* part in her daughter's decision to become a social worker.
a. an essential   b. a dominating   c. an esoteric   d. a small

_____ 14. The artist drew an amazingly lifelike portrait with only a few *deft* strokes of his pencil.
a. classical   b. defiant   c. skillful   d. noncommunicative

_____ 15. Ms. Alvarez made a firm *commitment* to give up smoking.
a. pledge   b. assumption   c. lie   d. program

Number correct _____ (total 15)

Using Review Words in Context

Using context clues, determine which word from the list below best completes each sentence in the passage. Write the word in the blank. Each word is used only once.

associate	cycle	formidable	primitive	subtle
bulbous	dynamic	incessant	scores	velocity
conspicuous	effects	predominantly	sediment	voluptuous

Carlsbad Caverns

Today most people _____ southern New Mexico with the desert, but two hundred million years ago the whole area was under water. This warm, shallow sea was populated by _____ of different species of marine life. Most of these species had shells that were made _____ of calcite, or limestone. Over the next hundred and forty million years, the shells of dead creatures and minerals from the water itself collected to form a thick limestone _____ at the bottom of the sea. Then, sixty million years ago, the violent upheaval of the earth's surface that formed the Rocky Mountains lifted the entire area above sea level. This series of events created a massive limestone block from which nature's master sculptor, water, created one of its most awe-inspiring works—Carlsbad Caverns.

Water is a relentless reshaper of the earth's surface. The earth's water supply is in a _____ equilibrium. This means that, although water undergoes a continuous _____ of change and movement—falling as rain, seeping into the earth as ground water, flowing into rivers to the sea, and eventually evaporating into the atmosphere, where it forms clouds and again falls as rain—the total amount remains constant. As water seeps into earth that is rich in limestone, it dissolves that mineral. In southeastern New Mexico the _____ seepage of water over the centuries hollowed out huge underground caves that today resemble honeycombs. Water continued to drip into these caves, losing carbon dioxide to the underground atmosphere and leaving behind minute deposits of limestone.

This depositing of limestone is a _____ process, occurring with almost imperceptible _____ . Yet, the _____ of this buildup—the massive formations that adorn Carlsbad Caverns—provide _____ and undeniable evidence of the immense age of the earth. Starting as thin tubes, calcite deposits grow down from the ceiling of the cave into icicle like formations called *stalactites*. Water that drips from the walls and ceiling of the cave collects on its floor, slowly building up formations called *stalagmites*.

In Carlsbad Caverns, the stalactites and stalagmites form an amazing array of shapes, from pencil-thin formations called *soda straws*, to _____ , knobby pillars, to beautiful, _____ flowing draperies, to whole Chinese temples and elephants complete with tusks. One large chamber of the caverns, four thousand feet long and over six hundred feet wide, is a vast enchanted forest of stone sculpture. The sheer size of this underground art gallery is an eloquent testimony to the _____ power of water and time.

Paintings on the cave walls near the entrance indicate that _____ people once used the caverns. We have no way of knowing how far into the interior they ventured or how far the caves themselves extend, because there are still many unexplored areas. However, even if every inch of Carlsbad Caverns is mapped some day, there will always be something new to see, because with every drip of water, this fantastic underground landscape continues to change.

Number correct _____ (total 15)

Part B   Review Word Reinforcement

Using Language and Thinking Skills

True-False Decide whether each statement is true or false. Mark **T** for True and **F** for False.

_____ 1. If Russia and China are *adjacent,* they share a common border.

_____ 2. A morning hello is considered *esoteric* conversation.

_____ 3. Most light bulbs are *bulbous.*

_____ 4. Paul Bunyan is a *mythological* character.

_____ 5. The U.S. places an *export* tax on everything that comes into the country.

_____ 6. Oceans cover more than 70 percent of the earth's surface; therefore, our planet's surface is *predominantly* water.

_____ 7. A *theory* is an explanation of how or why something happens.

_____ 8. A river can be a *tributary.*

_____ 9. *Sediment* is usually found on the top of a lake or pond.

_____ 10. A mother can practice *paternalism.*

_____ 11. Measurement of air pressure is an essential part of *hydrological* studies.

_____ 12. Superman is a *paragon* of virtue.

_____ 13. Freedom is an *abstract* concept.

_____ 14. A speedometer does not measure *velocity*.

_____ 15. A seed of a plant is an *embryo*.

Number correct _____ (total 15)

Practicing for Standardized Tests

Analogies Write the letter of the word pair that best expresses a relationship similar to that expressed in the original pair.

_____ 1. CLASS : CLASSIC ::   (A) effect : affected   (B) community : communal (C) cycle : cyclic   (D) myth : realistic   (E) abstraction : abstract

_____ 2. HYDROMETER : LIQUID ::   (A) dam : water   (B) wings : air (C) barometer : air pressure   (D) thermometer : illness   (E) running : stopwatch

_____ 3. BULBOUS : SHAPE ::   (A) paternal : father   (B) contemporary : relic (C) convertible : auto   (D) portable : export   (E) energetic : energy

_____ 4. SCIENTIST : THEORY ::   (A) artist : painting   (B) plumber : pipe (C) illusion : magician   (D) student : school   (E) teacher : class

_____ 5. SURGEON : DEFT ::   (A) farmer : paternal   (B) professor : mythological (C) coward : mettlesome   (D) soldier : pacific (E) clown : comical

_____ 6. ASSOCIATE : ASSOCIATION ::   (A) allege : proof   (B) retain : detention (C) confront : confrontation   (D) embrace : affection (E) sing : opera

_____ 7. CONCRETE : ABSTRACT ::   (A) theoretical : hypothetical (B) primitive : primeval   (C) refined : distinguished   (D) initial : primary   (E) mettlesome : timid

_____ 8. SIMULTANEOUS : CONCURRENT ::   (A) permanent : fleeting (B) temporary : transient   (C) subtle : obvious   (D) primitive : sophisticated   (E) active : passive

_____ 9. DOMINATE : CONTROL ::   (A) retain : expel   (B) divorce : unite (C) like : love   (D) grieve : mourn   (E) reward : punish

_____ 10. CRUDE : REFINED ::   (A) timid : meek   (B) despondent : disconsolate (C) voluptuous : sensuous   (D) integral : essential   (E) nonchalant : agitated

Number correct _____ (total 10)

Synonyms Write the letter of the word whose meaning is closest to that of the capitalized word.

_____ 1. ALLEGEDLY: (A) factually   (B) timorously   (C) obviously (D) supposedly   (E) persistently

_____ 2. ASSOCIATE: (A) assume   (B) affect   (C) connect   (D) retain (E) embrace

141

_____ 3. COMPONENT: (A) cycle (B) element (C) tributary (D) theorem
(E) nutrient

_____ 4. DEFT: (A) skilled (B) formal (C) malformed (D) clumsy (E) timid

_____ 5. DOMINATE: (A) commit (B) disdain (C) agitate (D) rule (E) obligate

_____ 6. ESOTERIC: (A) common (B) disdainful (C) obvious (D) fleeting
(E) profound

_____ 7. FORMIDABLE: (A) conspicuous (B) menacing (C) laughable
(D) comforting (E) prolonged

_____ 8. INTEGRAL: (A) necessary (B) uniform (C) interior (D) initial
(E) numerous

_____ 9. PARAGON: (A) despot (B) ideal (C) embryo (D) dynamo (E) simile

_____ 10. VOLUPTUOUS: (A) primitive (B) voluntary (C) ascetic
(D) luxurious (E) supercilious

Number correct _____ (total 10)

Antonyms Write the letter of the word that is most nearly _opposite_ in meaning to
the capitalized word.

_____ 1. ABSTRACT: (A) exquisite (B) concrete (C) malformed
(D) incessant (E) theoretical

_____ 2. ADJACENT: (A) fat (B) bleak (C) neighboring (D) similar
(E) distant

_____ 3. COMMUNAL: (A) political (B) mutual (C) private (D) associated
(E) tyrannical

_____ 4. CONSPICUOUS: (A) obvious (B) dynamic (C) ostentatious
(D) pretentious (E) imperceptible

_____ 5. EXPORT: (A) dispose (B) buy (C) detain (D) import (E) deport

_____ 6. DISTINGUISHED: (A) contemporary (B) famous (C) ordinary
(D) voluptuous (E) formidable

_____ 7. INCESSANT: (A) continual (B) dynamic (C) timorous (D) hostile
(E) intermittent

_____ 8. NONCHALANT: (A) anxious (B) defiant (C) indifferent
(D) disdainful (E) subtle

_____ 9. PRIMITIVE: (A) mythological (B) primeval (C) alien
(D) futuristic (E) esoteric

_____ 10. TIMID: (A) agitated (B) shy (C) committed (D) cynical
(E) assured

Number correct _____ (total 10)

Spelling and Wordplay

Fill-Ins Spell the target word correctly in the blanks to the right of its definition.

1. reconstruction: <u>r</u> __ __ __ __ __ __ <u>t</u> __ __

2. continual: __ __ <u>c</u> <u>e</u> __ __ __ __

3. hug: __ __ __ __ __ <u>c</u> __

4. model: <u>p</u> __ __ __ __ __ __

5. essential: <u>i</u> __ __ __ __ __ __ __

6. to control: <u>d</u> __ __ __ __ <u>i</u> __ __ __

7. consequence: __ <u>f</u> <u>f</u> __ __ __

8. public: <u>c</u> __ __ __ __ __ __ __

9. cruel use of power: __ <u>p</u> __ <u>r</u> __ __ __ __ <u>i</u> __ __

10. not obvious: __ __ __ __ <u>l</u> <u>e</u> __

11. modern: <u>c</u> __ __ __ __ __ __ __ __ __ __ <u>r</u> __

12. next to: __ __ <u>j</u> __ __ __ __ <u>t</u>

13. dreaded: <u>f</u> __ __ __ __ __ __ __ <u>l</u> <u>e</u>

14. part: <u>c</u> __ <u>m</u> __ __ __ __ __

15. supposedly: __ <u>l</u> __ __ <u>g</u> __ __ __ __ <u>y</u>

Number correct _____ (total 15)

Part C Related Words Reinforcement

Using Related Words

Finding Examples In the blank write the word below that best describes each situation.

abstraction	allegation	commune	dehydrate	dynamo
hydrology	myth	nutrition	simile	tenacious

_____ 1. a forceful and energetic leader

_____ 2. a group of people living and working together

_____ 3. accusing someone without having definite proof

_____ 4. the story of Hercules

_____ 5. comparing the sun to a red rubber ball

143

_____ 6. an idea in a philosophical discussion

_____ 7. scientists gathering information to help them predict and control floods

_____ 8. refusing to give up until you have solved the geometry problem

_____ 9. planning the menus for the school cafeteria

_____ 10. exercising hard on a hot day without having anything to drink

Number correct _____ (total 10)

Reviewing Word Structures

The Latin Roots _prime, temp, port,_ and _ten_ In the blank write the review word that best completes each sentence. The word must contain the root noted in parentheses.

1. The flat tire _____ us for two hours. (ten)

2. We decorated the house in bright _____ colors for the children's party. (prime)

3. Although the carpenter's pounding was disturbing, we knew that it was just

   a _____ inconvenience. (temp)

4. Why does Jason bring his _____ television to the beach when he could be enjoying the natural scenery? (port)

5. Wilderness camping gives one some idea of what life was like for

   _____ man. (prime)

6. Sometimes it's easier to discuss your problems with a _____ than with your parents or teachers. (temp)

7. One hundred and sixty million years ago, dinosaurs moved through the

   _____ forests. (prime)

8. Because we had studied so much material over the school term, it was difficult

   to _____ it all for the final examination. (ten)

9. At the airport you can have a _____ help you carry your luggage. (port)

10. People who have been charged with a crime are held in _____ at the county jail while awaiting trial. (ten)

Number correct _____ (total 10)

Number correct in Unit _____ (total 110)

Vocab Lab 3

FOCUS ON: Political Science

For a change of pace, take a look at the following words used in the field of political science.

bipartisan (bī pär′ tə z'n, -s'n) adj. of, representing, or supported by two parties. ● All members of the Senate joined in a *bipartisan* movement to support the clean-air bill.

boycott (boi′ kät) v. to refuse to buy, use, or participate in; n. the act of boycotting. ● The mayor and her allies *boycotted* the meeting to show disapproval of the issue.

bureaucracy (byoo räk′ rə sē) n. a government made up of departments managed by appointed officials with specialized functions and operating according to fixed rules. ● In a *bureaucracy* several people usually must approve a decision before any action can be taken.

coalition (kō′ ə lish′ ən) n. a temporary pact between groups. ● By forming a *coalition*, several neighborhood groups produced enough votes to pass a ban on handguns.

filibuster (fil′ ə bus′ tər) n. the act of blocking the passage of a bill by making long speeches and introducing irrelevant issues; v. the use of such methods to obstruct a bill. ● To demonstrate their disapproval of the bill, the senators joined in a *filibuster* that lasted three days and nights.

fiscal (fis′ kəl) adj. referring to public or private revenues, debt, or taxation. ● The gas company published a complete financial statement at the end of the *fiscal* year.

impeachment (im pēch′ mənt) n. a formal charge of misconduct against a public official. ● The House of Representatives must initiate the proceedings for *impeachment* of officials of the federal government.

jurisdiction (joor′ is dik′ shən) n. the authority to hear and decide legal cases; the range of authority. ● Judge Black's *jurisdiction* extended only to the city limits, so he could not hear cases involving crimes committed in other locations.

lobby (läb′ ē) v. to try to influence legislators to vote in a certain way; n. a group that lobbies. ● Students and faculty at the university *lobbied* at the state capitol for more education funds.

mandate (man′ dāt) n. the wishes of the public as shown by their votes; an order given by someone in authority. ● Governor Fogbound interpreted his landslide election as a *mandate* for his tax-reform program.

mediate (mē′ dē āt′) v. to act as a go-between in settling a dispute. ● The political science professor agreed to *mediate* between the students and the administration in settling the disagreement about course requirements.

patronage (pā′ trən ij, pat′ rən-) n. the distribution of political appointments or other favors by a government official. ● After appointing his neighbor as a village trustee, the village president was accused of *patronage*.

quorum (kwôr′ əm) n. the minimum number of people who must be present at a meeting for official business to be conducted. ● Our club charter says that five people constitute a *quorum*, so we were forced to cancel last week's meeting when only four people showed up.

repeal (ri pēl′) v. to officially withdraw or cancel. ● Congress voted to *repeal* the controversial amendment.

tariff (tar′ if) n. a government tax, usually placed upon imports or exports. ● Grocers hoped that the *tariff* on imported food items would be lifted.

Sentence Completion Complete each sentence by using one of the words from the preceding list. Each word is used only once.

1. Many citizens want to _____ the new tax law, and therefore they have staged a series of protest marches.

2. The incumbent's landslide victory was a _____ from the voters.

3. As soon as Elinor arrives, we will have a _____ for our meeting.

4. To show displeasure at the company's firing of two hundred employees, the mayor urged citizens to _____ the company's products.

5. Various consumer groups _____ in Washington, D.C., in hopes of influencing the legislators' votes.

6. The new governor promises that he will eliminate the _____ system and that his appointments will be based only on merit.

7. During the presidential debate, each candidate was asked to make a statement about government debts and other _____ matters.

8. Ms. Haskell was not surprised when her call to the IRS was transferred three times. "What else do you expect from a _____ ?" she asked.

9. A judge has the _____ in a court of law.

10. _____ is the most serious action that can be taken when a public official is suspected of misconduct.

11. The city appointed a university professor to _____ the dispute.

12. The committee had two chairpersons, one from each political party, to assure _____ representation.

13. A _____ of nurses and administrators has been formed in order to seek more federal aid to meet the medical needs of the elderly.

14. Because they strongly disagreed with the proposed legislation, several senators decided to stage a _____ .

15. A high _____ often discourages people from buying goods cheaply abroad and bringing them back to the United States.

Number correct _____ (total 15)

FOCUS ON: *Multiple Meanings of Words*

Everyone knows the meaning of *run*. Track stars, politicians, traffic police, lingerie salespeople, baseball players, mechanics, and gamblers all use this word. However, *run* means something different to each of them.

Many words have multiple meanings. To determine which meaning is intended in a particular situation, you must consider the context in which the word is used. Consider another example. Look at how the word *walk* is used in the following sentence:

To help students plan their futures, the guidance counselor invited people from various *walks* of life to speak at a Career Day seminar.

Try to determine what *walk* means in the context in which it is used in the sentence. The word appears to be a synonym for *occupation*, *profession*, or *activity*. To make sure, turn to the dictionary. A sample entry from *Webster's New World Dictionary* for *walk* is shown below:

walk (wôk) *vi.* [OE. *wealcan,* to roll < IE. base *wel-,* to turn, roll, from which also comes L. *volvere*] **1.** to move along on foot at a normal pace by placing one foot (or, with four-footed animals, two feet) on the ground before lifting the other (or others) **2.** to appear after death *[ghosts are said to *walk* in this old house]* **3.** to follow a certain course, way of life, etc. *[let us *walk* in peace]* ☆**4.** *Baseball* to get a walk ☆**5.** *Basketball same as* TRAVEL — *vt.* **1.** to go through, along, over, etc. by walking *[to *walk* the deck]* **2.** to cause (a horse, dog, etc.) to walk, as for exercise **3.** to push (a bicycle, etc.) while walking alongside **4.** to go along with (a person) on a walk *[I'll *walk* you home]* **5.** to bring to a specified state by walking *[to *walk* oneself to exhaustion]* ☆**6.** *Baseball a)* to give a walk to (a batter) *b)* to force (a run) *in* by doing this when the bases are loaded —*n.* **1.** the act of walking **2.** a stroll or hike *[an afternoon *walk*]* **3.** a route taken in walking **4.** a distance to walk *[an hour's *walk* from here]* **5.** the pace of one who walks **6.** a way of walking *[I knew her by her *walk*]* **7.** a particular position in life, area of activity, etc. *[people from all *walks* of life]* **8.** a path set apart for walking *[the park has gravel *walks*]* **9.** an enclosure for grazing or exercising animals ☆**10.** *Baseball* an advancing to first base on four balls (see BALL, *n.* 7) —**walk (all) over** [Colloq.] **1.** to defeat completely **2.** to rule over in a harsh or bullying way — **walk away from** to get ahead of easily —**walk away with 1.** to steal **2.** to win easily —**walk off 1.** to go away, esp. without warning **2.** to get rid of (fat, etc.) by walking —**walk off with 1.** to steal **2.** to win (something), esp. easily —**walk out** ☆to go on strike —☆**walk out on** [Colloq.] to leave; desert; abandon — **walk'ing** *adj., n.*

Note that there are meanings listed for the verb (vi.) and (vt.) form of *walk* and for the noun (n.) form, as well as for idiomatic phrases. Since *walk* is used as a noun in the sentence, concentrate on the noun meanings only. Number seven, "a particular position in life, area of activity, etc.," is the meaning that applies to the sample sentence. This process is a quick, easy way of determining the specific sense of a word that has multiple meanings.

Determine Meanings Use the process outlined on the preceding page and a dictionary to determine the meanings of the italicized words in the sentences below. Write the meaning on the answer line.

1. The bishop's *see* is in Portugal.

   _____

2. The hunter is training his dog to *point* and to retrieve game.

   _____

3. My mother visited a *medium* to see if she could find her missing ring.

   _____

4. That is a very *free* translation of the Spanish song lyrics.

   _____

5. He was poisoned by coal *damp*.

   _____

Number correct _____ (total 5)

Writing Sentences Write a sentence using a different meaning of each of the italicized words in **Determining Meanings.** Try to use some of the more uncommon meanings.

1. *see:* _____

   _____

2. *point:* _____

3. *medium:* _____

4. *free:* _____

   _____

5. *damp:* _____

   _____

6. *crib:* _____

7. *chuck:* _____

8. *down:* _____

9. *iron:* _____

10. *sheet:* _____

Number correct _____ (total 10)

Number correct in Vocab Lab _____ (total 30)

148

UNIT 13

Part A *Target Words and Their Meanings*

1. agency (ā′ jən sē) n.
2. analytical (an′ ə lit′ i k′l) adj.
3. chaos (kā′ äs) n.
4. facility (fə sil′ ə tē) n.
5. fermentation (fur′ mən tā′ shən, -men-) n.
6. forerunner (fôr′ run′ ər) n.
7. formulate (fôr′ myə lāt′) v.
8. inquiry (in′ kwə rē, -kwī-′; in kwīr′ ē) n.
9. isolate (ī′ sə lāt′, is′ ə-) v.
10. mystic (mis′ tik) n., adj.
11. original (ə rij′ ə n'l) adj., n.
12. perceptive (pər sep′ tiv) adj.
13. physiology (fiz′ ē äl′ ə jē) n.
14. precursor (pri kur′ sər) n.
15. rigorous (rig′ ər əs) adj.
16. spirit (spir′ it) n.
17. sublime (sə blīm′) adj.
18. supernatural (soo′ pər nach′ ər əl) adj., n.
19. uncompromising (un käm′ prə mī′ zin) adj.
20. unrestrained (un ri strānd′) adj.

Inferring Meaning from Context

For each sentence write the letter of the word or phrase that is closest to the meaning of the word or words in italics. Use context clues to help you determine the correct answer.

_____ 1. The director of the employment *agency* told the job applicant that his company specialized in helping recent college graduates find work.

a. service b. school c. opportunity d. statistics

_____ 2. She used an *analytical* approach to solve the complex problem, first breaking it down into simpler parts, and then considering each part separately.

a. confusing b. systematic c. impractical d. flawed

_____ 3. The bargain hunters waited patiently in line for the store to open, but once the doors were unlocked, they began pushing and running in all directions, creating total *chaos*.

a. serenity b. creativity c. bankruptcy d. disorder

_____ 4. Members of the new gym are entitled to use all of its *facilities*, including an Olympic pool, basketball courts, a weight room, a quarter-mile running track, a steam room, and a sauna.

a. obligations b. resources c. prerequisites d. skills

_____ 5. Alcohol is produced by the *fermentation* of sugars in grains, a process that changes complex molecules into simpler substances.

a. isolation b. molecular breakdown c. substitution d. production

_____ 6. The hot, humid weather on Wednesday afternoon was the *forerunner* of the violent thunderstorms that struck on Wednesday night.
a. sign   b. cause   c. result   d. model

_____ 7. The speaker tried to *formulate* in logical steps her plan for revitalizing the neighborhood so that the audience could easily follow her reasoning.
a. argue against   b. make fun of   c. express in a systematic way
d. interrupt

_____ 8. *An inquiry* was being conducted to determine who had stolen the social security checks from the post office.
a. A classification   b. A conviction   c. A cause   d. An investigation

_____ 9. The research team is working hard to *isolate* the virus that causes AIDS; but, separating the organism from similar microorganisms is difficult.
a. destroy   b. transform   c. set apart   d. weaken

_____ 10. *Mystics* in the Middle Ages believed that they could have spiritual experiences through supernatural insight rather than by using their senses and intellect.
a. Scholars   b. Teachers   c. People who thought they had extraordinary powers   d. People who lived alone

_____ 11. The *original* plan had been to have the graduation party at the beach, but we had to change plans when the weather became cold and rainy.
a. secondary   b. unanimous   c. new   d. first

_____ 12. The painter was extraordinarily *perceptive*, seeing subtle differences in color, shape, and light that less observant people did not notice.
a. aware   b. critical   c. suspicious   d. forgetful

_____ 13. To gain a better understanding of the *physiology* of intestinal ulcers, some scientists have used computers to simulate the chemical changes that occur during digestion.
a. normal size   b. waste materials   c. mental factors   d. vital processes and function

_____ 14. The Model T Ford, the first mass-produced automobile, was *a precursor of* today's sleek, fast cars.
a. something that prepares the way for   b. a result of   c. a cause of
d. one way of dealing with

_____ 15. The swimming coach insists on *a rigorous* training program for her athletes because she believes that physical discipline is essential for maximum performance.
a. an easygoing   b. an enjoyable   c. an optional   d. a strict

_____ 16. Scholars agree that Fitzgerald's novel *The Great Gatsby* successfully captures the *spirit* of the 1920's, convincingly portraying what life was like during that era.
a. essential quality   b. mental skills   c. patriotism   d. religion

_____ 17. Watching a sunset can be *a sublime* experience.

    a. a forgettable b. an awe-inspiring c. a boring d. a social

_____ 18. The fortuneteller boasted that she could communicate with *supernatural* forces and even told stories about her encounters with ghosts.

    a. underground b. otherworldly c. unhealthy d. wealthy

_____ 19. The trial lasted so long because the opposing lawyers were *uncompromising*; neither was willing to make any concession to the other.

    a. eager to find a middle ground b. talking constantly c. inflexible
    d. underpaid

_____ 20. As the *unrestrained* laughter at Frank's joke echoed throughout the hall, students gathered around to find out what had caused such hilarity.

    a. quiet b. uncontrolled c. brief d. oppressive

Number correct _____ (total 20)

Part B   *Target Words in Reading and Literature*

You should now have a general idea of the meaning of each target word. Examine the shades of meaning these words have in the following excerpt.

Chemistry Versus Alchemy

Charles H. Simpson

The following essay describes the achievements of Jan Baptista van Helmont, a scientist of the seventeenth century, who was a pioneer in the study of gases. Although he was influenced by the unscientific medieval beliefs of his time, he was a careful experimenter, and his contributions laid the groundwork for later significant discoveries about the behavior of gases.

The link between the alchemist[1] and modern chemistry was forged by Jan Baptista van Helmont in the work he did during the early part of the seventeenth century. In the light of today's knowledge, van Helmont appears as a strange mixture of a man; but very likely he was a true product of his times. A chemist, **physiologist**, and physician, he was also a **mystic** and an   5 alchemist. Living in a period that was not far removed from the Middle Ages, his thoughts were influenced both by the past and by the new **spirit** of **inquiry** that was appearing throughout Europe. He believed in the philosopher's stone;[2] yet, he was deeply influenced by the work of William

---

[1] alchemist: a person who practiced alchemy, a form of chemistry studied in the Middle Ages; alchemists tried to change metals such as iron or lead into gold and attempted to find a substance that would keep people young

[2] philosopher's stone: an imaginary stone that alchemists thought would change base metals into gold

Harvey, Galileo, and Francis Bacon.[3] In the years following 1600, he   10
conducted a medical practice in Vilvorde, near Brussels, chiefly in the service
of the poor.

In the course of his chemical researches he became aware of the
existence of gases that were distinct from atmospheric air. He observed that
the gas given off by burning charcoal was the same as that produced in the   15
course of **fermentation** and noted that it differed subtly from the atmosphere.
He found that the same gas was present in mineral springs and in mines and
caverns, and saw that it was produced by the action of acids on chalk. He
called it "gas sylvestre," wild (or **unrestrained**) gas. He was the first to use
the term *gas*. In fact, he invented the word, deriving it from the Greek **chaos.**   20
He used *chaos* in connection with air rather than in its **original** meaning of
primordial[4] matter.

Van Helmont's wild gas, which he described correctly, was carbon dioxide.
Yet he cannot be regarded as the discoverer of carbon dioxide because he
had no means of collecting and keeping it, no **analytical facilities**, no method   25
of identifying it.

Though he lacked techniques for analysis, van Helmont's curiosity led him
to recognize many different gases. He was probably the first to observe
chlorine as a gas when he warmed Aqua Regia (a mixture of nitric and
hydrochloric acids); he burned sulfur to produce sulfur dioxide; and he   30
prepared nitric oxide nearly one hundred and fifty years before Priestley[5]
isolated it and studied its properties. All of these are included in van
Helmont's catalog of gases, as wild gas, windy gas (air), fat gas, dry or
sublimed gas. He used the term *gas* to describe any aeriform[6] substance

---

[3] Harvey, Galileo, Bacon: legendary figures in the history of science; Harvey discovered the
circulation of blood in the human body, Galileo proved Copernicus's theory that the earth and
the other planets revolve around the sun, and Bacon provided the philosophical basis for the
scientific method

[4] primordial: existing from the beginning; primitive

[5] Joseph Priestley: an eighteenth-centruy English scientist and theologian who discovered
oxygen.

[6] aeriform: airlike

lacking definite shape or volume and capable of infinite expansion.   35

Van Helmont was the first to show scientifically the material character of gases and their variety. He was, in truth, the **forerunner** of the eighteenth-century pneumatic[7] chemists. He was a **perceptive** observer and a careful experimenter. But he had a tendency to look backward instead of forward.   40

His roots were deep in alchemy, and he longed to interpret his scientific experience in terms of the past and as the workings of **supernatural agencies**. Perhaps, because he was more interested in medicine than in chemistry, he found it easier to look for old nostrums[8] than to seek out the **rigorous, uncompromising** explanations of science. He believed that water   45 was the chief, if not the only, constituent of all matter (a theory propounded by Thales[9] in 645 B.C.); yet, he **formulated** a clinical theory of digestion in the human body and is generally regarded as the **precursor** of the iatrochemical (healing chemicals) school of medicine.

---

[7] pneumatic: dealing with gases
[8] nostrums: oversimplified explanations, solutions, or cures
[9] Thales of Miletus: a sixth-century Greek philosopher who attempted to find natural, rather than supernatural explanations for natural phenomena

Refining Your Understanding

For each of the following items, consider how the target word is used in the passage. Write the letter of the word or phrase that best completes each sentence.

_____ 1. Van Helmont "appears as a strange mixture of a man" to us today because he was both a *mystic* (line 5) and a   a. scientist   b. moralist   c. philosopher.

_____ 2. When the author uses the phrase "the new *spirit* of inquiry" (lines 7–8), the meaning of *spirit* he probably intends is   a. soul   b. principle or attitude   c. ghost.

_____ 3. When the author says that van Helmont had "no *analytical facilities*" (line 25), he is referring to the scientist's   a. lack of mental ability   b. careless experimental methods   c. lack of laboratory techniques and equipment.

_____ 4. Van Helmont wanted to explain his scientific observations "as the workings of *supernatural agencies*" (lines 42–43) because   a. he lacked curiosity   b. he was a careless observer   c. he believed that there was a religious explanation for every natural event.

_____ 5. As "the *precursor* of the iatrochemical . . . school of medicine" (lines 48–49), van Helmont helped to   a. synthesize religion and science   b. pave the way for modern medicine   c. resist scientific explanations of human digestion.

Number correct _____ (total 5)

Part C   *Ways to Make New Words Your Own*

This section presents a variety of activities reinforcing the target words.

Using Language and Thinking Skills

True-False   Decide whether each statement is true or false. Write **T** for True and **F** for False.

_____ 1. A *perceptive* person notices significant details in his or her surroundings.

_____ 2. *Physiology* is the study of the human mind and emotions.

_____ 3. If you were asked to *formulate* a statement about the causes of the Great Depression, you would try to express your ideas in a systematic way.

_____ 4. An *uncompromising* person often yields to other people's opinions.

_____ 5. Someone with an *analytical* mind would be likely to study a problem by breaking it down into separate parts.

_____ 6. A *mystic* denies the importance of religious experience.

_____ 7. A boring or routine task can best be described as *sublime*.

_____ 8. If a police official began an *inquiry* into a recent crime, you could safely assume that the criminal had been caught and the case was closed.

_____ 9. Playing a *rigorous* game of tennis can be a good workout.

_____ 10. Someone who lives alone in a remote area would not feel *isolated*.

Number correct _____ (total 10)

Finding the Unrelated Word   Write the letter of the word that is not related in meaning to the other words in the set.

_____ 1. a. supernatural   b. natural   c. worldly   d. normal

_____ 2. a. serenity   b. calmness   c. chaos   d. tranquility

_____ 3. a. precursor   b. personification   c. herald   d. forerunner

_____ 4. a. original   b. primary   c. authoritative   d. initial

_____ 5. a. biology   b. physiology   c. anatomy   d. skeleton

_____ 6. a. uncontrolled   b. discreet   c. immoderate   d. unrestrained

_____ 7. a. sublime   b. ongoing   c. incessant   d. continual

_____ 8. a. socialize   b. integrate   c. isolate   d. associate

_____ 9. a. formulate   b. draw up   c. state   d. change

_____ 10. a. means   b. agency   c. instrument   d. goal

Number correct _____ (total 10)

154

Understanding Multiple Meanings Each box in this exercise contains a boldfaced word with its various definitions. Read the definitions and then the sentences that use the word. Write the letter of the definition that applies to each sentence. The definitions may be used more than once.

---

spirit
a. the life principle or soul (n.)
b. a supernatural being, such as a ghost, an angel, or a demon (n.)
c. an essential principle, a predominant characteristic, a mood, an attitude, or a quality (n.)
d. enthusiasm and loyalty (n.)
e. courage, vigor, or determination (n.)

_____ 1. Canada gave the famine-stricken country several shiploads of grain in a *spirit* of good will and humanitarian cooperation.

_____ 2. Some people refused to approach the old house because of rumors that a *spirit* inhabited it.

_____ 3. The ancient Greek philosophers defined the human *spirit* as an intangible and immortal source of life.

_____ 4. The cheerleaders were chosen for their gymnastic ability and school *spirit*.

_____ 5. The coach told us that the game with the conference champions would be a true test of our *spirit*.

---

facility
a. the ease of doing something (n.)
b. a skill or ability (n.)
c. a building or special room in which some activity can be done (n.)
d. the means by which something can be accomplished (n.)

_____ 6. May Shin has a special *facility* for playing the piano.

_____ 7. Because the Soviet Union has poor transportation *facilities*, some of its farm produce never reaches the market.

_____ 8. The old sewage-disposal building was torn down to make room for a new *facility*.

_____ 9. The *facility* with which Jennifer recited the entire poem was incredible.

_____ 10. A new laundry *facility* has been added to our apartment complex.

Number correct _____ (total 10)

155

Practicing for Standardized Tests

Analogies Write the letter of the word pair that best expresses a relationship similar to that expressed in the original pair.

_____ 1. FORERUNNER : PRECURSOR :: (A) enigma : mystery (B) birth : life (C) facility : difficulty (D) purchase : sale (E) forehand : backhand

_____ 2. ALCOHOL : FERMENTATION :: (A) velocity : speed (B) rust : oxidation (C) ruin : restoration (D) hydrogen : water (E) wood : fire

_____ 3. DETECTIVE : PERCEPTIVE :: (A) author : handy (B) scholar : studious (C) teacher : wealthy (D) farmer : punctual (E) tyrant : compassionate

_____ 4. ENTHUSIASM : SPIRIT :: (A) painting : watercolor (B) inquiry : question (C) tributary : shore (D) voter : ballot (E) oats : grain

_____ 5. ORDERLY : CHAOS :: (A) courageous : hero (B) loyal : patriot (C) original : origin (D) perceptive : observer (E) oppressive : freedom

_____ 6. PHYSIOLOGY : SCIENCE :: (A) despot : tyranny (B) astronomy : astrology (C) psychology : mind (D) democracy : government (E) doctor : nurse

_____ 7. RESPONSE : INQUIRY :: (A) discovery : search (B) heir : descendant (C) declaration : allegation (D) decision : choice (E) examination : test

_____ 8. FORMULATE : PLAN :: (A) organize : party (B) isolate : seclusion (C) irritate : irritation (D) imitate : mimicry (E) undulate : wave

_____ 9. RIGOROUS : HARSH :: (A) trusting : cynical (B) uncompromising : easygoing (C) analytical : illogical (D) unrestrained : uninhibited (E) cooperative : competitive

_____ 10. ISOLATE : UNITE :: (A) remember : recall (B) love : like (C) irritate : soothe (D) teach : tutor (E) plant : sow

Number correct _____ (total 10)

Word's Worth: chaos

Chaos comes from the Greek word _khaos_, which means "gulf," "abyss," or "empty space." In Greek mythology, Chaos was a state of formless confusion, an eternally dark and utterly empty space that existed before there were gods and before the universe itself came into being. Chaos gave birth to two children, Erebus (Darkness) and Nyx (Night). Nyx, in turn, gave birth to Death, War, Famine, and other dreadful "grandchildren" of Chaos.
However, Chaos was not a totally negative power. Erebus mysteriously gave birth to Gaea (Earth) and Eros (Love), two creative forces that ultimately produced order, harmony, and humanity itself.

Spelling and Wordplay

Crossword Puzzle Read each clue to determine what word will fit in the corresponding squares. There are several target words in the puzzle.

ACROSS

1. A process of molecular conversion that can produce alcohol or curdle milk
11. Using reason to break something down into its parts
12. A household pet
13. Colloq. *advertisement*
15. Frozen water
16. Majestic
18. Abbr. *Lieutenant*
19. Slang *Hello*
20. Third person singular of *to be*
21. To set apart
25. Spanish for *yes*
26. Systematic study
28. Contraction of *I should*
29. Objective case of *I*
30. An investigation
33. The soul
35. A series of names or words
37. 2,000 lbs.
39. To be excessively or foolishly fond of
40. Any physical substance
43. To trudge
44. Agent's place of business

DOWN

1. Skill
2. Passes a bill into law
3. To estimate the value of
4. Abbr. *Middle Latin*
5. Organ of sight
6. Abbr. *New Testament*
7. Abbr. *Titanium*
8. Abbr. *Alternating Current*
9. Opposite of *Heads*
10. Abbr. *Illinois*
13. First person singular of *to be*
14. To trace from or to a source
16. A piece of land used for a particular purpose
17. Prefix meaning "having two" or "twice"
19. Possesses
22. First; earliest
23. Past tense of *to lead*
24. Abbr. *Each*
27. A youngster
29. A person interested in spiritual matters
30. Roman numeral two
31. Abbr. *Northern Territory*
32. ___ ___ ___ Grande River
33. Abbr. *State*
34. Stately display of splendor
36. Abbr. *Tellurium*
38. Abbr. *Equal Rights Amendment*
41. Toward
42. Abbr. *Touchdown*

Part D Related Words

A number of words are closely related to the target words you have studied. Use your knowledge of the target words and of word parts to determine the meanings of these words.

1. agent (ā′ jənt) n.	12. mystify (mis′ tə fī′) v.
2. analyze (an′ ə līz′) v.	13. mystique (mis tēk′) n.
3. chaotic (kā ät′ ik) adj.	14. origin (ôr′ ə jin, är′-) n.
4. compromise (käm′ prə mīz′) n., v.	15. originate (ə rij′ ə nāt′) v.
5. facilitate (fə sil′ ə tāt′) v.	16. perception (per sep′ shən) n.
6. formula (fôr′ myə lə) n.	17. restrain (ri strān′) v.
7. inquire (in kwīr′) v.	18. restraint (ri strānt′) n.
8. isolation (ī′ sə lā′ shən, is′ ə-) n.	19. rigor (rig′ ər) n.
9. mysterious (mis tir′ ē əs) adj.	20. self-restraint (self ri strānt′) n.
10. mystery (mis′ tə rē, -trē) n.	21. spiritual (spir′ i chōō wəl, -chōōl) adj. n.
11. mysticism (mis′ tə siz′m) n.	22. sublimate (sub′ lə māt′) v.

Understanding Related Words

Verb Match Match each verb in the list below with its definition. Write the letter of the matching word in the blank. Use your dictionary if necessary.

_____ 1. to make easier		a. analyze
_____ 2. to adjust by mutual concession		b. compromise
_____ 3. to divert; to express an impulse in another way		c. facilitate
_____ 4. to perplex or bewilder		d. formulate
_____ 5. to examine critically by separating into elements		e. inquire
_____ 6. to hold back		f. isolate
_____ 7. to begin or initiate		g. mystify
_____ 8. to ask about or search into		h. originate
_____ 9. to plan in an orderly way		i. restrain
_____ 10. to separate from others		j. sublimate

Number correct _____ (total 10)

Turn to **The Letter g** on page 219 of the **Spelling Handbook**. Read the rule and complete the exercise provided.

Analyzing Word Parts

The Latin Suffix *-ate* The target words *formulate* and *isolate* and the related words *facilitate, originate,* and *sublimate* include the Latin suffix *-ate*, meaning "to make." These words and others that share the *-ate* suffix are listed below, along with the meanings of their roots.

Word	Root	Meaning
aerate	*aer*	air
fabricate	*fabrica*	product
facilitate	*facilis*	to make
formulate	*forma*	form
graduate	*gradus*	grade
isolate	*insula*	island
liberate	*liber*	free
originate	*oriri*	to arise
punctuate	*punctus*	a point
sublimate	*sublimare*	to elevate

In the blank write the word from the first column above that best completes each of the following sentences. Use a dictionary to check your work.

_____ 1. Hospital policy requires that we _?_ any patient who has a contagious disease.

_____ 2. The commercial claims that the mineral waters _?_ in a pure underground spring.

_____ 3. The landscaper said that we should _?_ the soil because oxygen is necessary for a healthy lawn.

_____ 4. If you _?_ your collection jar in standard units, you can measure the amount of rainfall received in your area.

_____ 5. The revolutionary army hopes to _?_ its jailed leaders.

_____ 6. A good writer must know not only how to spell words and construct and _?_ sentences, but he or she also must have worthwhile ideas to express.

_____ 7. The construction company will _?_ temporary shelters for the people left homeless by the earthquake.

_____ 8. Our teacher said that we should _?_ our answers carefully before raising our hands to speak.

_____ 9. The new procedures for collecting glass, cans, and newspapers will _?_ recycling in our community.

_____ 10. As children become socialized, they learn to _?_ many of their selfish impulses and become contributing members of a group.

Number correct _____ (total 10)

Number correct in Unit _____ (total 85)

159

The Last Word

Writing

Perceptive people notice details and relationships that less observant people miss. At times you might have wished that certain people were less perceptive because it seemed that they could almost read your mind. However, perception is a skill and, like any other skill, it can be developed. A good way to improve your perceptive ability is to practice focusing your attention closely and carefully on the world around you. As an introductory exercise, pick an object in your classroom, such as the top of your desk, the bulletin board, the ceiling, your hand, or the back of the head of the student sitting in front of you. Observe that object as if you were seeing it for the first time, and write a two- or three-paragraph description that does not name the object but paints such a vivid visual image that the reader will recognize it immediately.

Speaking

Describe a *rigorous* experience you have had, an event that pushed you to your limit. The experience can be physical—such as competing in a fifty-mile bike race on a scorching summer day—or mental—such as taking an extremely difficult math test. Did this experience motivate you to perform better than you expected, or did you fail to meet the challenge? Discuss what you learned from undergoing this experience and how you might react differently the next time.

Group Discussion

Because we must interact with other people in almost every situation and activity in life, we often cannot do things our own way. Instead, we must find a *compromise*, a solution that is acceptable to everyone involved. Divide the class into small groups to discuss the following questions about compromise. Then share your group's views with the class.

1. How do you work out a compromise? Does the strongest or most opinionated person always get his or her way? Why or why not?
2. Are there situations in which you should not compromise, regardless of what other people think? If so, give an example of such a situation.
3. Are good leaders effective because they impose their will on other people or because they are good compromisers? Explain your answer.

UNIT 14

Part A *Target Words and Their Meanings*

1. accessibility (ak ses′ə bil′ə tē) n.
2. bewilderment (bi wil′dər mənt) n.
3. concede (kən sēd′) v.
4. crystallize (kris′ tə līz′) v.
5. erode (i rōd′) v.
6. ethnic (eth′nik) adj.
7. heritage (her′ə tij) n.
8. homogeneity (hō′mə jə nē′ə tē) n.
9. impose (im pōz′) v.
10. invalid (in val′ id) adj. (in′ və lid) n.
11. liberation (lib′ə rā′shən) n.
12. metaphor (met′ə fôr′, -fər) n.
13. mutable (myōōt′ə b'l) adj.
14. phenomenon (fi näm′ə nän′, -nən) n.
15. prejudicial (prej′ə dish′əl) adj.
16. quota (kwō′tə) n.
17. repression (ri presh′ən) n.
18. specter (spek′tər) n.
19. taunt (tônt, tänt) v., n.
20. wary (wer′ē) adj.

Inferring Meaning from Context

For each sentence write the letter of the word or phrase that is closest to the meaning of the word or words in italics. Use context clues to help you.

_____ 1. The Brisbane Hotel, which is centrally located, has a steady business because of its *accessibility to* travelers.

a. availability to   b. importance to   c. historical significance to
d. appearance for

_____ 2. The instructional manual for the new computer software created *bewilderment* because no one could make sense of the directions.

a. confusion   b. satisfaction   c. terror   d. confidence

_____ 3. Everyone expected the candidate to *concede* defeat after early election returns showed that victory was not possible.

a. deny   b. avoid   c. fight   d. acknowledge

_____ 4. The brutal actions of the dictator forced the reformers to *crystallize* their opposition, and soon protest marches became common.

a. forget about   b. regret   c. deny   d. give a definite form to

_____ 5. The farmer planted trees along the hillside to ensure that the soil would not *erode*; the tree roots kept the soil from being washed away by rains.

a. become acidic   b. wear away   c. become diseased   d. get wet

_____ 6. The Cultural Diversity Festival featured music and dance from different countries, as well as a rich variety of *ethnic* foods, including Mexican, Caribbean, Polish, and Greek dishes.

a. original   b. fattening   c. donated   d. national

_____ 7. The Constitution and the Declaration of Independence are priceless documents of our national *heritage*; they have enriched America.

a. boundaries   b. conflicts   c. estate   d. tradition

_____ 8. Although young adults take pride in their individuality, their fashions show a remarkable *homogeneity*; blue jeans, for example, have become a uniform.

a. uniqueness   b. color   c. sameness   d. freshness

_____ 9. The government will *impose* heavy taxes on some foreign goods coming into this country, raising the prices of those items.

a. place   b. cancel   c. limit   d. release

_____ 10. Any claim that the world is flat is obviously *invalid*; the claim contradicts all evidence, including photographs of the earth from outer space.

a. the product of a sick mind   b. false   c. an intentional lie   d. true

_____ 11. The U.S. Embassy continued negotiations with the terrorists in order to secure the *liberation* of the hostages who were held captive in Beirut.

a. imprisonment   b. silence   c. freedom   d. respect

_____ 12. When Joan complained to her boss that she was tired of being a slave to her job, the boss did not appreciate her *metaphor* and sarcastically remarked that real slaves worked much harder than she did.

a. appearance   b. comparison   c. work habits   d. closed-mindedness

_____ 13. The human species changes little from generation to generation; human culture, however, is quite *mutable*, as evidenced by the altered roles of women in the last two decades.

a. interesting   b. formidable   c. changeable   d. unchanging

_____ 14. Michael Jordan is a *phenomenon* among basketball players; such a talented athlete might appear only once in a generation.

a. funny person   b. rare happening   c. spokesman   d. thoughtful person

_____ 15. The lawyer for the defense argued that the newspaper and television reports about the grisly crime had created a *prejudicial* atmosphere. The townspeople had already decided that the defendant was guilty.

a. fair-minded   b. biased   c. fearful   d. degrading

_____ 16. The number of immigrants who can be legally admitted to the United States is determined by a *quota*. Each country is assigned a fixed number of people who may migrate to our country.

a. lottery   b. measurement of income   c. special allotment   d. system of testing

_____ 17. Many governments use the military as a means of *repression*. The military subdues opposition, inhibits free speech, and denies civil liberties.

a. glorifying the government   b. protecting citizen freedoms   c. civil defense   d. restraining by force

_____ 18. The movie chillingly portrayed the children's terrifying encounter with the *specter* by using special effects that made the ghost seem real.

a. vivid memories   b. alien creature   c. spirit   d. madman

_____ 19. A small group of hometown spectators *taunted* the referees until the insults became so disruptive that the home team was penalized.

a. ignored   b. physically abused   c. ridiculed   d. cheered for

_____ 20. Because they are unsure of whom to trust, children who are physically abused often become *wary of* all adults.

a. friendly with   b. fearless with   c. aware of   d. suspicious of

Number correct _____ (total 20)

Part B   Target Words in Reading and Literature

You should now have a general idea of the meaning of each target word. Refine your understanding by examining the shades of meaning these words have in the following excerpt.

Climbing All Over the Family Trees

Stefan Kanfer

In the spring of 1977, the television series "Roots" presented a history of blacks in Africa and America—and stimulated interest by blacks and nonblacks alike in searching for their pasts. In the following essay, from Time *magazine, the writer offers reasons for this interest in ancestors and in the past.*

Democracy makes every man forget his ancestors. So thought de Tocqueville, the observer who for more than a century trapped the American character in his shrewd *apercus*[1] That character is too **mutable** to stay contained. Today it is frantically climbing family trees. After Haley's comet[2], not only blacks but all **ethnic** groups saw themselves whole, traceable across oceans and centuries to   5
the most remote ancestral village.

But the hunt for origins has been building for a decade. Leery of a **homogeneity** that could suffocate the individual, **wary** of **quota** systems that specified "Black, Hispanic, Other," Americans began to perceive themselves beyond the melting pot. They met their fears with a fever of ethnicity and a   10
quest for forgotten countries and families.

The recent "white roots" **phenomenon** is a reversal of U.S. tradition. In other periods immigration was the sincerest form of flattery. Many of the populations that came to the U.S. were in flight from their past. To them the concept of a new world was no **metaphor**: for the first time they were free of regal decrees and   15

---
[1] apercus: French for *insight*

[2] Haley's comet: The writer is referring to the popularity of the television series *Roots,* based on the book by Alex Haley. The phrase alludes to Halley's comet, a famous comet that appears in the sky approximately every seventy-five years.

military **repression**, released from the **specters** of famine and caste. In fact, the importance of lineage[3] had been **eroding** since the Middle Ages. Rising middle classes demanded recognition of performance, not tradition. The Industrial Revolution identified the worker, like his machinery, with the job. Voltaire **crystallized** the sentiments of the *arrivistes*[4]: "Who serves his country well has no need of ancestors." His was a romantic ideal, however; only in America were immigrants truly unhooked from history. In his classic study *The Uprooted*, Oscar Handlin observed: "The immigrants could not **impose** their own ways upon society; but neither were they constrained to conform to those already established. To a significant degree, the newest Americans had a wide realm of choice."

The realm came at painful cost. Immigrants **conceded** more than the **accessibility** of the old familiar places and persons. They lost an unrecoverable currency[5]: their language. **Prejudicial taunts** drove immigrant children to absorb

20

25

---

[3] lineage: direct descent from an ancestor
[4] arrivistes: French for *social climbers*
[5] currency: used here as a metaphor—The writer seems to be comparing the loss of one's language to losing money, i.e., currency.

the style and speech of Americans. Their elders were caught between 30
memories of the land they had left and **bewilderment** at a nation whose
mainstream they could not enter.

Now all that is altering. Americans have become like those adoptees who
demanded the long-denied knowledge of **heritage**. Families anxious for
stability and identity reach out for the past with bloodlines and charts. 35
Pedigrees[6] as long as the Duke of Norfolk's are abruptly trotted out by
commoners. What was **invalid** a generation ago is invaluable today. Says
Michael Arlen, who recovered his Armenian heritage in *Passage to Ararat*:
"There is a good chance now the clearheaded, impatient young will set their
fathers free." 40

However, the act of **liberation** may be difficult. The standard appurtenances[7]
of modern life—birth and death certificates, tax records—are sometimes
unrecoverable. Family trees have a tendency to run down to the soil.

---

[6] pedigree: family tree or record of ancestry
[7] appurtenance: something added to a more important thing; adjunct

Refining Your Understanding

For each of the following items, consider how the target word is used in the
passage. Write the letter of the word or phrase that best completes each sentence.

_____ 1. According to the author, Americans are now "leery of . . . *homogeneity*"
(lines 7–8) because they   a. no longer believe in the American ideals of
freedom and equality   b. are afraid that they might lose their
individuality   c. think they are superior to everyone else.

_____ 2. Kanfer states that for the immigrants the "new world was no *metaphor*"
(line 15) because the new world   a. provided many opportunities for a
better life   b. lost its appeal after they arrived   c. encouraged interest
in family histories.

_____ 3. When the author speaks of "the *specters* of famine and caste" (line 16)
he is referring to   a. visions of ghosts induced by hunger   b. the dread
of famine and social castes   c. warnings of what might happen in
America.

_____ 4. When the author says that "immigrants *conceded* more than the
accessibility of the old familiar places and persons," (lines 27–28) he
means that the immigrants   a. gave up a great deal in coming to this
country   b. admitted that choosing to immigrate had been a mistake
c. acknowledged that they were inferior to other Americans.

_____ 5. Examples of *"prejudicial taunts"* (line 29) would be   a. ethnic songs on
the radio   b. ridicule directed at an ethnic group   c. ethnic foods
without English names.

Number correct _____ (total 5)

Part C Ways to Make New Words Your Own

This section presents a variety of reinforcement activities that will help you make these words part of your permanent vocabulary.

Using Language and Thinking Skills

Finding the Unrelated Word Write the letter of the word that is not related in meaning to other words in the set.

_____ 1. a. constant b. changeable c. variable d. mutable

_____ 2. a. bewilderment b. confusion c. clarity d. perplexity

_____ 3. a. mock b. taunt c. respect d. deride

_____ 4. a. standard b. phenomenon c. rarity d. exception

_____ 5. a. wary b. cautious c. trusting d. suspicious

_____ 6. a. approachability b. remoteness c. availability d. accessibility

_____ 7. a. restraining b. repression c. encouragement d. silencing

_____ 8. a. waste b. endure c. disintegrate d. erode

_____ 9. a. truthful b. untrue c. invalid d. illogical

_____ 10. a. dissimilarity b. variety c. mixture d. homogeneity

_____ 11. a. impose b. force c. invite d. command

_____ 12. a. ration b. allotment c. quota d. limitlessness

_____ 13. a. shape b. scatter c. form d. crystallize

_____ 14. a. rootlessness b. legacy c. tradition d. heritage

_____ 15. a. acknowledge b. deny c. concede d. admit

Number correct _____ (total 15)

Practicing for Standardized Tests

Analogies Write the letter of the word pair that best expresses a relationship similar to that expressed in the original pair.

_____ 1. SPECTER : FEAR :: (A) poetry : prose (B) repression : tyranny (C) injury : pain (D) comparison : metaphor (E) hostility : tolerance

_____ 2. LIBERATION : EMANCIPATION :: (A) enigma : mystery (B) leader : despot (C) note : paper (D) game : golf (E) medicine : prescription

_____ 3. HOMOGENEITY : HETEROGENEITY :: (A) quota : limit (B) introvert : extrovert (C) theory : proof (D) uniform : badge (E) classic : class

_____ 4. LAND : ERODE ::   (A) river : swim   (B) steel : brace   (C) cake : frost
(D) iron : rust   (E) subdivision : construct

_____ 5. ETHNIC : ETHNICITY ::   (A) antagonistic : indifference   (B) true :
probability   (C) cynical : trust   (D) passive : activity   (E) hostile :
hostility

_____ 6. BULLY : TAUNT ::   (A) cynic : idealize   (B) tyrant : pacify
(C) scientist : experiment   (D) patient : nurse   (E) door : lock

_____ 7. PREJUDICIAL : UNBIASED ::   (A) mindless : ignorant   (B) mutable :
changeable   (C) dynamic : lethargic   (D) insincere : pretentious
(E) hostile : wary

_____ 8. HERITAGE : INHERIT ::   (A) idol : idolize   (B) person : characterize
(C) untruth : invalidate   (D) court : legalize   (E) alien : immigrate

_____ 9. IMPOSE : TAX ::   (A) enforce : regulation   (B) taunt : abuse
(C) validate : dilemma   (D) revolt : law   (E) isolate : isolation

_____ 10. POET : METAPHOR ::   (A) puzzle : enigma   (B) artist : color
(C) river : stream   (D) athlete : sport   (E) cup : water

Number correct _____ (total 10)

Spelling and Wordplay

Word Maze Find and circle each target word in this maze.

E	K	S	B	L	F	A	M	E	T	A	P	H	O	R	accessibility
B	N	E	I	M	P	O	S	E	W	A	R	Y	C	E	bewilderment
E	O	Z	N	M	R	E	M	O	T	E	T	T	P	T	concede
W	I	I	V	U	M	Z	A	I	N	I	P	I	H	C	crystallize
I	S	L	A	T	R	I	L	P	L	T	R	E	E	E	erode
L	S	L	L	A	Q	M	G	I	E	N	E	N	N	P	ethnic
D	E	A	I	B	C	U	B	R	O	U	J	E	O	S	heritage
E	R	T	D	L	Q	I	O	M	A	A	U	G	M	B	homogeneity
R	P	S	H	E	S	D	N	T	A	T	D	O	E	G	impose
M	E	Y	Y	S	E	R	O	H	A	X	I	M	N	T	invalid
E	R	R	E	M	O	S	E	F	T	L	C	O	O	W	liberation
N	J	C	O	N	D	E	C	E	N	E	I	H	N	D	metaphor
T	C	J	V	X	T	H	E	R	I	T	A	G	E	J	mutable
A	I	N	O	I	T	A	R	E	B	I	L	U	V	M	phenomenon
D	C	O	N	C	E	D	E	O	N	E	K	U	H	C	prejudicial

accessibility
bewilderment
concede
crystallize
erode
ethnic
heritage
homogeneity
impose
invalid
liberation
metaphor
mutable
phenomenon
prejudicial
quota
repression
specter
taunt
wary

Part D   Related Words

A number of words are closely related to the target words you have studied. Use your knowledge of the target words and of word parts to determine the meanings of these words. (For information about word parts analysis, see pages 6–12.)

1. accede (ak sēd′) v.
2. access (ak′ses) n.
3. accessible (ak ses′ə b′l) adj.
4. bewilder (bi wil′dər) v.
5. crystal (kris′t′l) adj., n.
6. erosion (i rō′zhən) n.
7. heterogeneous (het′ər ə jē′nē əs, het′rə-; -jēn′yəs) adj.
8. homogeneous (hō′mə jē′nē əs, häm′ə-) adj.
9. immutable (i myōōt′ə b′l) adj.
10. imposition (im′pə zish′ən) n.
11. inaccessible (in′ək ses′ə b′l) adj.
12. inherit (in her′it) v.
13. inheritance (in her′it əns) n.
14. invalidate (in val′ə dāt′) v.
15. liberate (lib′ə rāt′) v.
16. metaphorical (met′ə fôr′i k′l) adj.
17. mutation (myōō tā′shən) n.
18. mutual (myōō′choo wəl) adj.
19. phenomenal (fi näm′ə n′l) adj.
20. repress (ri pres′) v.
21. spectral (spek′trəl) adj.
22. valid (val′id) adj.

Turn to **The Prefix ex-** on page 206 and **The Prefix in-** on page 207 of the **Spelling Handbook**. Read the rules and complete the exercises provided.

Understanding Related Words

Matching Ideas Each of the words listed below applies to one of the situations that follow. In the blank write the word that best describes the situation.

accede	erosion	immutable	inheritance	phenomenal
bewilder	heterogeneous	imposition	liberate	valid

_____ 1. From his beach house, Mr. Carson can see the surf wearing away the shoreline.

_____ 2. The football coach took great pride in his ability to create plays that left the opposition in hopeless confusion.

_____ 3. Upon the death of her grandparents, Karla will become the owner of their bungalow.

_____ 4. The summer camp has children of all ages, races, and economic backgrounds.

_____ 5. Because the robber was armed and dangerous, the bank teller gave in to her demand for money.

_____ 6. Whenever my cousin's family stays overnight at our house, my two brothers and I have to sleep on the floor.

_____ 7. The private school's dress code cannot be changed; its rules will hold as long as the current principal remains.

_____ 8. Current photos laminated onto bus passes ensure that the passes are being used by the proper owner.

_____ 9. When Allied troops marched triumphantly into Paris, the French citizens celebrated their release from Nazi oppression.

_____ 10. When Mount St. Helens exploded, it spread volcanic ash all over the Pacific Northwest.

Number correct _____ (total 10)

True-False Decide whether each statement is true or false. Write **T** for True and **F** for False.

_____ 1. In a community that is known for its _homogeneous_ population, you would expect to find a diverse mixture of people.

_____ 2. If a species has undergone a _mutation_, the new species will be no different than its ancestors.

_____ 3. A good debater will present solid evidence to _invalidate_ his or her own position.

_____ 4. When you _repress_ a laugh, you hold it back.

_____ 5. If you were dependent on a wheelchair, you would find that buildings without ramps are often _inaccessible_.

Number correct _____ (total 5)

Analyzing Word Parts

The Latin Root _liber_ _Libere_ is a Latin adverb meaning "freely," "frankly," or "like a free man." It comes from the Latin verb _liber,_ which means "free." The five English words listed below are all derived from the root _liber._ Match each word with the appropriate definition.

_____ 1. liberator   a. giving freely; tolerant of views differing from one's own

_____ 2. liberal   b. an African country founded by freed slaves from the United States

_____ 3. liberalize   c. a person who frees an individual or a group from an enemy or from tyranny

_____ 4. Liberia   d. a person who advocates unrestricted civil rights

_____ 5. libertarian   e. to reduce or eliminate restrictions

Number correct _____ (total 5)

Number correct in Unit _____ (total 70)

The Last Word

Writing

Sometimes a *taunt* can be good fun. Two friends, for example, may taunt each other without meaning any harm. At other times, however, a taunt may be mean-spirited and even hateful. Use examples from your own experience to describe the difference between a friendly taunt and a mean taunt.

Speaking

Most of us have heard good ghost stories, perhaps told while sitting around a campfire on a moonless summer night. Share your favorite story of a ghost, or *specter*—or create your own spine-tingling tale.

Group Discussion

Immigration in the United States is based on a *quota* system, which limits the number of immigrants that may come to the United States from any one country. Some people criticize the quota system and argue that we should have an "open-door" policy, allowing anyone to enter our country. Try to find out more information about our *quota* system and the open-door alternative. Then discuss whether quotas should be maintained, altered, or abolished altogether.

UNIT 15

Part A Target Words and Their Meanings

1. allot (ə lät′) v.
2. baffle (baf′ ′l) v.
3. cower (kou′ ər) v.
4. disadvantaged (dis′ əd van′ tijd) adj.
5. dismiss (dis mis′) v.
6. elaborate (i lab′ ər it) adj. (i lab′ ə rāt′) v.
7. enduring (in door′ iŋ) adj.
8. entice (in tīs′) v.
9. functional (fuŋk′ shən əl) adj.
10. illiterate (i lit′ ər it) adj.
11. intellectual (in′ t′l ek′ choo wəl) adj., n.
12. introvert (in′ trə vʉrt′) v., n.
13. laborious (lə bôr′ ē əs) adj.
14. mentor (men′ tər) n.
15. optimistic (äp′ tə mis′ tik) adj.
16. prospect (präs′ pekt) n., v.
17. reform (ri fôrm′) v., n.
18. spontaneity (spän′ tə nē′ ə tē) n.
19. substantive (sub′ stən tiv) adj.
20. summarily (sə mer′ ə lē) adv.

Inferring Meaning from Context

For each sentence write the letter of the word or phrase that is closest to the meaning of the word or words in italics. Use context clues to help you determine the correct answer. (For information about how context helps you understand vocabulary, see pages 1–5.)

_____ 1. Ms. Tabor *allotted* four weeks for us to complete our science projects, but several of us were finished in two weeks.
   a. rejected b. worked c. condensed d. provided

_____ 2. Roy C. Sullivan must have been *baffled* by his resistance to lightning; although most people who are struck by lightning are killed, he was struck seven times—and survived!
   a. unconcerned b. angered c. puzzled d. unconvinced

_____ 3. The terrifying roar made even Leo, the powerful lion, *cower* in a corner.
   a. strut b. cringe from fear c. relax d. fall asleep

_____ 4. Eliza thought that she was *disadvantaged* because she was an only child and had to spend much of her time alone.
   a. unfortunate b. lucky c. popular d. distinguished

_____ 5. The judge *dismissed* the bribery charges, suggesting that they had been made up by people who were prejudiced against the defendant.
   a. increased b. rejected c. supported d. misunderstood

_____ 6. Brian's explanation of how evaporation takes place was very *elaborate*; he explained every aspect of the process completely.
   a. brief b. alien c. limited d. detailed

171

_____ 7. Novelist Laura Ingalls Wilder believed that only one kind of happiness was worth seeking because it was *enduring*—"love and kindness and helping each other and just plain being good."
a. legal   b. temporary   c. impossible to achieve   d. lasting

_____ 8. The restaurant owner tried to *entice* people to eat at her restaurant by offering two meals for the price of one.
a. tell   b. coax   c. force   d. trick

_____ 9. A table with folding legs can be very *functional*, having a variety of uses.
a. fashionable   b. dangerous   c. practical   d. expensive

_____ 10. Although Americans have ample opportunity to become good readers, millions are still *illiterate*.
a. in poverty   b. introverted   c. unable to read   d. bookworms

_____ 11. Marius prefers *intellectual* activities, such as reading and visiting art galleries, to less serious or more physical pursuits.
a. illiterate   b. academic   c. moral   d. artistic

_____ 12. Grandfather was *an introvert*; he preferred to be alone.
a. a person who kept to himself   b. a person preoccupied with possessions   c. an active person   d. an outgoing person

_____ 13. Picking the stems off ten quarts of strawberries is a *laborious* task.
a. tiresome   b. complex   c. effortless   d. stimulating

_____ 14. Ms. Barelli was Jason's *mentor*; he often sought her advice.
a. student   b. menace   c. counselor   d. enemy

_____ 15. Ten years ago many Americans believed that war with the Soviet Union was inevitable; but today they are much more *optimistic* about peace.
a. confused   b. hopeful   c. skeptical   d. disturbed

_____ 16. If we continue to abuse our environment, we will face the *prospect* of persistent foul air and polluted water.
a. likelihood   b. perspective   c. enigma   d. loss

_____ 17. Susan B. Anthony is especially noted for helping *reform* the U.S. voting system in the late 1800's so that women, as well as men, could vote.
a. dispense with   b. divert   c. damage   d. improve

_____ 18. People enjoy Gloria's *spontaneity* and the excitement of never knowing what she'll do next.
a. maturity   b. thoughtfulness   c. free and natural behavior
d. planned and thoughtful actions

_____ 19. Club members expected that the changes in their constitution would be minor, but the changes in the revision were, in fact, *substantive*.
a. considerable   b. dishonest   c. imperceptible   d. unexpected

_____ 20. After the judge read the verdict, the prisoner was marched *summarily* out of the courtroom, even before photographers could take a photo.
a. slowly   b. defiantly   c. nonchalantly   d. hastily

Number correct _____ (total 20)

Part B *Target Words in Reading and Literature*

You should now have a general idea of the meaning of each target word. Refine your understanding by examining the shades of meaning these words have in the following article.

Confessions of a Misspent Youth

Mara Wolynski

What would you think of a school in which students were never tested, were forbidden to be bored, and were never made to compete with each other? The author attended such a school. The following passage examines the effects this experience had on her later life.

The idea of permissive education appealed to my mother in 1956 when she was a Bohemian[1] and I was four. In Greenwich Village, she found a private school whose beliefs were hers and happily enrolled me. I know it was an act of motherly love, but it might have been the worst thing she ever did to me. At this school—I'll call it Sand and Sea . . . I soon became an exemplar[2] of educational freedom—the freedom not to learn   5

We had certain hours **allotted** to various subjects, but we were free to **dismiss** anything that bored us. In fact, it was school policy that we were forbidden to be bored or miserable or made to compete with one another. There were no tests and no hard times. When I was bored with math, I was excused and allowed to   10 write short stories in the library. The way we learned history was by trying to recreate its least important elements. One year, we pounded corn, made tepees, ate buffalo meat, and learned two Indian words. That was early American history. Another year we made **elaborate** costumes, clay pots, and papier-maché[3] gods. That was Greek culture. Another year we were all   15 maidens and knights in armor because it was time to learn about the Middle Ages. We drank our orange juice from tin-foil goblets but never found out what the Middle Ages were. They were just "The Middle Ages."

I knew that the Huns[4] drank a quart of blood before going to war, but no one ever told us who the Huns were or why we should know who they were. And   20 one year, the year of ancient Egypt, when we were building our pyramids, I did a

---

[1] Bohemian: a person who lives in a free, unconventional way
[2] exemplar: an example; a typical specimen
[3] papier-maché: a material made of paper pulp and glue
[4] Huns: a warlike Asian tribe that invaded Europe in the fourth and fifth centuries

thirty-foot-long mural for which I **laboriously** copied hieroglyphics[5] onto the sheet of brown paper. But no one ever told me what they stood for. They were just there and beautiful.

We spent great amounts of time being creative because we had been told by our incurably **optimistic mentors** that the way to be happy in life was to create. Thus, we didn't learn to read until we were in the third grade because early reading was thought to discourage creative **spontaneity.** The one thing they taught us very well was to hate **intellectuality** and anything connected with it. Accordingly, we were forced to be creative for nine years. And yet Sand and Sea has failed to turn out a good artist. What we did do was to continually form and re-form interpersonal relationships and that's what we thought learning was all about, and we were happy. At ten, for example, most of us were **functionally illiterate**, but we could tell that Raymond was "acting out" when, in the middle of what passed for English, he did the twist on top of his desk. Or that Nina was **"introverted"** because she always **cowered** in the corner.

When we finally were graduated from Canaan[6], however, all the happy little children fell down the hill. We felt a profound sense of abandonment. So did our parents. After all that tuition money, let alone the loving freedom, their children faced high school with all the glorious **prospects** of the poorest slum-school kids. And so it came to be. No matter what school we went to, *we* were the underachievers and the culturally **disadvantaged**. . . .

25

30

35

40

---

[5] hieroglyphics: pictures or symbols representing words, syllables, or sounds used by the ancient Egyptians

[6] Canaan: the Promised Land of the Israelites; the author ironically suggests that the school was not the wonderful educational place it promised it would be

"We were thrilled with Freddy's last ashtray."

During my own high-school years, the school psychologist was **baffled** by my lack of **substantive** knowledge. He suggested to my mother that I be given a battery of psychological tests to find out why I was blocking out information. The thing was, I wasn't blocking because I had no information to block. Most of my Sand and Sea classmates were also **enduring** the same kinds of hardships that accompany severe handicaps. My own reading comprehension was in the lowest eighth percentile, not surprisingly. I was often asked by teachers how I had gotten into high school. However, I did manage to stumble *not* only through high school but also through college (first junior college — rejected by all four-year colleges, and then New York University), hating it all the way as I had been taught to. I am still amazed that I have a B.A. . . .

Now I see my twelve-year-old brother (who is in a traditional school) doing college-level math, and I know that he knows more about many other things besides math than I do. And I also see traditional education working in the case of my fifteen-year-old brother (who was **summarily** yanked from Sand and Sea, by my **reformed** mother, when he was eight so that he wouldn't become like me). Now, after seven years of real education, he is making impressive film documentaries for a project on the Bicentennial. A better learning experience than playing Pilgrim for four and a half months, and Indian for four and a half months, which is how I imagine they spent this year at Sand and Sea.

And now I've come to see that the real job of school is to **entice** the student into the web of knowledge and then, if he's not enticed, to drag him in. I wish I had been.

Refining Your Understanding

For each of the following items, consider how the target word is used in the passage. Write the letter of the word or phrase that best completes each sentence.

_____ 1. The author uses the word *mentors* (line 26) as a synonym for
a. students   b. teachers   c. parents.

_____ 2. From the context, you might gather that *functionally illiterate* (lines 33–34) probably means   a. completely unable to read   b. unable to comprehend directions   c. unable to read well enough to do a certain job.

_____ 3. The author felt that she and her classmates from Sand and Sea were culturally *disadvantaged* (line 42) because   a. they had to study ancient Egypt   b. they were forced to be creative   c. they hadn't really learned anything in the school.

_____ 4. "*Substantive* knowledge" (line 44) probably refers to   a. basic and essential knowledge of a subject   b. intuition   c. grammar.

_____ 5. The fact that the author's mother was *reformed* (line 58) shows that she a. came to believe in the type of education offered by Sand and Sea b. became unhappy with Sand and Sea   c. didn't believe Mara's brother had sufficient intellectual potential for Sand and Sea.

Number correct _____ (total 5)

Part C *Ways to Make New Words Your Own*

This section presents a variety of reinforcement activities that will help you make these words part of your permanent vocabulary.

Using Language and Thinking Skills

Finding Examples Write the letter of the situation that best demonstrates the meaning of each word.

_____ 1. **functional**

    a. A painting of a rural scene

    b. An old, well-running car that has no luxury features

    c. A ruffle on a dress

_____ 2. **disadvantaged**

    a. A child growing up in a poor home with no books

    b. A program for students with exceptional ability in science

    c. A person using his or her last dollar to play the lottery

_____ 3. **prospect**

    a. A pleasant memory

    b. A challenging physics problem

    c. A good job opportunity

_____ 4. **enduring**

    a. Surrendering to enemy forces

    b. Failing to finish an assignment on time

    c. Putting up with the pain until the doctor arrives

_____ 5. **introvert**

    a. A self-conscious person at a party

    b. A person with mild brain damage

    c. A person who is interested in the politics of his or her community

_____ 6. **spontaneity**

    a. Practicing a piano solo

    b. Inviting friends over for a party at the last minute

    c. Slipping and falling down the stairs

_____ 7. **optimistic**

    a. Not worrying about the harvest even though rain is scarce

    b. Giving up after reading a story problem for math

    c. Rushing to get to a store before the merchandise is sold out

_____ 8. **dismiss**

    a. Arrive just as your train pulls out of the station

    b. Make your brother leave the room when you get a phone call

    c. Ask your friends to come to a surprise birthday party

_____ 9. **illiterate**

    a. A poor excuse

    b. A person who is bored with reading

    c. A person who signs a personal check with an *X*

_____ 10. **elaborate**

    a. A sudden inspiration

    b. A royal British wedding

    c. A simple black dress

Number correct _____ (total 10)

Practicing for Standardized Tests

Antonyms   Write the letter of the word that is most nearly *opposite* in meaning to the capitalized word.

_____ 1. OPTIMISTIC: (A) cheerful   (B) subtle   (C) glad   (D) lax   (E) pessimistic

_____ 2. BAFFLE: (A) clarify   (B) surprise   (C) appall   (D) muffle   (E) puzzle

_____ 3. SUMMARILY: (A) briefly   (B) concisely   (C) confusedly
(D) leisurely   (E) immediately

_____ 4. ENDURING: (A) lasting   (B) fleeting   (C) permanent   (D) enhancing
(E) durable

_____ 5. FUNCTIONAL: (A) useless   (B) elaborate   (C) accessible
(D) practical   (E) homogeneous

_____ 6. LABORIOUS: (A) rigorous   (B) difficult   (C) simultaneous
(D) effortless   (E) brutal

_____ 7. INTROVERT: (A) extrovert   (B) masochist   (C) convert   (D) despot
(E) tyrant

_____ 8. ENTICE: (A) taunt   (B) lure   (C) discourage   (D) ensure   (E) coax

_____ 9. INTELLECTUAL: (A) scholarly   (B) abstract   (C) classical
(D) mindless   (E) contemporary

_____ 10. COWER: (A) cringe   (B) tremble   (C) threaten   (D) strut   (E) cancel

Number correct _____ (total 10)

Word's Worth: mentor

Mentor was originally a character in Homer's *Odyssey*, the ancient Greek poem that describes Odysseus's ten years of wandering after the fall of Troy. In his absence, Odysseus entrusted his family and property to the care of his loyal friend Mentor. Mentor did his job so well that thousands of years later his name has become a synonym for someone who is a wise and trusted counselor.

Spelling and Wordplay

Crossword Puzzle Read each clue to determine what word will fit in the corresponding squares. There are several target words in the puzzle.

ACROSS

1. Complex
8. Abbr. Louisiana
10. Word of laughter
11. Colloq. *Elevated Railroad*
12. Standard
13. Abbr. *District of Columbia*
15. Horizontally level
16. Prefix: Two
17. Abbr. *Univ. of Ohio*
18. Abbr. *Office of Oceanography*
19. Contraction of *I am*
21. — — — s and pans
22. Abbr. *Right of Way*
23. Abbr. *Room Temperature*
24. Abbr. *Chemical Engineering*
25. Abbr. Railroad
26. Abbr. (L.) That Is
27. Affirmative word
28. Abbr. *Overseas Investors Services*
30. Abbr. Net Register
31. To discharge
33. Old French coin
34. Precious stone
36. Abbr. Out of Print
37. Abbr. *Postal Union Mail*
38. Prefix: Undo
39. To erase
41. Abbr. *Eastman School of Music*
43. Abbr. *National Rifle Association*
45. Abbr. *Alternating Current*
46. Cheerful
49. Thick, sticky black material
51. Not off
52. Colloq. *Advertisement*
54. 3.14159265
55. Organ of hearing
57. Useful
62. Abbr. *Saint*
63. Impulsive activity

DOWN

1. Lasting
2. Stick out your tongue and say "— —"
3. Puzzled
4. Changes or improvements
5. To distribute shares
6. Tempts
7. To provide with weapons
8. Difficult
9. Past participle of *alight*
14. Cringed
20. Untidy condition
21. To hunt for gold
27. Exclamation of pain
29. Immediately
32. Shapes something
35. Trusted teacher
39. Hoover or Aswan
40. Prefix: Three
42. Sounds
44. — — — Tin Tin
47. Skill in dealing with people
48. Murderer of Abel
50. A gentle touch (two words)
53. Female deer
56. On, in, near, or by
57. Abbr. *Family Practice*
58. See 17 Across
59. Abbr. *Newport News*
60. Abbr. (Chem.) *Tantalum*
61. Abbr. (Chem.) *Nickel*

Part D   Related Words

A number of words are closely related to the target words you have studied. Use your knowledge of the target words and of word parts to determine the meanings of these words. (For information about word parts analysis, see pages 6–12.) Learning these related words expands your vocabulary and helps you learn the target words more thoroughly.

1. advantage (əd van′ tij) n.
2. endure (in door′) v.
3. extrovert (eks′trə vurt′) n.
4. function (fuŋk′ shən) n., v.
5. introverted (in′ trə vurt′ ed) adj.
6. literate (lit′ər it) adj.
7. optimal (äp′ tə məl) adj.
8. optimum (äp′ tə məm) n., adj.
9. prospective (prə spek′ tiv) adj.
10. prospector (präs′pek tər) n.
11. reformer (ri fôr′ mər) n.
12. spontaneous (spän tā′ nē əs) adj.
13. substance (sub′ stəns) n.
14. substantial (səb stan′ shəl) adj.
15. summary (sum′ ə rē) adj., n.
16. summation (sə mā′ shən) n.

Turn to **The Letter c** on page 218 of the **Spelling Handbook.** Read the rule and complete the exercise provided.

Understanding Related Words

Sentence Completion   In the blank write the word below that best completes each sentence.

advantage	function	literate	prospector	substantial
endure	introverted	optimal	reformer	summation

1. One _____ that the colonists had over the British in the Revolutionary War was their familiarity with the territory.

2. One of Benjamin Franklin's most popular proverbs is a _____ of how to maintain economic health: "A penny saved is a penny earned."

3. Jane Pierce, the wife of President Franklin Pierce, was so _____ that she did not even attend her husband's inaugural ball.

4. Beethoven certainly made _____ use of his talent, composing his *Ninth Symphony* when he was totally deaf.

5. If you lived at the North Pole, you would have to _____ 186 days each year in which the sun never rises.

6. Although a clock's main _____ is to record the exact time, early clocks had only an hour hand.

7. Since all the gold in the world would fit into a single block less than eight feet square, a _____ who finds a nugget of gold should be excited.

8. Although most people wouldn't think that paperweights have _____ value, a glass paperweight was auctioned for $20,000 in 1970.

9. Ralph Nader is a social _____ who has become the champion of U.S. consumers in areas such as automobile safety and pollution control.

10. In Colonial America the number of _____ people was highest in New England and lowest in the South.

Number correct _____ (total 10)

Analyzing Word Parts

The Latin Root *lit* The target word *illiterate*, the related word *literate*, and other words, such as *literal*, *literary*, and *literature*, come from the Latin word *littera*, meaning "letter." All five of these words refer to some aspect of reading or writing. Write your own definitions of these words based on an analysis of this root and other word parts. Then check the definitions in a dictionary and make any necessary changes.

Word   Definition

1. illiterate: _____

2. literal: _____

3. literary: _____

4. literate: _____

5. literature: _____

Number correct _____ (total 5)

The Prefix *dis-* The target words *disadvantaged* and *dismiss* include the prefix *dis-*, a negative prefix meaning "apart from" or "away from." Listed below are ten words that include the prefix *dis-* and ten definitions. Write the letter of each word in the blank in front of its definition.

_____ 1. to send away   a. disadvantage

_____ 2. refusing to follow orders   b. discourage

_____ 3. an unhealthy state   c. discredit

_____ 4. a handicap   d. disease

_____ 5. to put out of place   e. disembark

_____ 6. to cause to lose hope   f. disgrace

_____ 7. to leave a ship or airplane   g. dislocate

_____ 8. that can be thrown away   h. dismiss

_____ 9. to cast doubt on   i. disobedient

_____ 10. to bring shame upon   j. disposable

Number correct _____ (total 10)

Number correct in Unit _____ (total 70)

The Last Word

Writing

Write an imaginative story that includes one item from each column.

Characters	Incidents	Conditions
reformer	allotting tax refunds	with laborious effort
mentor	cowering in a corner	at a reform rally
intellectual	prospecting for gold	in an elaborate manner
introvert	enduring the impossible	with an optimistic attitude
extrovert	elaborating on a subject	in a burst of spontaneity
illiterate	baffling an audience	for the disadvantaged
prospector	dismissing the obvious	summarily

Speaking

Research a program that teaches basic reading and writing skills to the illiterate members of your community. Explain the program's intended audience and purpose, and its method of teaching. If possible, give some examples of the program's successes.

Group Discussion

Surveys tell us that one out of five Americans is functionally illiterate. Discuss the meaning of this statement. Use the following steps to guide your discussion.
1. Define the phrase "functionally illiterate."
2. Discuss the multiple causes of illiteracy.
3. Describe at least three effects this problem has on American society.
4. Outline a creative approach that might help solve this problem in your community.

UNIT 16:   Review of Units 13–15

Part A   Review Word List

Unit 13 Target Words

1. agency
2. analytical
3. chaos
4. facility
5. fermentation
6. forerunner
7. formulate
8. inquiry
9. isolate
10. mystic
11. original
12. perceptive
13. physiology
14. precursor
15. rigorous
16. spirit
17. sublime
18. supernatural
19. uncompromising
20. unrestrained

Unit 13 Related Words

1. agent
2. analyze
3. chaotic
4. compromise
5. facilitate
6. formula
7. inquire
8. isolation
9. mysterious
10. mystery
11. mysticism
12. mystify
13. mystique
14. origin
15. originate
16. perception
17. restrain
18. restraint
19. rigor
20. self-restraint
21. spiritual
22. sublimate

Unit 14 Target Words

1. accessibility
2. bewilderment
3. concede
4. crystallize
5. erode
6. ethnic
7. heritage
8. homogeneity
9. impose
10. invalid
11. liberation
12. metaphor
13. mutable
14. phenomenon
15. prejudicial
16. quota
17. repression
18. specter
19. taunt
20. wary

Unit 14 Related Words

1. accede
2. access
3. accessible
4. bewilder
5. crystal
6. erosion
7. heterogeneous
8. homogeneous
9. immutable
10. imposition
11. inaccessible
12. inherit
13. inheritance
14. invalidate
15. liberate
16. metaphorical
17. mutation
18. mutual
19. phenomenal
20. repress
21. spectral
22. valid

Unit 15 Target Words

1. allot
2. baffle
3. cower
4. disadvantaged
5. dismiss
6. elaborate
7. enduring
8. entice
9. functional
10. illiterate
11. intellectual
12. introvert
13. laborious
14. mentor
15. optimistic
16. prospect
17. reform
18. spontaneity
19. substantive
20. summarily

Unit 15 Related Words

1. advantage
2. endure
3. extrovert
4. function
5. introverted
6. literate
7. optimal
8. optimum
9. prospective
10. prospector
11. reformer
12. spontaneous
13. substance
14. substantial
15. summary
16. summation

Inferring Meaning from Context

For each sentence write the letter of the word or phrase that is closest in meaning to the word or words in italics.

_____ 1. It was *an analytical* and reasoned discussion.
a. a wary   b. a boisterous   c. a liberating   d. a probing

_____ 2. The single-family houses in that new development are too *homogeneous.*
a. uncompromising   b. dilapidated   c. similar   d. isolated

_____ 3. Grandfather Johnson's gold watch is a cherished *heritage* in our family.
a. compromise   b. tradition   c. quota   d. function

_____ 4. Some sculptors prefer to work in marble because it will not *erode.*
a. nurture   b. ignite   c. crystallize   d. wear away

_____ 5. We enjoy performing *ethnic* dances from different countries.
a. cultural   b. immutable   c. sublime   d. enduring

_____ 6. Ben's *perception* of the situation was excellent.
a. repression   b. isolation   c. awareness   d. misreading

_____ 7. I *repressed* a yawn.
a. imitated   b. held back   c. observed   d. let out

_____ 8. Because the chemical had a *mutable* nature, the scientist had to work quickly while the chemical was in its liquid state.
a. fair   b. easy   c. rigid   d. changeable

_____ 9. We watched the gymnast's *phenomenal* ability to bend backwards and touch his feet.
a. laborious   b. bewildered   c. supernatural   d. exceptional

_____ 10. Detective Sato was *baffled* by the unsolved murder case.
a. bewildered   b. reformed   c. enticed   d. unrestrained

_____ 11. Terry has *a facility* for speaking to groups.
a. an agency   b. a skill   c. a good job   d. a quota

_____ 12. The detective *formulated* a theory about the murder case after many days of investigating leads.
a. dismissed   b. conceded   c. remembered   d. composed

_____ 13. The oily rags burst into flames due to *spontaneous* combustion.
a. natural   b. elaborate   c. rigorous   d. mutable

_____ 14. Once exposed to the air, the gel begins to *crystallize.*
a. ferment   b. take a definite form   c. isolate parts   d. sublimate

_____ 15. Nancy made a *valid* point in the debate.
a. inquiring   b. well-reasoned   c. unfounded   d. bewildering

Number correct _____ (total 15)

Using Review Words in Context

Using context clues, determine which word from the list below best completes each sentence in the story. Write the word in the blank. Each word will be used once.

agent   baffling   concede   enticing   inaccessible
inherit   inheritance   inquiries   invalid   mystery
optimistic   prospect   prospector   self-restraint taunted

The Rich Uncle

Leonard received word that his Great-Uncle Charlie had died. Apparently, Charlie had been a bedridden _____ for years. Although they had never met, Leonard was Charlie's only relative and stood to _____ his entire estate.

Leonard knew that Great-Uncle Charlie and his brother, Great-Uncle Fred, had emigrated to America about 1900. As an ambitious young immigrant, Charlie wanted to go to Alaska and _____ for gold. By nature, Charlie was _____ and planned on making a fortune in the gold fields. His brother Fred, on the other hand, was a cautious type, always showing a great deal of _____ . Fred refused to go to Alaska. "The gold fields are so far from civilization that they're almost _____ ," said Fred. "Why, we could be alone for months at a time!"

Charlie would not _____ to Fred. He _____ Fred, shouting, "Only a fool would refuse to go!" But not even Charlie's _____ descriptions of adventure and riches would make Fred change his mind. They separated, to remain apart for the rest of their lives.

Whether or not Charlie ever found gold had remained an unsolved family _____ . Over the years, _____ were made about Charlie, but Fred's family was never able to uncover much information. They did have a single photo of Charlie in Alaska. It pictured a grinning, dirty _____ , Charlie, waving his pick in the air triumphantly. This photo, of course, made the family mystery even more _____ . The _____ representing Charlie's estate eventually contacted Leonard and made an appointment to meet with him to settle the estate. Leonard was almost beside himself with curiosity about his upcoming _____ . Leonard finally asked, "How much do I get?"

The estate representative smiled as she gave Leonard one tiny gold nugget valued at $49.63.

Number correct _____ (total 15)

Practicing for Standardized Tests

Analogies Write the letter of the word pair that best expresses a relationship similar to that expressed in the original pair.

_____ 1. GHOST : SUPERNATURAL ::   (A) Zeus : mythological   (B) tributary : hydroelectric   (C) test tube : experimental   (D) embryo : adult (E) spirit : enthusiastic

_____ 2. CHORE : LABORIOUS ::   (A) tool : primitive   (B) puzzle : mysterious (C) organization : chaotic   (D) reader : illiterate   (E) component : whole

_____ 3. CHAOS : ORDER ::   (A) endurance : perseverance   (B) forerunner : precursor   (C) prospect : opportunity   (D) separation : isolation (E) enticement : rejection

_____ 4. FERMENTATION : WINE ::   (A) thunder : lightning   (B) carbonation : bubbles   (C) pessimist : fear   (D) hero : bravery   (E) invalid : injury

_____ 5. INFLICT : IMPOSE ::   (A) taunt : tease   (B) clarify : mystify (C) confront : cower   (D) repress : reform   (E) verify : invalidate

_____ 6. EARTHQUAKE : PHENOMENON ::   (A) ancestor : heritage (B) watershed : tributary   (C) crystal : sugar   (D) formula : secret (E) biology : science

_____ 7. BAFFLED : MYSTERY ::   (A) elated : repression   (B) taunted : introvert   (C) haunted : specter   (D) liberated : tyrant   (E) eroded : mountainside

_____ 8. COWER : FRIGHTENED ::   (A) reform : rigid   (B) isolate : unified (C) concede : victorious   (D) rejoice : happy   (E) entice : offensive

_____ 9. TEACHER : MENTOR ::   (A) specter : movie   (B) chaos : reform (C) scholar : barbarian   (D) hermit : introvert   (E) inquiry : statement

_____ 10. SALESMAN : QUOTA ::   (A) portion : allotment   (B) agency : staff (C) policeman : badge   (D) commuter : train   (E) fisherman : limit

Number correct _____ (total 10)

Antonyms Write the letter of the word that is most nearly _opposite_ in meaning to the capitalized word.

_____ 1. OPTIMISTIC: (A) mystic   (B) idealistic   (C) pessimistic (D) timorous   (E) incessant

_____ 2. INVALID: (A) mythical   (B) worthless   (C) tender   (D) enduring (E) legitimate

_____ 3. INTROVERT: (A) extrovert   (B) reformer   (C) specter (D) arbitrator   (E) loner

—— 4. SUBLIME: (A) splendid (B) unimpressive (C) esoteric (D) ethnic
(E) sublimated

—— 5. ORIGINAL: (A) initial (B) metaphorical (C) rigorous
(D) spontaneous (E) last

—— 6. PREJUDICIAL: (A) biased (B) cowering (C) fair (D) rigorous
(E) paternal

—— 7. ILLITERATE: (A) functional (B) baffled (C) ignorant
(D) educated (E) optimistic

—— 8. MUTABLE: (A) alterable (B) temperamental (C) mutual
(D) ambiguous (E) fixed

—— 9. PRECURSOR: (A) forerunner (B) follower (C) prospect
(D) commitment (E) compromiser

—— 10. LIBERATION: (A) diversion (B) repression (C) emancipation
(D) agitation (E) determination

Number correct _____ (total 10)

Synonyms Write the letter of the word whose meaning is closest to that of the
capitalized word.

—— 1. MENTOR: (A) teacher (B) commitment (C) spirit (D) forerunner
(E) contemporary

—— 2. ETHNIC: (A) erosive (B) culinary (C) cultural (D) effective
(E) theoretical

—— 3. INQUIRY: (A) judgment (B) composition (C) reform
(D) investigation (E) ambiguity

—— 4. ENTICE: (A) reject (B) lure (C) embrace (D) assume (E) defy

—— 5. REPRESS: (A) retain (B) dismiss (C) liberate (D) restrain
(E) integrate

—— 6. FORMULATE: (A) stimulate (B) function (C) destroy (D) attain
(E) develop

—— 7. ALLOT: (A) deter (B) alter (C) assign (D) endure (E) assume

—— 8. HOMOGENEITY: (A) similarity (B) difference (C) indifference
(D) rigidity (E) mystique

—— 9. WARY: (A) resolved (B) cautious (C) unrestrained (D) trusting
(E) introverted

—— 10. RIGOROUS: (A) effective (B) deft (C) righteous (D) demanding
(E) gory

Number correct _____ (total 10)

Spelling and Wordplay

Word Pyramid Build a word pyramid by following the code at the base of the pyramid.

G E N E __ __ __
        13 6 2

G E N E __ __ __ __ __
        1 7 10 4 15

__ __ __ __ G E N E __ __ __
5 10 8 10   10 14 12

G E N E __ __ __ __ __ __
        11 1 13 6 10 9

G E N E __ __ __ __ __ __ __
        1 7 10 4 6 12 13

__ __ __ __ __ __ G E N E __ __ __
5 3 13 3 11 10   10 14 12

G E N E __ __ __ __ __ __ __ __
        1 7 10 4 6 2 1 7

A C E G H I L M N O R S T U Y
1 2 3 4 5 6 7 8 9 10 11 12 13 14 15

The root *gene* comes from the Latin *gens,* meaning "race" or "clan." It is usually found in words referring to family and ancestry. For the following items, write the word that is being defined. Choose from among the words in the pyramid.

1. made up of similar parts; uniform: _____

2. dealing with heredity and the way animals and plants pass on certain

   characteristics to offspring: _____

3. all the people born during the same time period: _____

4. a person who studies family histories: _____

5. different in structure; dissimilar: _____

Number correct _____ (total 5)

Part C   Related Words Reinforcement

Using Related Words

True-False   Determine whether each statement is true or false. Write **T** for True and **F** for False.

_____ 1. Being placed in *isolation* means that you have a chance to meet many more people.

_____ 2. A good magician will *bewilder* his audience.

_____ 3. Playing on their home court is an *advantage* for most teams.

_____ 4. Sticking to a diet necessitates *self-restraint*.

_____ 5. Grass planted on a hillside will promote *erosion*.

_____ 6. A *spontaneous* remark is one that is thought about and planned beforehand.

_____ 7. One is *sublimating* when he or she suppresses a desire to hit someone and later vents anger by kicking a wall.

_____ 8. The moon is easily *accessible* now to most tourists.

_____ 9. An employer would probably not hire a *prospective* applicant.

_____ 10. *Mysticism* is based on scientific principles.

_____ 11. "All the world's a stage" is a *metaphorical* expression.

_____ 12. You might feel you couldn't win if the conditions for doing so were *optimal*.

_____ 13. The girl's *mystique* made her life an open book to all.

_____ 14. You would fail an exam if ninety percent of your answers were *valid*.

_____ 15. Something that is *immutable* does not change.

_____ 16. The goal of a good encyclopedia is to *mystify* its readers.

_____ 17. A *mutual* agreement is usually one-sided.

_____ 18. An *extrovert* is more interested in other people and things than in his or her own thoughts and feelings.

_____ 19. Going uphill will *facilitate* one's running ease.

_____ 20. Crashing a party is usually an *imposition* on the host.

_____ 21. Your meal was *substantial* if it was meager and beneath your standards.

_____ 22. You could call a group of students *homogeneous* if they came from many different countries and spoke many different languages.

_____ 23. Some of the *rigors* of pioneer life included hard labor, unsophisticated tools, and the isolation of the prairie.

_____ 24. A person sentenced to prison is considered *liberated*.

_____ 25. A salesperson would celebrate if she reached her *optimum* sales goal.

_____ 26. Martin Luther King, Jr., was a *reformer*.

_____ 27. Top-secret government information is *inaccessible* to the general public.

_____ 28. A *literate* person would be unable to read even simple directions.

_____ 29. If your friend *accedes* to your request, he agrees to it.

_____ 30. A *heterogeneous* group of people would look and act very much alike.

Number correct _____ (total 30)

Reviewing Word Structures

The Word Parts *dis-* and *-ate* Review the prefix *dis-* on page 180 and the suffix *-ate* on page 159. For each sentence below, the italicized words can be replaced by a word from the following list. Write the correct word in the appropriate blank.

disadvantaged   dismiss   facilitate   formulate   originate

_____ 1. Why did Ms. Gallup *send away* her third-grade class ten minutes early?

_____ 2. That organization helps all kinds of children, especially those who are *not accustomed to having many advantages*.

_____ 3. Where did the expression "I'm from Missouri. Show me." *come from?*

_____ 4. That cost-saving measure will *make more efficient* our company's mailing system.

_____ 5. The mathematician tried to *develop* an equation that would solve a troubling inconsistency in gravitational theory.

Number correct _____ (total 5)

Number correct in Unit _____ (total 100)

Vocab Lab 4

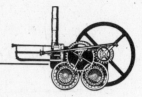

FOCUS ON: Engineering

Engineering is the application of science for useful purposes. Engineering is divided into chemical, electrical, environmental, materials, and mechanical engineering. Broaden your vocabulary by learning the following words.

Chemical

distillation (dis′ tə lā′ shən) n. the process of purifying a solid or liquid by heating it until it forms a gas, and condensing the gas. ● The scientist compared the weights of the solutions before and after *distillation*.

fusion (fyo͞o′ zhən) n. the process of joining or uniting. ● The *fusion* of particles in the nucleus of an atom releases enormous quantities of energy.

polymer (päl′ i mər) n. a chemical compound made up of giant, long, chainlike molecules formed by the chemical linking of many smaller molecules. ● The new *polymer* created in the chemical reaction was similar to the original compound.

Electrical

electroplate (i lek′ trə plāt′) v. to deposit a metal coating on something by using an electric current; n. anything so plated. ● The company decided to *electroplate* the picture frame with a thin coating of silver.

photoelectric cell (fōt′ ō i lek′ trik) n. a device that either produces a current or allows a current to flow when a light shines on it. ● Most elevator doors operate on a *photoelectric cell*, commonly called an electric eye.

transformer (trans fôr′ mər) n. a device that increases or decreases voltage as electric energy is transferred from one circuit to another. ● The repairman said that the wiring was fine and that the problem seemed to be in the *transformer*.

Environmental

pollutant (pə lo͞ot′ nt) n. a substance that makes something unclean or impure. ● Cigarette smoke is a deadly *pollutant*.

radioactivity (rā′ dē ō ak tiv′ ə tē) n. the rays or high energy and atomic particles given off when the core of an atom disintegrates. ● The small doses of *radioactivity* that the body absorbs during an X-ray procedure probably are not harmful.

recycling (rē sī′ k'l iŋ) n. the process of treating used materials so that they can be recovered for human use. ● *Recycling* is an effective way of coping with the vast amounts of waste produced each day.

Materials

assay (as′ ā, a sā′; for v. a sā′, ə-) n. a process used to determine the amount of metal or valuable minerals in a substance; v. to make an assay of; analyze. ● The prospectors will not know how much gold the ore contains until an *assay* is performed.

metallurgy (met′ 'l ûr′ jē) n. the science of separating metals from ore and preparing them for use. ● Manufacturing industries rely heavily on the findings of *metallurgy*.

190

smelt (smelt) v. to separate metals from impurities by melting or fusing ore. ● The huge furnaces in ironworks are used to *smelt* raw ore.

Mechanical

pulley (pōōl′ ē) n. a simple machine made of a wheel and a rope or chain. ● Using a *pulley* enables people to lift many times more weight than they can lift unaided.

torque (tôrk) n. a force that causes rotation. ● As a result of *torque*, a wheel turns easier when force is applied farther from the center.

turbine (tûr′ bin, -bīn) n. an engine driven by steam, water, or air pressure acting on the curved vanes of a wheel on a shaft. ● Many jet planes are driven by *turbine* engines.

Sentence Completion Complete each sentence below by using the appropriate word from the focus list. Each word is used only once.

1. The pressure generated by flowing water can be used to spin the blades

   of _____ engines.

2. Atomic fission, in which atoms are split apart, does not produce nearly as

   much energy as does atomic _____ , in which particles are joined.

3. The backpackers found what they thought was silver ore, but they could not

   be sure until a(n) _____ was performed.

4. One reason the city council voted to make _____ mandatory
   was that all the waste disposal sites in the area were full.

5. Special furnaces must be used to _____ ore so that the usable
   metals can be separated from the impurities.

6. One engineer suggested redesigning the drive shaft of the car to increase

   the _____ .

7. The _____ that is produced in nuclear reactions is potentially
   harmful and must be carefully channelled and contained.

8. To produce a thick metallic coating on a piece of silverware, you can

   _____ the object by using a strong current and a concentrated
   metallic solution.

9. The miniature electric train came with a _____ that lowered
   the voltage of the current coming from the electric outlet.

10. Since the piano would not fit through the front door, the movers used

    a _____ to lift it through the large, second-story window.

    Number correct _____ (total 10)

FOCUS ON: *Language Usage*

Developing your vocabulary means more than just learning the meanings of words. It means learning how and where and when to use them. Not every English speaker uses the same language. In fact, no individual speaker even uses the same language all the time. Appropriate English usage depends on the person, the historical time and geographic location, the specific situation, and the audience.

Language Levels

People who have mastered good English usage have mastered standard English. This is the English that is used in professional writing and speaking, is taught in schools, and is understood throughout the United States. However, users of standard English also know several nonstandard variations that are appropriate in particular situations, and they use each correctly.

Standard English has two levels—formal and informal. Formal English is used in writing and in serious or ceremonial situations. Informal, or colloquial, English is used in casual writing and in conversation. Jargon and idioms are two of the several types of special usage that are part of informal language. **Jargon** is specialized vocabulary usage shared by people in the same occupation or profession. The expression *grand slam*, for example, is part of baseball jargon. An **idiom** is an expression or group of words that cannot be literally translated. For example, if you define each of the words in the idiom *to cut the mustard*, the meaning produced differs from the meaning of the idiom as a whole.

Usage Labels

People learn how to use the various levels of language correctly by observing how other people use them and by using the levels themselves. However, there is a convenient source of information on language usage—the dictionary. Not only does a dictionary list the meanings of words, but it also indicates how they are used. Some of the most common usage labels you will find in the dictionary are shown below:

- *obsolete (obs.)*—used previously but not now. For example, the use of *quaint* to mean "cunning" or "crafty."
- *archaic*—used previously but now only in certain situations. The use of *doth* for *does* is an archaic form.
- *dialect (dial.)*—used regularly only in a specific geographic area or areas. For example, people in certain parts of the United States use the word *goober* for *peanut*.
- *British, Canadian, Scottish (Brit., Canad., Scot.)*—used in the language of another English-speaking country but not in American English. *Queue* is a British term for a line of persons waiting to be served.
- *colloquial (colloq.)*—used in conversational speech and writing. The use of *catch* to mean "a hidden qualification or tricky condition" is colloquial usage.
- *slang*—used only in very informal situations. *Cool* or *neat* when meant as forms of approval are slang. (Note: After a usually brief popularity, slang often disappears or becomes part of the standard language. The words *mob* and *bully* were once considered slang.)

Rewriting Sentences Rewrite the following informal sentences in formal English. Answers will vary; suggested answers below.

1. I'm broke.

   _____

2. I'll have to split before three.

   _____

3. Randy always was a real wiseacre.

   _____

4. Your analysis hit the nail on the head.

   _____

5. Before the performance, the director told the starring actress to break a leg.

   _____

   _____

Number correct _____ (total 5)

Matching Write the correct usage label in the blank next to each word. Use your dictionary to check your work.

_____ 1. boondocks

_____ 2. leave (meaning to allow)

_____ 3. head-shrinker

_____ 4. petrol

_____ 5. quoth

Number correct _____ (total 5)

Number correct in Vocab Lab _____ (total 20)

The following questions test your comprehension of words studied in the first half of this book. Test questions have been written in a way that will familiarize you with the typical standardized test format. As on most standardized vocabulary tests, questions are divided into the following categories: *antonyms, analogies,* and *sentence completion.*

Antonyms

Each question below consists of a word in capital letters, followed by five lettered words or phrases. Choose the word or phrase that is most nearly *opposite* in meaning to the word in capital letters. Some of the questions require you to distinguish fine shades of meaning, consider all the choices before deciding which is best.

_____ 1. ARBITRARY: (A) simple (B) objective (C) outlandish (D) difficult (E) unpleasant

_____ 2. DIFFUSE: (A) hostile (B) obtuse (C) concentrated (D) distant (E) dark

_____ 3. UNALTERABLE: (A) embarrassing (B) poor (C) steadfast (D) changeable (E) binding

_____ 4. DIMINUTIVE: (A) huge (B) timely (C) tuneful (D) corrective (E) weary

_____ 5. PERENNIAL: (A) serious (B) chronic (C) exotic (D) flowery (E) fleeting

_____ 6. ADAPTABLE: (A) inborn (B) rigid (C) immune (D) theatrical (E) strong

_____ 7. ENIGMATIC: (A) clear (B) diseased (C) negative (D) automatic (E) original

_____ 8. DIVERSITY: (A) shallowness (B) deformity (C) uniformity (D) anger (E) depth

_____ 9. ASCETIC: (A) clean (B) self-indulgent (C) surgical (D) beautiful (E) foolish

_____ 10. BENIGN: (A) youthful (B) bereaved (C) relieved (D) harmful (E) uncontrollable

_____ 11. PACIFIC: (A) distant (B) shallow (C) cosmic (D) ephemeral (E) belligerent

_____ 12. SERENE: (A) agitated (B) invisible (C) virtuous (D) difficult (E) cynical

_____ 13. INTERMINABLE: (A) single (B) clinging (C) brief (D) elevated (E) unbearable

_____ 14. TAUT: (A) firm (B) lax (C) teachable (D) bleak (E) serene

_____ 15. INITIAL: (A) beginning (B) first (C) brief (D) written (E) ending

_____ 16. TRANSIENT: (A) fleeting (B) momentary (C) stunted (D) perpetual (E) convulsive

_____ 17. BLEAK: (A) bright (B) depressing (C) formal (D) rejected (E) relentless

_____ 18. FLEETING: (A) transitory (B) passing (C) prolonged (D) reflexive (E) imperceptible

_____ 19. SPURIOUS: (A) faint (B) relentless (C) authentic (D) doubtful (E) diverted

_____ 20. METTLESOME: (A) courageous (B) placid (C) malformed (D) brave (E) afraid

_____ 21. MERGER: (A) enterprise (B) classification (C) separation (D) encouragement (E) constituency

_____ 22. TYRANNY: (A) freedom (B) cheerfulness (C) finality (D) fidelity (E) good fortune

_____ 23. INFINITESIMAL: (A) unnamed (B) unknown (C) external (D) immense (E) experimental

_____ 24. RECEDE: (A) succeed (B) undo (C) progress (D) reap (E) proclaim

_____ 25. EVOKE: (A) suppress (B) persist (C) refuse (D) entrust (E) examine

Number correct _____ (total 25)

Analogies

Each question below consists of a pair of words or phrases, followed by five lettered pairs of words or phrases. Select the lettered pair that _best_ expresses a relationship similar to that expressed in the original pair.

_____ 1. ALIEN : UNKNOWN ::   (A) cynic : disdainful (B) authority : punctual (C) convict : admired (D) tyrant : deposed (E) author : flexible

_____ 2. DISPUTE : ARBITRATOR ::   (A) game : player (B) truth : witness (C) contest : judge (D) director : drama (E) agreement : protector

_____ 3. DIVERT : ATTENTION ::   (A) reroute : traffic (B) entertain : performer (C) advertise : advertisement (D) cook : restaurant (E) campaign : election

_____ 4. SEPARATION : ESTRANGEMENT ::   (A) divorce : marriage (B) education : instruction (C) luck : gambling (D) mail : delivery (E) song : singer

_____ 5. RIDDLE : ENIGMA :: (A) sphinx : Egypt (B) pun : fun (C) proverb : saying (D) mail : delivery (E) dating : parties

_____ 6. AUTHORITY : SPECIALIST :: (A) teacher : principal (B) dilemma : solution (C) actor : stage (D) sculptor : clay (E) constituent : voter

_____ 7. TIGHTROPE : TAUT :: (A) light : luminous (B) estuary : desertlike (C) granite : resilient (D) turtle : swift (E) alien : familiar

_____ 8. EVOKE : FEELING :: (A) whisper : secret (B) respond : clue (C) cleanse : water (D) conform : diversity (E) cook : stove

_____ 9. SUSTAIN : PROLONG :: (A) idolize : reject (B) initiate : begin (C) dispose : retain (D) compensate : withdraw (E) argue : meditate

_____ 10. POLICEMAN : APPREHEND :: (A) instinct : follow (B) lawyer : testify (C) professor : lecture (D) relic : restore (E) parasite : benefit

_____ 11. IDOL : IDLE: :: (A) lawyer : legal (B) course : coarse (C) masochist : painful (D) star : famous (E) hospital: surgical

_____ 12. SAILBOAT : NAUTICAL :: (A) hero : cowardly (B) ghost : living (C) prayer : spiritual (D) moon: solar (E) sea : angry

_____ 13. TERMINATE : END :: (A) argue: agree (B) dribble: guard (C) authorize : permit (D) drive : sail (E) nullify : legislate

_____ 14. FOOD : SUSTENANCE :: (A) author : book (B) despot : tyranny (C) cynic : optimist (D) apprehension : fear (E) petal : blossom

_____ 15. ARROWHEAD : RELIC :: (A) answer : enigma (B) array : disarray (C) dilemma : solution (D) apple : fruit (E) argument : estrangement

_____ 16. SWOON : FAINT :: (A) study : graduate (B) alienate : unite (C) initiate : continue (D) convulse : shake (E) persist : relent

_____ 17. OBLIGATION : OPTION :: (A) duty : service (B) requirement : choice (C) respect : kindness (D) draft : military (E) selection : force

_____ 18. DESPOTISM : GOVERNMENT :: (A) hostility : law (B) girl : woman (C) Democrat : Republican (D) president : company (E) terrier : dog

_____ 19. PRETENTIOUS : OSTENTATIOUS :: (A) enigmatic : mysterious (B) ultimate : initial (C) democratic : political (D) placid : tempestuous (E) diffuse : concentrated

_____ 20. CHILD : NAIVETÉ :: (A) athlete : competitor (B) prophet : foresight (C) teller : bank (D) historian : past (E) doctor : diagnosis

_____ 21. SPURIOUS : COUNTERFEITER :: (A) predictable : politics (B) stunted : giant (C) tenuous : leader (D) nautical : farmer (E) educated : professor

_____ 22. METTLESOME : COWARD :: (A) brave : hero (B) authoritative : despot (C) hostile : pacifist (D) impartial : judge (E) disquieting : confrontation

_____ 23. RECORDS : ARCHIVES ::   (A) talent : intelligence   (B) past : future
(C) stopwatch : time   (D) growth: immaturity   (E) demonstration :
exhibition

_____ 24. LAMP : ILLUMINATION ::   (A) needle : thread   (B) plug : socket
(C) microphone : amplification   (D) piano : instrument   (E) rainfall :
drought

_____ 25. WAVES : UNDULATE ::   (A) mountains : climb   (B) sunlight : conceals
(C) snakes : slither   (D) food : forage   (E) flowers : pollinate

Number correct _____ (total 25)

Sentence Completion

Each sentence below has one or two blanks. Each blank indicates that
something has been omitted. Beneath the sentence are five lettered words or sets
of words. Choose the word or set of words that *best* fits the meaning of the
sentence as a whole.

_____ 1. The _?_ course in English is 101 and it is a necessary _?_ to English 102.
(A) initial . . . prerequisite   (B) ostentatious . . . conversion   (C) benign
. . . alternate   (D) diminutive . . . ultimatum   (E) unalterable . . .
classification

_____ 2. The gymnast's _?_ in performing rigorous routines shows that _?_ size
may be offset by gigantic will.
(A) formality . . . authoritative   (B) peculiarity . . . adaptable
(C) hostility . . . uniform   (D) persistence . . . diminutive   (E) diversion
. . . comprehensive

_____ 3. The _?_ in the directions for setting up the equipment led to two
completely different arrangements.
(A) conviction   (B) ambiguity   (C) uniformity   (D) code
(E) transfusion

_____ 4. The bubbling brook and clear blue sky were so _?_ they could _?_ even
the most troubled soul.
(A) transitory . . . dispose   (B) meditative . . . agitate   (C) disquieting
. . . convert   (D) somber . . . reject   (E) serene . . . pacify

_____ 5. Atsuko's heated _?_ with Susan over the _?_ and careless way she did the
club's bookkeeping was heard all the way down the hall.
(A) convulsion . . . unpretentious   (B) confrontation . . . lax
(C) conversion . . . tenuous   (D) dilemma . . . cynical   (E) turmoil . . .
unrelenting

_____ 6. Union representatives delivered the following _?_: increase wages or be
prepared for a strike.
(A) stunt   (B) ultimatum   (C) circumstance   (D) merger   (E) paradox

_____ 7. During the seemingly _?_ lecture, many members of the audience were lost in their own _?_.
(A) deliberate . . . illusion   (B) relentless . . . serenity   (C) interminable . . . meditation   (D) arbitrary . . . diversion   (E) comprehensive . . . pacification

_____ 8. Following the accident settlement, the driver of the damaged car demanded immediate _?_ of all funds and payments due him.
(A) rejection   (B) derivation   (C) prolongation   (D) perception   (E) disposition

_____ 9. It was easy to _?_ laughter from the children, who were basically uninhibited and _?_.
(A) evoke . . . unpretentious   (B) entrust . . . enterprising   (C) force . . . rejected   (D) infuse . . . unalterable   (E) derive . . . adaptive

_____ 10. The _?_ for survival is strong in virtually all animals and humans.
(A) mettle   (B) instinct   (C) personification   (D) obligation   (E) alter ego

_____ 11. The flaw in the diamond was so _?_ that several jewelers overlooked it in their appraisal.
(A) persistent   (B) tenuous   (C) enhancing   (D) imperceptible   (E) luminous

_____ 12. After the _?_ of the two previously _?_ companies, management policies were set to govern the newly created corporation.
(A) estrangement . . . hostile   (B) merger . . . independent   (C) adaptation . . . arbitrary   (D) constitution . . . diminutive   (E) initiation . . . enterprising

_____ 13. Only a _?_ would make such a point of wearing blue jeans and tennis shoes when everyone else was dressed formally.
(A) arbitrator   (B) cynic   (C) constituent   (D) despot   (E) nonconformist

_____ 14. Fortunately, tests after the surgery proved that the tumor was _?_.
(A) benign   (B) comprehensive   (C) frigid   (D) resilient   (E) persistent

_____ 15. The main character in the story lives in a modest apartment and is quite _?_ even though his wealth would allow him any luxury.
(A) virtuous   (B) brooding   (C) benign   (D) unpretentious   (E) serene

Number correct _____ (total 15)

Number correct in Unit _____ (total 65)

198

The following questions test your comprehension of words studied in the second half of the book. As on most standardized vocabulary tests, questions are divided into the following categories: *antonyms, analogies,* and *sentence completion.*

Antonyms

Each question below consists of a word in capital letters, followed by five lettered words or phrases. Choose the word or phrase that is most nearly *opposite* in meaning to the word in capital letters. Some of the questions require you to distinguish fine shades of meaning; consider all the choices before deciding which is best.

_____ 1. CONSPICUOUS: (A) conscious (B) concealed (C) unconscious (D) central (E) tenacious

_____ 2. ABSTRACT: (A) concrete (B) obsolete (C) vague (D) inconsiderate (E) indestructible

_____ 3. DYNAMIC: (A) anonymous (B) proper (C) heavenly (D) powerful (E) sluggish

_____ 4. INTEGRAL: (A) incomprehensible (B) untimely (C) nonessential (D) financial (E) essential

_____ 5. SUBTLE: (A) lowly (B) elevated (C) deep (D) obvious (E) careful

_____ 6. PORTABLE: (A) stationary (B) windowless (C) uncomfortable (D) thin (E) movable

_____ 7. TENACIOUS: (A) tough (B) weak (C) elderly (D) hungry (E) strong

_____ 8. DESPONDENT: (A) corresponding (B) expansive (C) depressed (D) hopeful (E) temporary

_____ 9. DEFIANCE: (A) compliance (B) enjoyment (C) daring (D) extravagance (E) rigor

_____ 10. DEFT: (A) aloud (B) doubtful (C) clumsy (D) crazy (E) defective

_____ 11. TIMID: (A) bold (B) late (C) early (D) tenuous (E) similar

_____ 12. DISDAIN: (A) refrain (B) abstain (C) respect (D) expect (E) reject

_____ 13. RIGOROUS: (A) heightened (B) joyful (C) easy (D) royal (E) false

_____ 14. ACCESSIBLE: (A) immobile (B) unapproachable (C) nonviolent (D) invalid (E) unavoidable

_____ 15. INVALID: (A) unworthy (B) wealthy (C) antisocial (D) questionable (E) legitimate

_____ 16. INCESSANT: (A) lasting (B) prolonged (C) brief (D) stupid (E) steady

_____ 17. ERODE: (A) corrode (B) restore (C) steal (D) destroy (E) avoid

_____ 18. WARY: (A) careless   (B) overdressed   (C) hot   (D) careful   (E) brave

_____ 19. IMMUTABLE: (A) legal   (B) unsure   (C) stable   (D) loud   (E) alterable

_____ 20. HETEROGENEOUS: (A) visible   (B) purposeless   (C) similar
(D) disappearing   (E) varied

_____ 21. CONSOLATION: (A) revelation   (B) boredom   (C) comfort
(D) fondness   (E) distress

_____ 22. STIMULATE: (A) run   (B) erode   (C) soothe   (D) urge   (E) trust

_____ 23. ANONYMOUS: (A) famous   (B) animated   (C) joyful   (D) depressed
(E) melancholy

_____ 24. DOMINATION: (A) expulsion   (B) power   (C) deprivation
(D) subordination   (E) declaration

_____ 25. PRIMITIVE: (A) good   (B) bad   (C) early   (D) modern   (E) older

Number correct _____ (total 25)

Analogies

Each question below consists of a pair of words or phrases, followed by five lettered pairs of words or phrases. Select the lettered pair that *best* expresses a relationship similar to that expressed in the original pair.

_____ 1. BOOKS : ILLITERATE ::   (A) paintings : literate   (B) films : blind
(C) water : tributary   (D) heroes : mythology   (E) analysis : intellectual

_____ 2. ALLEGE : CLAIM ::   (A) judge : arrest   (B) defend : prosecute
(C) speculate : wonder   (D) accuse : try   (E) arrest : imprison

_____ 3. HISTORY : MYTH ::   (A) fact : fiction   (B) answer : question
(C) book : story   (D) assumption : theory   (E) fairy tale : fable

_____ 4. NUTRIENTS : GROWTH ::   (A) component : part   (B) body :
development   (C) calories : measurement   (D) vitamins : health
(E) oxygen : air

_____ 5. PRIMEVAL : CONTEMPORARY ::   (A) prehistoric : modern
(B) embryonic : undeveloped   (C) streamlined : efficient   (D) similar :
duplicate   (E) beautiful : functional

_____ 6. PARAGON : MODEL ::   (A) good : evil   (B) beauty : admiration
(C) medal : courage   (D) sainthood : attainment   (E) mentor : advisor

_____ 7. CAUSE : EFFECT ::   (A) accident : car   (B) snow : cold   (C) illness :
fever   (D) spring : weather   (E) danger : condition

_____ 8. TYRANT : DOMINATE ::   (A) train : sail   (B) prison : steal
(C) prince : govern   (D) disease : diagnose   (E) life preserver : sink

_____ 9. FORMIDABLE : AWESOME ::   (A) voluptuous : ascetic   (B) initial :
following   (C) valid : false   (D) optimistic : hopeful   (E) cloudy : clear

____ 10. MENTOR : AID :: (A) teacher : help (B) mystic : religion (C) agent : reform (D) specter : spirit (E) analysis : intellectual

____ 11. FAMILIES : COMMUNITY :: (A) church : faith (B) nations : treaty (C) states : country (D) marriage : children (E) relatives : parents

____ 12. RIGOROUS : LABORIOUS :: (A) dominant : subtle (B) accessible : isolated (C) enduring : momentary (D) uncompromising : relentless (E) flavorful : nutritious

____ 13. ISOLATE : UNITE :: (A) erode : restore (B) join : merge (C) separate : divorce (D) insulate : improve (E) taunt : compliment

____ 14. SCORE : TWENTY :: (A) fifty : half dollar (B) dozen : twelve (C) money : dollars (D) mile : kilometer (E) era : century

____ 15. ORIGINAL : SUCCEEDING :: (A) early : late (B) second : third (C) first : next (D) now : then (E) final : last

____ 16. BAFFLED : ENIGMA :: (A) amused : joke (B) committed : commitment (C) exported : product (D) consoled : grief (E) proposed : theory

____ 17. IMMUTABLE : CHANGEABLE :: (A) fickle : disloyal (B) inedible : cooked (C) written : permanent (D) mutual : simultaneous (E) unalterable : mutable

____ 18. LIBERATION : BONDAGE :: (A) warden : prison (B) knowledge : ignorance (C) education : intelligence (D) emancipation : proclamation (E) freedom : liberator

____ 19. COWARD : COWERING :: (A) civilian : compromising (B) tyrant : liberating (C) commitment : committing (D) professor : teaching (E) illiterate : reading

____ 20. ADJACENT : REMOTE :: (A) deft : athletic (B) enticing : coaxing (C) optimistic : pessimistic (D) despondent : brooding (E) accessible : attainable

____ 21. GHOST : SPECTER :: (A) comet : phenomenon (B) witch : Halloween (C) tradition : heritage (D) scale : weight (E) mechanic : garage

____ 22. HEIR : INHERITANCE :: (A) canoe : portage (B) river bed : rock (C) paycheck : salary (D) winner : award (E) estate : mansion

____ 23. WIND : VELOCITY :: (A) air : temperature (B) snow : fall (C) humidity : air (D) barometer : pressure (E) rain : gauge

____ 24. RELISH MALICIOUSLY : GLOAT :: (A) accede : oppose (B) sublimate : repress (C) entice : repel (D) write : publish (E) walk : run

____ 25. HYDROMETER : LIQUID :: (A) books : literacy (B) velocity : speedometer (C) water : erosion (D) whole : sectors (E) barometer : air pressure

Number correct _____ (total 25)

Sentence Completion

Each sentence below has one or two blanks, indicating that something has been omitted. Below the sentence are five lettered words or sets of words. Choose the word or set of words that *best* fits the meaning of the sentence as a whole.

_____ 1. Mr. Chun _?_ us each one share in his company and told us that he was _?_ that the present one-dollar value per share would grow to at least ten dollars per share in the next year.
(A) consoled . . . nonchalant   (B) assured . . . despondent   (C) allotted . . . optimistic   (D) imposed . . . spontaneous   (E) conceded . . . hopeful

_____ 2. Marion behaves so _?_ that she makes her staff feel lowly and resentful.
(A) spiritually   (B) timorously   (C) nonchalantly   (D) superciliously
(E) disconsolately

_____ 3. The fireworks display was so _?_ and carefully worked out that even the most _?_ among us were unafraid.
(A) formulated . . . literate   (B) chaotic . . . distinguished   (C) accessible . . . introverted   (D) elaborate . . . timid   (E) spontaneous . . . wary

_____ 4. Although the instructor's _?_ made sense to everyone, her examples were so _?_ that few could comprehend their meaning.
(A) commitment . . . invisible   (B) theory . . . esoteric   (C) myth . . . oppressive   (D) integrity . . . subtle   (E) bewilderment . . . substantive

_____ 5. Mr. Sanchez was _?_ in his _?_ of a person's character.
(A) uncompromising . . . embrace   (B) degraded . . . metaphor   (C) invalid . . . restraint   (D) analytical . . . facility   (E) perceptive . . . judgment

_____ 6. The _?_ filthy conditions in the _?_ operating room led to countless cases of infection.
(A) appallingly . . . primitive   (B) superciliously . . . communal
(C) allegedly . . . contemporary   (D) summarily . . . prospective
(E) disconsolately . . . adjacent

_____ 7. Although Jeannette felt great pride as her name was added to the honor roll, she tried to be _?_.
(A) intellectual   (B) distinguished   (C) brave   (D) harsh   (E) nonchalant

_____ 8. As they developed stronger self-government, the colonies began to resent the _?_ with which the governing country treated them.
(A) bewilderment   (B) paternalism   (C) assurance   (D) integrity
(E) detention

_____ 9. Gina could not _?_ her diet any longer: the buffet was too _?_ to pass up.
(A) endure . . . enticing   (B) dismiss . . . enduring   (C) sublimate . . . tenacious   (D) facilitate . . . spontaneous   (E) repress . . . phenomenal

_____ 10. Each salesperson was _?_ one thousand dollars for travel expenses.
(A) awarded   (B) saving   (C) wasting   (D) allotted   (E) taxed

Number correct _____ (total 10)

Number correct in Unit _____ (total 60)

202

SPELLING HANDBOOK

Knowing the meanings of words is of prime importance in using language correctly. However, another important skill is knowing how to spell the words you use. Good spelling goes hand-in-hand with vocabulary development.

Almost everyone has at least some problems with spelling. If you have trouble spelling, be encouraged to know that many others like yourself have learned to spell by following these suggestions:

1. **Proofread everything you write.** Everyone at one time or another makes errors caused by carelessness or haste. By reading through all that you write, you will be able to catch many of your errors.

2. **Learn to look at the letters in a word.** Spelling errors are errors in choosing or arranging the letters that compose a word. Learn to spell a word by examining various letter combinations contained in the different parts of the word. Then memorize these combinations for future use.

3. **Pronounce words carefully.** It may be that you misspell certain words because you do not pronounce them carefully. For example, if you write *probly* instead of *probably*, it is likely that you are mispronouncing the word. Learning how to pronounce words, and memorizing certain letter combinations that create particular sounds, will help you spell many of the words in our language.

4. **Keep a list of your own "spelling demons."** Although you may not think about it, most of the words that you use you *do* spell correctly. It is usually a few specific words that give you the most trouble. Keep a list of the words you typically have trouble spelling. Then look for patterns in your misspelled words. By learning the correct patterns and concentrating on spelling the words on your list correctly, you will show quick improvement.

5. **Use memory helps, called mnemonic devices, for words that give you trouble.** *Stationery* has an *e* as in *letter*; there is *a rat* in *separate*; *Wednesday* contains *wed*.

6. **Memorize and apply the spelling rules given in this Spelling Handbook.** Make sure you understand these rules. Then use the rules so that they will become automatic.

Words with Prefixes

The Addition of Prefixes

When a prefix is added to a word, the spelling of the word remains the same. (For further information about word parts, see pages 6-12.)

con- + junction = conjunction	*ex-* + port = export
dis- + charge = discharge	*de-* + hydrate = dehydrate
re- + cycle = recycle	*in-* + visible = invisible

A prefix can be added to a root as well as to a word. A root is a word part that cannot stand alone; it must be joined to other parts to form a word. A root can be joined with many different prefixes to form words with different meanings. **However, the spelling of the root remains the same.**

de- + tain = detain	*per-* + sist = persist
re- + tain = retain	*re-* + sist = resist
con- + tain = contain	*con-* + sist = consist

Exercise Complete each sentence with two words from the list below that have the same root.

assurance	detain	imposition	persuaded	retain
composition	dissuaded	insurance	proceed	succeed

1. We received the _____ of our _____ company that it would pay for the damages to our car.

2. My friends _____ me to go to the party, but the bad

   weather _____ me at the last minute.

3. If theater customers _____ their ticket stubs, the manager will

   not _____ them at the door upon their attempting to reenter the theater.

4. If you _____ in your classes at school, you will be able

   to _____ with your education.

5. Angie thought that writing a _____ was an _____ .

Number correct _____ (total 5)

The Prefix *ad-*

When some prefixes are added to certain words, the spelling of the prefix changes. The prefix *ad-* changes in the following cases to create a double consonant.

ac- before *c*	*al-* before *l*	*ar-* before *r*
af- before *f*	*an-* before *n*	*as-* before *s*
ag- before *g*	*ap-* before *p*	*at-* before *t*

Examples:

ad- + pall = appall   *ad-* + tain = attain
ad- + sure = assure   *ad-* + fect = affect

Exercise Add the prefix *ad-* to each of the roots or base words below. Change the spelling of the prefix as appropriate.

1. *ad-* + count = _____

2. *ad-* + ray = _____

3. *ad-* + prove = _____

4. *ad-* + tend = _____

5. *ad-* + sign = _____

6. *ad-* + fix = _____

7. *ad-* + sortment = _____

8. *ad-* + gression = _____

9. *ad-* + firm = _____

10. *ad-* + cuse = _____

11. *ad-* + nounce = _____

12. *ad-* + point = _____

13. *ad-* + low = _____

14. *ad-* + fect = _____

15. *ad-* + tract = _____

Number correct _____ (total 15)

The Prefix *com-*

The spelling of the prefix *com-* does not change when it is added to roots or to words that begin with the letters *m*, *p*, or *b*.

com- + mon = common   *com-* + ponent = component
com- + municate = communicate   *com-* + bustion = combustion

The prefix *com-* changes to *con-* when added to words that begin with the letters *c, d, g, j, n, q, s, t,* and *v*.

com- + tinent = continent   *com-* + sole = console
com- + gratulate = congratulate *com-* + spicuous = conspicuous

The prefix *com-* changes to *col-* when added to roots or words beginning with *l* to create a double consonant.

com- + lect = collect   *com-* + lide = collide

The prefix *com-* changes to *cor-* when added to roots or words beginning with *r* to create a double consonant.

com- + rode = corrode   com- + rupt = corrupt

Exercise Add the prefix *com-* to each of the roots or base words below. Change the spelling of the prefix as appropriate.

1. *com-* + solidate = _____

2. *com-* + tact = _____

3. *com-* + vict = _____

4. *com-* + respond = _____

5. *com-* + pete = _____

6. *com-* + cede = _____

7. *com-* + league = _____

8. *com-* + pose = _____

9. *com-* + sequence = _____

10. *com-* + quest = _____

11. *com-* + stitute = _____

12. *com-* + fess = _____

13. *com-* + prehend = _____

14. *com-* + duct = _____

15. *com-* + serve = _____

Number correct _____ (total 15)

The Prefix ex-

The spelling of the prefix *ex-* does not change when joined to vowels or to the consonants *p, t, h,* or *c*.

ex- + press = express   ex- + ception = exception
ex- + terior = exterior   ex- + it = exit
ex- + hausted = exhausted   ex- + ample = example

Exception: *Ex-* becomes *ec-* before *c* in the word *eccentric*.

The prefix *ex-* changes to *ef-* before *f*.

ex- + fort = effort   ex- + fective = effective

The prefix *ex-* changes to *e-* before most other consonants.

ex- + rosion = erosion   ex- + vaporate = evaporate
ex- + migrant = emigrant   ex- + lection = election

No common English words begin with the letters *exs*. When the prefix *ex-* is joined to roots that begin with the letter *s*, the *s* is dropped.

ex- + spect = expect   ex- + sist = exist

The Prefix *in-*

The spelling of the prefix *in-* does not change except in the following cases:

(a) The prefix *in-* changes to *im-* before *m, p,* or *b*.

in- + mutable = immutable   in- + position = imposition
in- + migration = immigration   in- + becile = imbecile

(b) The prefix *in-* changes to *il-* before *l* to create a double consonant.

in- + legible = illegible   in- + lusion = illusion

(c) The prefix *in-* changes to *ir-* before *r* to create a double consonant.

in- + regular = irregular   in- + rational = irrational

Exercise A The Prefixes *in-* and *ex-* can be added to each of the roots or base words listed below. Write the words formed by adding these prefixes. Change the spellings of the prefixes, the roots, or the base words as appropriate.

1. *in-* + hale = _____

2. *in-* + fuse = _____

3. *in-* + press = _____

4. *in-* + migrate = _____

5. *in-* + stinct = _____

6. *ex-* + hale = _____

7. ex- + fuse = _____

8. *ex-* + press = _____

9. *ex-* + migrate = _____

10. *ex-* + stinct = _____

Number correct _____ (total 10)

Exercise B Add the prefix *in-* or *ex-* to each of the roots or base words below. Change the spelling of the prefix as appropriate.

1. *in-* + herit = _____

2. *in-* + legal = _____

3. *in-* + volve = _____

4. *in-* + dulge = _____

5. *ex-* + vade = _____

6. *in-* + fect = _____

7. *in-* + accessible = _____

8. *ex-* + plain = _____

9. *ex-* + scape = _____

10. *in-* + pound = _____

11. *in-* + mobile = _____

12. *ex-* + clude = _____

13. *ex-* + ceed = _____

14. *ex-* + communicate = _____

15. *in-* + rigate = _____

Number correct _____ (total 15)

Words with Suffixes

Words Ending in *y*

When a suffix is added to a word ending in *y* preceded by a consonant, the *y* is usually changed to *i*.

mystery + *-ous* = mysterious   classify + *-ed* = classified
controversy + *-al* = controversial   classify + *-es* = classifies
peculiarity + *-es* = peculiarities   defy + *-ance* = defiance

There are two exceptions:

(a) When *-ing* is added, the *y* does not change.

classify + *-ing* = classifying   unify + *-ing* = unifying
carry + *-ing* = carrying   defy + *-ing* = defying

(b) Some one-syllable words do not change the *y*.

dry + *-ness* = dryness   shy + *-ness* = shyness

When a suffix is added to a word ending in *y* preceded by a vowel, the *y* usually does not change.

array + *-ed* = arrayed   destroy + *-er* = destroyer
enjoy + *-able* = enjoyable   joy + *-ful* = joyful

Exceptions: day + *-ly* = daily   gay + *-ly* = gaily

Exercise A   In these sentences, find each misspelled word and write the correct spelling on the line following the sentence.

1. Melissa's fears were allayed when she heard the dayly news.

   _____

2. I carryed my applycation to the employment office.

   _____

3. The families on the block are trieing to find a relyable dog walker.

   _____

4. A parent's insecurityes are often transmitted to his or her children.

   _____

5. The victoryous team relyed on its offense.

   _____

6. Crying hysterically, the victims told the scaryest storyes we had ever heard.

   _____

7. Are you implying that I am guiltyer than you?

   _____

8. The historycal novels on sale are good buys.

   _____

9. The deliveries of necessitys answered our prayers.

   _____

10. The spys have detected several irregular activitys.

   _____

Number correct _____ (total 15)

Exercise B   Add the suffixes indicated and write the new words.

1. agency + *-es* = _____

2. holy + *-est* = _____

3. tragedy + *-es* = _____

4. pacify + *-ed* = _____

5. mystify + *-ed* = _____

6. personify + *-ing* = _____

7. enjoy + *-ment* = _____

8. hurry + *-ing* = _____

9. inquiry + *-es* = _____

10. play + *-ful* = _____

11. worry + -ed = _____

12. primary + -ly = _____

13. tally + -ing = _____

14. pay + -able = _____

15. glory + -ous = _____

Number correct _____ (total 15)

The Final Silent e

When a suffix beginning with a vowel is added to a word ending in a silent _e_, the _e_ is usually dropped.

elevate + -ion = elevation   infinite + -ive = infinitive
diverse + -ity = diversity   virtue + -ous = virtuous
enterprise + -ing = enterprising   condense + -er = condenser
examine + -ation = examination   probe + -ed = probed

When a suffix beginning with a consonant is added to a word ending in a silent _e_, the _e_ is usually retained.

ultimate + -ly = ultimately   remote + -ness = remoteness
estrange + -ment = estrangement   shame + -less = shameless
subtle + -ty = subtlety   resource + -ful = resourceful

Exceptions:

true + -ly = truly   whole + -ly = wholly
argue + -ment = argument   awe + -ful = awful

Exercise A In these sentences, find each misspelled word and write the correct spelling on the line following the sentence.

1. As the elevator climbed, everyone felt the excitment riseing.

_____

2. Hostility is the primary motiveation of most criminals.

_____

3. The adversity she is experiencing is shapeing her personality.

_____

4. The advocates of the proposeal are examining the regulateions.

_____

5. The accusations against the driver made him feel truely aweful.

_____

6. Alice's strangness was barely noticed, except by her relatives.

_____

7. Our guideance counselor spoke with each student in the class about scheduleing and attendance.

_____

8. Graduation ceremonies usually include a commencment address given by one of the students.

_____

9. A resourceful lawyer asks probeing questions of her opposition.

_____

10. The amazing account of the children's involvement was unbelieveable.

_____

11. The announcement informed the performers of an additional rehearseal.

_____

12. One requirment of each student is participation in a reciteal.

_____

13. By the second month of his summer job, Tim had a reputation for latness.

_____

14. The fameous author signed copies of her recently condensed novel.

_____

15. Management acknowledges the scarceity of enterprising workers.

_____

Number correct _____ (total 20)

Exercise B Add the suffixes indicated and write the new words.

1. approve + -al = _____

2. tolerate + -ion = _____

3. prime + -er = _____

4. enhance + -ment = _____

5. dote + -age = _____

6. regulate + -ed = _____

7. probe + -ing = _____

8. serene + -ity = _____

9. speculate + -ive = _____

10. console + -ing = _____

11. irate + -ly = _____

12. associate + -ion = _____

13. time + *-less* = _____

14. recycle + *-ed* = _____

15. motive + *-ate* = _____

16. move + *-ment* = _____

17. discharge + *-ed* = _____

18. response + *-ible* = _____

19. taste + *-ful* = _____

20. elevate + *-ing* = _____

Number correct _____ (total 20)

Doubling the Final Consonant

In words of more than one syllable, double the final consonant before adding a suffix beginning with a vowel only if both of the following conditions exist:

1. The word ends with a single consonant preceded by a single vowel.
2. The word is accented on the last syllable.

com mit′ + *-ed* = com mit′ted   re fer′ + *-al* = re fer′ral
com mit′ + *-al* = com mit′tal   per mit′ + *-ing* = per mit′ting
re gret′ + *-ed* = re gret′ted   de ter′ + *-ence* = de ter′rence

Note in the examples above that the syllable accented in each new word is the same syllable that was accented before adding the suffix.

If the newly formed word is accented on a different syllable, the final consonant is not doubled.

re fer′ + *-ence* = ref′er ence   pre fer′ + *-ence* = pref′er ence

Exercise Each word below is divided into syllables. Determine which syllable in each word is accented, and insert the accent mark. Add the suffix indicated, noting if the accent moves to a different syllable. Then write the new word.

1. re mit + *-ed* = _____ + *-ing* = _____

2. in fer + *-ed* = _____ + *-ence* = _____

3. a bet + *-ed* = _____ + *-ing* = _____

4. sub mit + *-ed* = _____ + *-ing* = _____

5. in her it + *-ed* = _____ + *-ing* = _____

6. ed it + *-ed* = _____ + *-or* = _____

7. im pel + *-ed* = _____ + *-ing* = _____

8. ex it + *-ed* = _____ + *-ing* = _____

9. lev el + *-ed* = _____ + *-ing* = _____

10. be fit + -ed = _____ + -ing = _____

11. e mit + -ed = _____ + -ing = _____

12. ex cel + -ed = _____ + -ing = _____

13. rav el + -ed = _____ + -ing = _____

14. dif fer + -ed = _____ + -ing = _____

15. de fer + -ed = _____ + -ing = _____

Number correct _____ (total 15)

Words Ending in *ize* or *ise*

The suffix *-ize* is added to words to form verbs meaning "to make or become."

visual + *-ize* = visualize   (to make into a visual image)

theory + *-ize* = theorize   (to make a theory)

The *-ise* ending is less common. It is usually part of the base word itself rather than a suffix.

devise   surprise   televise   advertise

Exercise Decide whether *ize* or *ise* should be added to each word or letter group. Then write the complete word.

1. social   _____

2. rev   _____

3. idol   _____

4. immortal   _____

5. adv   _____

6. revital   _____

7. comprom   _____

8. disgu   _____

9. conceptual   _____

10. magnet   _____

11. desp   _____

12. sympath   _____

13. burglar   _____

14. terror   _____

15. exerc   _____

Number correct _____ (total 15)

The Suffix -ion

The suffix -ion changes verbs to nouns.

suggest + -ion = suggestion   equate + -ion = equation

discuss + -ion = discussion   separate + -ion = separation

attract + -ion = attraction   create + -ion = creation

In the examples above, -ion is either added directly to the verb form, or the final e is dropped before -ion is added.

Some verbs, when made into nouns, have irregular spellings.

compose + -ion = composition   dissuade + -ion = dissuasion

degrade + -ion = degradation   assume + -ion = assumption

In the case of words that do not adhere to regular spelling patterns, you must memorize their spellings.

Exercise A Add -ion to each of the following words.

1. stimulate _____

2. revise _____

3. deliberate _____

4. subtract _____

5. segregate _____

6. aggravate _____

7. affect _____

8. digest _____

9. convict _____

10. relate _____

11. afflict _____

12. repress _____

13. penetrate _____

14. oppress _____

15. associate _____

Number correct _____ (total 15)

Exercise B Each of the following nouns is formed by adding a variation of the -ion suffix to a verb. Write the verb form of each. Use a dictionary if needed.

1. erosion _____

2. competition _____

3. resumption _____

4. allegation _____

5. persuasion _____

6. perception _____

7. conversion _____

8. reduction _____

9. imposition _____

10. division _____

11. confrontation _____

12. abolition _____

13. abstention _____

14. recession _____

15. admission _____

Number correct _____ (total 15)

Other Spelling Problems

Words with *ie* and *ei*

When the sound is long *e* (*ē*), it is spelled *ie* except after *c*.
If the vowel combination sounds like a long *a* (*ā*), spell it *ei*.

i before e
thief   grief   niece   yield   brief
chief   achieve   relieve   piece

except after c
ceiling   perceive   deceit   conceive   receive   receipt

or when sounded as *a*
neighbor   sleigh   reign

Exceptions:
either   weird   seize   financier
neither   species   leisure

You can remember these words by combining them into the following sentence: *Neither financier seized either weird species of leisure.*

Exercise A Find the misspelled words in these sentences and spell them correctly on the line following the sentence.

1. The chief problem is the boy's belief that he does not have to yeild to anyone.

_____

2. I hope that receiving our card relieves Abby's greif.

_____

3. During the siege, the soldier's rations were siezed.

_____

4. Aunt Bertha spends her leisure time with her many neices.

_____

5. "What a wierd experience!" shrieked the participants.

_____

6. The financier saves niether receipts nor pieces of correspondence.

_____

7. We could not conceive of how Derek became so decietful.

_____

8. What a relief that the theif has been captured!

_____

9. The crack in the ceiling is almost impossible to percieve.

_____

10. Metalworkers achieved perfection in that sheild.

_____

Number correct _____ (total 10)

Exercise B Fill in the blanks with *ie* or *ei*.

1. h a n d k e r c h _ _ f
2. f _ _ l d
3. r e c _ _ v e
4. c o n c _ _ t
5. p _ r c e
6. n _ _ t h e r
7. p _ _ r
8. d e c _ _ v e
9. b r _ _ f
10. w _ _ l d

Number correct _____ (total 10)

Words with the "Seed" Sound

Only one English word ends in *sede:* supersede
Three words end in *ceed:* exceed proceed succeed
All other words ending with the sound of *seed* are spelled out *cede:*
accede   concede   precede   recede   secede

Exercise A In these sentences, find each misspelled word and write the correct spelling on the line following the sentence.

1. As the water receeds, the clean-up crews will proceed with their job.

   _____

2. In the succeding months, the organization anticipates that five groups will secede.

   _____

3. If the candidate conceeds that point, he will exceed his budget.

   _____

4. The preseding announcement superseded all previous ones.

   _____

5. The procedes from the fund-raiser exceeded our hopes.

   _____

6. In acceeding to her opponent's arguments, the debator lost all hopes of winning the debate.

   _____

7. By provision of the treaty, the unexplored land is to be ceeded to the nearest province.

   _____

8. To succede you must learn to proceed boldly.

   _____

9. An arbitrator will interceed on behalf of those who wish to secede.

   _____

10. If we succeed with our parade plans, the mayor's car will preceed the floats.

   _____

Number correct _____ (total 10)

Exercise B Put a check by the five correctly spelled words below.

1. succede _____   6. superceed _____

2. acceed _____   7. presede _____

3. recede _____   8. succeed _____

4. intercede _____   9. proceed _____

5. exceed _____   10. conceed _____

Number correct _____ (total 10)

The Letter c

When the letter *c* has a *k* sound, it is usually followed by the vowels *a, o, u,* or by any consonant except *y*.

*c*alendar   cir*c*ulate   *c*orrect   *cy*cle   distin*c*t

When the letter *c* has an *s* sound, it is usually followed by an *e*, an *i*, or a *y*.

*c*irculate   *cy*cle   inferen*c*e   prin*c*ipal

Exercise A Decide if the *c* in each word below has a *k* sound or an *s* sound. Write *k* or *s* in the blank.

1. deceit _____   11. clamp _____

2. capital _____   12. cylinder _____

3. recipe _____   13. current _____

4. fancy _____   14. trace _____

5. become _____   15. local _____

6. continent _____   16. force _____

7. decimal _____   17. officer _____

8. transcript _____ 18. mercy _____

9. crystallize _____ 19. focus _____

10. citation _____   20. culminate _____

Number correct _____ (total 20)

Exercise B Fill in the missing letter or letters in each word.

1. c _ r c _ m s t a n c e

2. c _ m p r e h e n d

3. c _ n s t i t u t e

4. p r e c _ _ d e

5. p r o c _ a i m

6. s u s c _ p t i b l e

7. p e c _ l i a r

8. c _ _ n i c

9. s o u r c _

10. a s c _ t i c

Number correct _____ (total 10)

The Letter g

When the letter g has a sound as in the word go, it is usually followed by the vowels a, o, u, or by any consonant except y.

gargle   guard   negligence   rigor

When the letter g has a j sound, it is usually followed by an e, an i, or a y.

gymnasium   negligence   origin   rigid

Exceptions: giggle gill girl give

Exercise A Decide if the g in each word below has a j sound or a sound as in the word go. Write j or go in the blank.

1. glamour _____
2. guide _____
3. vigil _____
4. page _____
5. gardenia _____
6. gape _____
7. pigeon _____
8. gyrate _____
9. gush _____
10. guy _____
11. gypsy _____
12. enrage _____
13. indigent _____
14. epigram _____
15. dragon _____
16. gourd _____
17. giant _____
18. eagle _____
19. germ _____
20. angel _____

Number correct _____ (total 20)

Exercise B Fill in the missing letter in each word.

1. o b l i g _ t e
2. a m b i g _ i t y
3. e n i g _ a
4. m e r g _
5. e g _
6. e s t r a n g _ m e n t
7. r e g _ l a t e
8. b e n i g _
9. e x c h a n g _
10. d e g _ e e

Number correct _____ (total 10)

219

Spelling Review

Exercise A Add the prefix or suffix indicated and write the new word.

1. *in-* + pose = _____
2. hostile + *-ity* = _____
3. *ex-* + voke = _____
4. *ad-* + ray = _____
5. *ex-* + port = _____
6. *in-* + legal = _____
7. *com-* + ponent = _____
8. assume + *-ion* = _____
9. *con-* + sent = _____
10. *ad-* + prove = _____
11. regulate + *-ion* = _____
12. *in-* + regular = _____
13. dissuade + *-ion* = _____
14. *ad-* + dress = _____
15. abominate + *-ion* = _____

Number correct _____ (total 15)

Exercise B Three of the words in each row follow the same spelling pattern. Circle the word that does not follow that pattern.

1. victorious   reliance   crying   drier
2. concentration   universal   assurance   estrangement
3. forgotten   submitting   committal   inference
4. devise   realize   surprise   revise
5. concentration   fascination   competition   illumination
6. dissimilar   invisible   depress   renter
7. admit   assure   attainment   approve
8. concentric   congratulate   compress   condense
9. immobile   invalid   inference   integer
10. export   erode   eviction   election

Number correct _____ (total 10)

220

Exercise C   In these sentences, find each misspelled word and write the correct spelling on the line following the sentence.

1. We regretted the tardyness of our replies.

   _____

2. Your daily task is makeing your bed and putting your clothes away.

   _____

3. In the attorney's opinion, capital punishment is a deterent to conmitting crime.

   _____

4. What a surprise! We never expected them to televize the play.

   _____

5. Niether an ilegible nor a mispelled request is acceptable.

   _____

6. To succede one must attain a level of effectivness even under truely adverse circumstances.

   _____

7. The breif downpour prevented the water from receeding.

   _____

8. To avoid an arguement, the candidate circulated a clear statment of her views.

   _____

9. "Procede," shouted the chief. "Tolerate no defyance!"

   _____

10. The baby's ceaseless crying was terrifing.

    _____

11. Transition to their new countrys is difficult for many immigrants.

    _____

12. The exspiration date of the license was December 1988.

    _____

13. Tubeing down the rapids feels awfully wierd.

    _____

14. The severity of Joan's shyness makes her seem totaly imature.

    _____

15. The spies are carrying classifyed information.

    _____

Number correct _____ (total 25)

Number correct in Handbook _____ (total 340)

Commonly Misspelled Words

abbreviate	characteristic	emphasize	laboratory
absence	colonel	enthusiastic	legitimate
accidentally	colossal	equipped	leisure
accommodate	column	especially	lieutenant
accompanying	commission	etiquette	literacy
achievement	committed	exaggerate	literature
acknowledge	committee	excellent	luxurious
acquaintance	competitive	exceptional	maintenance
all right	complexion	exhaust	maneuver
altogether	compulsory	exhilarate	marriage
amateur	conscience	existence	mathematics
analyze	conscientious	experience	medieval
annihilate	conscious	familiar	miniature
anonymous	consensus	fatigue	minimum
apologize	contemptible	February	mischievous
appearance	convenience	feminine	missile
appreciate	corps	financial	misspell
appropriate	correspondence	foreign	mortgage
arctic	courageous	forfeit	municipal
argument	criticism	fragile	necessary
arrangement	criticize	generally	nickel
ascent	cylinder	genius	noticeable
assassinate	dealt	government	nuclear
associate	decision	grammar	nuisance
attendance	definitely	guarantee	obstacle
audience	dependent	gymnasium	occasionally
auxiliary	descent	handkerchief	occur
awkward	description	height	occurrence
bachelor	despair	hindrance	opinion
bargain	desperate	humorous	optimistic
beginning	dictionary	imaginary	outrageous
believe	different	immediately	pamphlet
benefited	dining	implement	parallel
biscuit	diphtheria	incidentally	parliament
bookkeeper	disappear	inconvenience	particularly
bulletin	disappoint	incredible	pastime
bureau	disastrous	indispensable	permissible
business	discipline	inevitable	perseverance
cafeteria	dissatisfied	infinite	perspiration
calendar	efficient	influence	persuade
calorie	eighth	inoculation	picnicking
campaign	eligible	intelligence	pleasant
cellophane	eliminate	irrelevant	pneumonia
cemetery	embarrass	irresistible	possess
changeable	eminent	knowledge	possibility

222

practice
preference
preparation
privilege
probably
professor
pronunciation
propeller
prophecy
psychology
quantity
questionnaire
realize
recognize
recommend
reference
referred
rehearse

reign
repetition
representative
restaurant
rhythm
ridiculous
sandwich
schedule
scissors
secretary
separate
sergeant
similar
sincerely
sophomore
souvenir
specifically

specimen
strategy
strictly
subtle
success
sufficient
surprise
syllable
sympathy
symptom
tariff
temperament
temperature
thorough
together
tomorrow
traffic

tragedy
transferred
truly
Tuesday
twelfth
tyranny
unanimous
undoubtedly
unnecessary
vacuum
vengeance
vicinity
village
villain
weird
wholly
writing

Commonly Confused Words

The following section lists words that are commonly confused and misused. Some of these words are homonyms, words that sound similar but have different meanings. Study the words in this list and learn how to use them correctly.

accent (ak′ sent) n.—stress in speech or writing; v.—to pronounce with stress
ascent (ə sent′) n.—act of going up
assent (ə sent′) n.—consent; v.—to accept or agree

accept (ək sept′, ak-) v.—to agree to something or receive something willingly
except (ik sept′) v.—to omit or exclude; prep.—not including

adapt (ə dapt′) v.—to adjust, to make fitting or appropriate
adept (ə dept′) adj.—proficient
adopt (ə däpt′) v.—to choose as one's own, to accept

affect (ə fekt′) v.—to influence, to pretend
affect (af′ ekt) n.—emotion
effect (ə fekt′, i-) n.—result of an action
effect (ə fekt′, i-) v.—to accomplish or produce a result

all ready adj.—completely prepared
already (ôl red′ ē) adv.—even now; before the given time

any way adj., n.—in whatever manner
anyway (en′ ē wā′) adv.—regardless

appraise (ə prāz′) v.—to set a value on
apprise (ə prīz′) v.—to inform

bazaar (bə zär′) n.—market or fair
bizarre (bi zär′) adj.—odd

bibliography (bib′ lē äg′ rə fē) n.—list of writings on a particular topic
biography (bī äg′ rə fē) n.—written history of a person's life

coarse (kôrs) adj.—rough, crude
course (kôrs) n.—route, progression

costume (käs′ tōōm, -tyōōm) n.—special way of dressing
custom (kus′ təm) n.—usual practice or habit

decent (dē′ s'nt) adj.—proper
descent (di sent′) n.—fall; coming down
dissent (di sent′) n.—disagreement; v.—to disagree

desert (dez′ ərt) n.—arid region
desert (di zurt′) v.—to abandon
dessert (di zurt′) n.—sweet course served at the end of a meal

device (di vīs′) n.—a contrivance
devise (di vīz′) v.—to plan

elusive (i lōō′ siv) adj.—hard to catch or understand
illusive (i lōō′ siv) adj.—misleading, unreal

emigrate (em′ ə grāt′) v.—to leave a country and take up residence elsewhere
immigrate (im′ ə grāt′) v.—to enter a country to take up residence

farther (fär′ thər) adj., adv.—more distant (refers to space)
further (fur′ thər) adj., adv.—additional (refers to time, quantity, or degree)

flair (fler) n.—natural ability, knack for style
flare (fler) v.—to flame; to erupt; n.—a blaze of light

lay (lā) v.—to set something down or place something
lie (lī) v.—to recline; to tell untruths; n.—an untruth

moral (môr′ əl, mär′-) n.—lesson; adj.—relating to right and wrong
morale (mə ral′, mô-) n.—mental state of confidence, enthusiasm

personal (pur′ s'n əl) adj.—private
personnel (pur sə nel′) n.—body of people, usually employed in an organization

precede (pri sēd′) v.—to go before
proceed (prə sēd′, prō-) v.—to advance; to continue

profit (präf′ it) v.—to gain earnings; n.—benefits; income from investments
prophet (präf′ it) n.—predictor or fortuneteller

quiet (kwī′ ət) adj.—not noisy; n.—a sense of calm
quit (kwit) v.—to stop
quite (kwīt) adv.—very; totally; truly

step (step) n.—footfall; v.—to move the foot as in walking
steppe (step) n.—large, treeless plain

team (tēm) n.—group of people working together on a project
teem (tēm) v.—to swarm or abound

than (than, then; *unstressed* thən, thən) conj.—word used in comparison
then (then) adv.—at that time, next in order of time

thorough (thur′ ō, -ə) adj.—complete
through (thrōō) prep.—by means of; from beginning to end; adv.—in one side and out the other

Glossary

A

abstract (adj.) theoretical; difficult to understand (v.) to remove; to summarize; (n.) written summary; p. 103. *Related word:* abstraction; p. 112.

accessibility (n.) state of being easily reached or obtained; p. 161. *Related words:* accede, access, accessible, inaccessible; p. 168.

adapt (v.) to adjust; p. 23. *Related words:* adaptable, adaptation, adapter; p. 30.

adjacent (adj.) next to; having a common border with; p. 116.

agency (n.) firm empowered to act for another; p. 149. *Related word:* agent; p. 158.

agitate (v.) to shake up; to provoke; p. 33. *Related word:* agitation; p. 40.

alien (adj.) foreign; (n.) foreigner; p. 23. *Related word:* alienate; p. 30.

allegedly (adv.) supposedly; p. 103. *Related words:* allegation, allege; p. 112.

allot (v.) to distribute; to assign; p. 191.

alter ego (n.) second self; trusted friend; p. 33.

ambiguity (n.) uncertainty; vagueness; p. 33. *Related word:* ambiguous; p. 40.

analytical (adj.) reasoned; investigative; p. 149. *Related word:* analyze; p. 158.

appallingly (adv.) horribly; fearfully; p. 126. *Related word:* appall; p. 133.

apprehension (n.) anxious feeling; arrest; p. 77. *Related words:* apprehend, apprehensive; p. 84.

arbitrary (adj.) based on a whim or a notion; tyrannical; p. 13. *Related word:* arbitrator; p. 20.

array (n.) orderly grouping; display; (v.) to place in order; to dress splendidly; p. 23.

ascetic (adj.) severe; strict in behavior; (n.) one who practices self-denial; p. 56. *Related word:* asceticism; p. 63.

associate (v.) to join as a partner; to relate to; (n.) partner; colleague; (adj.) joined with others, usually in work; p. 116. *Related word:* association; p. 122.

assumption (n.) belief; something taken for granted; p. 103. *Related word:* assume; p. 112.

attainment (n.) achievement; accomplishment; p. 103.

authority (n.) commanding power to influence others' thoughts, opinions, or behavior; p. 33. *Related words:* authoritarian, authoritative, authorize; p. 40.

B

baffle (v.) to confuse; to puzzle; p. 171.

benign (adj.) kind; gentle; harmless; p. 56.

bewilderment (n.) confusion; puzzlement; p. 161. *Related word:* bewilder; p. 168.

bleak (adj.) not cheerful; gloomy; harsh; p. 77.

brood (v.) to worry; to hover over; (n.) the young of an animal or family; p. 56. *Related word:* brooding; p. 63.

bulbous (adj.) shaped like a bulb; p. 126.

C

capacity (n.) ability to contain or absorb; p. 67.

chaos (n.) turmoil; upheaval; confusion; p. 149. *Related word:* chaotic; p. 158.

circumstance (n.) condition; occurrence; p. 13.

classic (adj.) traditional; enduring; (n.) model of excellence; p. 103.

classify (v.) to group; to categorize; p. 23. *Related word:* classification; p. 30.

code (n.) set of principles or laws; rules; p. 33.

commitment (n.) obligation; pledge; promise; p. 103. *Related words:* commit, committee; p. 112.

communal (adj.) public; shared; p. 126. *Related words:* common, commune, communicate, communism, community; p. 133.

compensate (v.) to make up for; to repay; p. 67. *Related word:* compensation; p. 75

component (n.) element or part; (adj.) serving as one of the parts of a whole; p. 116.

comprehend (v.) to understand; to include; p. 13. *Related words:* comprehensible, comprehensive; p. 20.

concede (v.) to give up; to yield; to acknowledge; p. 161.

concentration (n.) strength or density; close attention; p. 13.

condense (v.) to make more compact; to say in fewer words; p. 56. *Related word:* condensation; p. 63.

conform (v.) to correspond to; to follow; p. 13. *Related words:* conformity, nonconformist; p. 20.

confrontation (n.) face-to-face meeting; p. 77. *Related word:* confront; p. 84.

consent (n.) approval; permission; (v.) to agree; p. 13.

considerable (adj.) large; of some importance; p. 33.

conspicuous (adj.) noticeable; obvious; p. 103.

constituency (n.) people represented by an elected official; voters; p. 33. *Related word:* constituent; p. 40.

constitute (v.) to make up; to form; p. 13. *Related word:* constitution; p. 20.

contemporary (adj.) happening at the same time; modern; (n.) one who is of the same age; p. 103. *Related word with the temp root:* temporary; p. 112.

conversion (n.) renovation; reversal; adaptation; p. 77. *Related word:* convert; p. 84.

conviction (n.) strong belief; p. 56.

convulsive (adj.) spasmodic; contracting uncontrollably; p. 67. *Related words:* convulse, convulsion; p. 75.

cower (v.) to shrink and tremble in fear; p. 171.

crystallize (v.) to take shape; to cause to form; p. 161. *Related word:* crystal; p. 168.

cycle (n.) series of events that recur regularly; p. 116. *Related word:* recycle; p. 122.

cynic (n.) fault-finding critic of human nature; p. 33. *Related word:* cynical; p. 40.

D

defiance (n.) resistance; bold opposition; p. 126. *Related word:* defy; p. 133.

deft (adj.) skillful in a quick and easy way; p. 126.

derive (v.) to get or to trace from a source; p. 67. *Related word:* derivation; p. 75.

despondent (adj.) dejected; discouraged; p. 126. *Related word:* despond; p. 133.

despotism (n.) government under an absolute ruler; p. 13. *Related word:* despot; p. 20.

diffuse (v.) to scatter; to spread out; (adj.) spread out; p. 13. *Related words with the fus root:* diffusion, fusion, infuse, transfusion; p. 20.

dilemma (n.) situation in which one must choose between equally unpleasant things; p. 33.

dimension (n.) size; scope; aspect; p. 33.

diminutive (adj.) small; shortened; (n.) very small person or thing; p. 23.

disadvantaged (adj.) underprivileged; poor; p. 171. *Related word:* advantage; p. 179.

disconsolately (adv.) dejectedly; cheerlessly; p. 126. *Related words with the consol root:* consolation, console; p. 133.

disdainful (adj.) proud; scornful; p. 126. *Related word:* disdain; p. 133.

dismiss (v.) to send away; to put out of mind; p. 171.

dispose (v.) to put in a certain order; to arrange; p. 77. *Related word:* disposition; p. 84.

disquieting (adj.) unsettling; disturbing; p. 77.

distinguished (adj.) famous; p. 126. *Related word:* distinguish; p. 133.

diverse (adj.) different; varied; p. 33. *Related words:* diversify, diversion, diversity, divert; p. 40.

dominate (v.) to rule or control; p. 103. *Related words:* domination, predominate; p. 112.

dynamic (adj.) forceful; vigorous; p. 103. *Related word:* dynamo; p. 112.

E

effect (n.) influence; result; meaning; (v.) to cause; to bring about; p. 116. *Related word:* affect; p. 122.

elaborate (adj.) ornate; detailed; (v.) to add details; to expand; p. 171.

embrace (v.) to hug; to accept readily; to take up or adopt; (n.) hug p. 126.

embryo (n.) egg; seed; early stage of development; p. 126. *Related word:* embryonic; p. 133.

enduring (adj.) lasting; permanent; p. 171. *Related word:* endure; p. 179.

enhance (v.) to make greater in value; p. 67. *Related word:* enhancement; p. 75.

enigma (n.) puzzle; mystery; p. 23. *Related word:* enigmatic; p. 30.

ensure (v.) to guarantee; to protect; p. 67.

enterprise (n.) project; activity; undertaking; p. 33. *Related word:* enterprising; p. 40.

entice (v.) to tempt; to attract; p. 171.

erode (v.) to wear away; p. 161. *Related word:* erosion; p. 168.

esoteric (adj.) understood by only a few; p. 103.

estate (n.) possessions; property; p. 103.

estrangement (n.) separation; p. 33. *Related word:* estrange; p. 40.

estuary (n.) mouth of a river where the tide meets the river current; inlet; p. 56.

ethnic (adj.) designating a group set apart by its customs, language, or religion; p. 161.

evoke (v.) to call forth; to bring to mind; p. 23.

export (n.) product moved from one country to another; (v.) to send out; (adj.) of or for exporting or exports; p. 116. *Related words with the* port *root:* deport, portable, portage, porter; p. 122.

exquisite (adj.) beautiful; flawless; p. 56.

F

facility (n.) ease; skill; p. 149. *Related word:* facilitate; p. 158.

fermentation (n.) the breakdown of complex molecules in organic compounds; p. 149.

fleeting (adj.) quickly passing; not lasting; p. 77. *Related word:* fleet; p. 84.

forerunner (n.) someone or something that comes before another; predecessor; p. 149.

formally *adv.* methodically; ceremonially; properly; p. 33. *Related word:* formality; p. 40.

formidable (adj.) hard to handle or overcome; difficult; p. 126.

formulate (v.) to devise; to develop; p. 149. *Related word:* formula; p. 158.

fragility (n.) state of being easily broken; p. 23.

frigid (adj.) extremely cold; p. 23. *Related word:* frigidity; p. 30.

functional (adj.) useful; practical; p. 171. *Related word:* function; p. 179.

G

gloat (v.) to exult smugly; to relish maliciously; p. 126.

grotesque (adj.) having a strange, bizarre appearance; p. 77.

H

heritage (n.) something passed down; p. 161. *Related words:* inherit, inheritance; p. 168.

homogeneity (n.) similarity; likeness; p. 161. *Related words with the* genus *root:* heterogeneous, homogeneous; p. 168.

hostility (n.) unfriendliness; ill will; warfare; p. 33. *Related word:* hostile; p. 40.

hydrological (adj.) relating to the study of water; p. 116. *Related words with the* hydro *root:* dehydrate, hydrology, hydrometer; p. 122.

I

idol (n.) object of worship; image of a god; p. 56. *Related words:* idolatry, idolize; p. 63.

illiterate (adj.) uneducated; ignorant; unable to read or write; p. 171. *Related word:* literate; p. 179.

illusion (n.) unreal or misleading image or appearance; p. 67. *Related word:* illusory; p. 75.

imperceptible (adj.) slight; subtle; difficult to perceive; p. 56. *Related words:* perceive, perception; p. 63.

impose (v.) to establish by force; to place a burden on; p. 161. *Related word:* imposition; p. 168.

impregnable (adj.) impenetrable; unshakable; p. 77.

incessant (adj.) constant; ceaseless; p. 116.

infinite (adj.) boundless; vast; p. 23. *Related words with the* fin *root:* finite, infinitesimal, infinity; p. 30.

initial (adj.) first; beginning; p. 67. *Related words:* initiate, initiation; p. 75.

inquiry (n.) question; investigation; p. 149. *Related word:* inquire; p. 158.

instinctively (adv.) naturally; innately; p. 77. *Related word:* instinct; p. 84.

integral (adj.) essential; whole; p. 116. *Related words:* integrate, integrity; p. 122.

intellectual (adj.) requiring intelligence; (n.) person who enjoys activities requiring thinking; p. 171.

interior (adj.) inner; (n.) inside; p. 23.

interminable (adj.) endless; p. 56. *Related words:* terminal, terminate; p. 63.

introvert (n.) person who is more interested in his or her own thoughts or feelings than in other people; p. 171. *Related words:* extrovert, introverted; p. 179.

invalid (adj.) having no force; null or void; (n.) one who is ill or disabled; p. 161. *Related words:* invalidate, valid; p. 168.

isolate (v.) to set apart from others; p. 149. *Related word:* isolation; p. 158.

L

laborious (adj.) calling for hard work; difficult; p. 171.

lax (adj.) loose; not strict; p. 67. *Related word:* laxity; p. 75.

liberation (n.) gaining of freedom; p. 161. *Related word:* liberate; p. 168.

luminous (adj.) bright; glowing; p. 56. *Related word:* illumination; p. 63.

M

malformation (n.) irregular formation of a part; deformation; p. 67.

masochist (n.) person who gets pleasure from inflicting pain on himself or herself; p. 67.

meditative (adj.) thoughtful; p. 56. *Related words:* meditate, meditation; p. 63.

memorable (adj.) impressive enough to be remembered; notable; p. 77.

mentor (n.) wise adviser; teacher; p. 171.

merge (v.) to join together; to unite; to combine; p. 23.

metaphor (n.) figure of speech that speaks of one thing as if it were another; p. 161. *Related word:* metaphorical; p. 168.

mettlesome (adj.) courageous; hardy; spirited; p. 67. *Related word:* mettle; p. 75.

mindless (adj.) showing little or no intelligence; stupid; p. 33.

mingle (v.) to blend; to mix; to socialize; p. 23.

mutable (adj.) changeable; p. 161. *Related words:* immutable, mutation, mutual; p. 168.

mystic (n.) one who claims to have had direct communion with God or with ultimate reality; (adj.) enigmatic; p. 149. *Related words:* mysterious, mystery, mysticism, mystify, mystique; p. 158.

mythological (adj.) legendary; p. 103. *Related words:* myth, mythology; p. 112.

N

naive (adj.) unsophisticated; gullible; p. 33. *Related word:* naiveté; p. 40.

nautical (adj.) of water, sailors, or ships; p. 56.

nonchalant (adj.) unconcerned; cool; indifferent; p. 126. *Related word:* nonchalantly; p. 133.

nutrient (adj.) nourishing; (n.) nourishing food element; p. 116. *Related words:* nutrition, nutritious; p. 122.

O

obligate (v.) to bind legally, morally, or by sense of duty; p. 13. *Related words:* obligation, obligatory; p. 20.

oppression (n.) harsh, unjust use of authority or power; p. 103. *Related word:* oppressive; p. 112.

optimistic (adj.) disposed to take a favorable view; p. 171. *Related words:* optimal, optimum; p. 179.

original (adj.) beginning; first; innovative; creative; (n.) source; p. 149. *Related words:* origin, originate; p. 158.

ostentatious (adj.) having a showy display of wealth; pretentious; p. 77.

P

pacific (adj.) peaceful; p. 56. *Related words:* pacification, pacify; p. 63.

paradoxical (adj.) puzzling; contrary to expectation; p. 33. *Related word:* paradox; p. 40.

paragon (n.) model; ideal; p. 126.

parasite (n.) living thing that nourishes itself on another organism; someone who lives at the expense of others and gives nothing in return; p. 23.

paternalism (n.) fatherlike system of control; p. 103. *Related word:* paternal; p. 112.

perceptive (adj.) observant; able to understand; quickly and easily; p. 149. *Related word:* perception; p. 158.

perennial (adj.) constant; enduring; (n.) plant having a life cycle of more than two years; p. 23.

persistent (adj.) determined; constant; p. 23. *Related words:* persist, persistence; p. 30.

personify (v.) to humanize an animal or object; p. 56. *Related word:* personification; p. 63.

phenomenon (n.) observable fact; rare occurrence; p. 161. *Related word:* phenomenal; p. 168.

physiology (n.) study of the functions of living things; p. 149.

placid (adj.) calm; peaceful; p. 56.

posterity (n.) future generations; p. 13.

precede (v.) to come before; p. 13. *Related words with the* cede *root:* antecedent, concede, proceed, recede; p. 20.

precursor (n.) forerunner; predecessor; p. 149.

predominantly (adv.) primarily; mostly; p. 103. *Related words:* domination, predominate; p. 112.

prejudicial (adj.) biased; tending to injure or harm; p. 161.

prerequisite (n.) requirement; p. 67. *Related word:* requisite; p. 75.

primitive (adj.) at or relating to an early stage of development; simple; p. 103. *Related words:* primary, prime, primeval; p. 112.

proclaim (v.) to announce publicly; p. 13.

prolong (v.) to lengthen; to extend; p. 67. *Related word:* prolongation; p. 75.

prone (adj.) inclined; tending; lying flat or face down; p. 13.

prospect (n.) likely chance for success; looking forward; anticipation; p. 171. *Related words:* prospective, prospector; p. 179.

Q

quota (n.) share or part assigned; limit; p. 161.

R

recurrence (n.) something that happens again; p. 116.

refined (adj.) elegant; cultured; p. 126. *Related word:* refine; p. 133.

reflexive (adj.) pertaining to a quick, automatic, or habitual reaction; p. 33.

reform (v.) to correct; to set straight; (n.) a correction of faults; p. 171. *Related word:* reformer; p. 179.

regard (v.) to look at steadily; to consider; (n.) a fixed look; consideration; respect; p. 77.

rejection (n.) discarding; refusal; p. 77. *Related words with the* jacere *root:* inject, project, reject; p. 84.

relentless (adj.) unyielding; persistent; p. 67. *Related words:* relent, unrelenting; p. 75.

relic (n.) object associated with a saint; keepsake; p. 77.

repression (n.) act of holding back by force; p. 161. *Related word:* repress; p. 168.

resentment (n.) feeling of hurt at being offended; bitterness; p. 77. *Related word:* resent; p. 84.

resilient (adj.) flexible; elastic; adaptable; p. 67. *Related word:* resilience; p. 75.

restoration (n.) process of bringing back to a former condition; p. 116. *Related word:* restore; p. 122.

retain (v.) to keep; to remember; p. 116. *Related words with the* ten *root:* detain, detention, tenacious, tenure; p. 122.

rigorous (adj.) harsh; severe; p. 149. *Related word:* rigor; p. 158.

S

score (n.) set of twenty; mark used for keeping account; (v.) to keep a record or account of, such as with marks; p. 126.

sector (n.) subdivision; segment; p. 103.

sediment (n.) matter that settles to the bottom of a liquid; p. 116.

serenity (n.) peace; calmness; p. 56. *Related word:* serene; p. 63.

simultaneous (adj.) occurring at the same time; p. 116. *Related word with the* sim *root:* simile; p. 122.

somber (adj.) drab; gloomy; grave; p. 56.

specter (n.) ghost; spirit; p. 161. *Related word:* spectral; p. 168.

spirit (n.) main principle; soul; enthusiasm; ghost; p. 149. *Related word:* spiritual; p. 158.

spontaneity (n.) instinctiveness; naturalness; p. 171. *Related word:* spontaneous; p. 179.

sprawl (v.) to spread out; to stretch out; p. 23.

spurious (adj.) not genuine; false; p. 77.

stimulate (v.) to animate; to spur on; to provoke; p. 116.

stunted (adj.) limited; dwarfed; p. 23. *Related word:* stunt; p. 30.

subdivision (n.) dividing of parts into smaller parts; a piece of land resulting from this; p. 13.

sublime (adj.) awe-inspiring; noble; great; p. 149. *Related word:* sublimate; p. 158.

subsequent (adj.) following; coming after; p. 13.

substantive (adj.) actual; large; basic; essential; p. 171. *Related words:* substance, substantial; p. 179.

subtle (adj.) delicate; hard to detect; p. 116.

summarily (adv.) done quickly; without going through the usual forms or channels; p. 171. *Related words:* summary, summation; p. 179.

superciliously (adv.) in a contemptuous manner; p. 126.

supernatural (adj.) beyond what is usual or normal; (n.) forces beyond nature; p. 149.

susceptible (adj.) easily influenced or affected by; p. 13.

sustain (v.) to maintain; to prolong; to support; p. 67. *Related word:* sustenance; p. 75.

swoon (v.) to faint; to feel strong emotion; p. 67.

T

taunt (v.) to ridicule; (n.) scornful remark; p. 161.

taut (adj.) tightly stretched; p. 67.

tendency (n.) inclination; disposition; p. 67. *Related word:* tend; p. 75.

tenuous (adj.) slender; flimsy; weak; p. 23.

theory (n.) idea; hypothesis; abstract thought; p. 103. *Related word:* theorem; p. 112.

thesis (n.) theory; research paper; statement of an idea; p. 103.

timorously (adv.) in a fearful or timid way; p. 126. *Related word:* timid; p. 133.

tolerant (adj.) accepting; patient with others; p. 56. *Related words:* intolerant, tolerate; p. 63.

transient (adj.) temporary; short-lived; (n.) person who moves about from one place to another; p. 77. *Related word:* transitory; p. 84.

tributary (n.) stream or river feeding into a larger body of water; (adj.) flowing or being channeled into a larger body; paying tribute; p. 116.

turmoil (n.) uproar; commotion; p. 77.

tyranny (n.) government ruled by absolute power; very cruel use of power; p. 13. *Related word:* tyrannical; p. 20.

U

ultimately (adv.) finally; p. 33. *Related word:* ultimatum; p. 40.

unalterable (adj.) unchangeable; firm; stable; p. 13.

uncompromising (adj.) not yielding; inflexible; p. 149. *Related word:* compromise; p. 158.

undulate (v.) to move in waves; p. 23.

uniform (adj.) having the same form; consistent; (n.) dress worn for group identification; p. 13. *Related words:* uniformity, unison; p. 20.

unpretentious (adj.) unassuming; not showy; p. 77. *Related word:* pretentious; p. 84.

unrestrained (adj.) uncontrolled; without boundaries or limits; p. 149. *Related words:* restrain, restraint, self-restraint; p. 158.

V

velocity (n.) speed; p. 116.

virtue (n.) morality; merit; p. 56. *Related word:* virtuous; p. 63.

voluptuous (adj.) sensual; luxurious; p. 126.

W

wary (adj.) cautious; on guard against; p. 161.

watershed (n.) area drained by a river system; an important turning point; p. 116.

Pronunciation Key

Symbol	Key Words	Symbol	Key Words
a	ask, fat, parrot	b	bed, fable, dub
ā	ape, date, play	d	dip, beadle, had
ä	ah, car, father	f	fall, after, off
		g	get, haggle, dog
e	elf, ten, berry	h	he, ahead, hotel
ē	even, meet, money	j	joy, agile, badge
		k	kill, tackle, bake
i	is, hit, mirror	l	let, yellow, ball
ī	ice, bite, high	m	met, camel, trim
		n	not, flannel, ton
ō	open, tone, go	p	put, apple, tap
ô	all, horn, law	r	red, port, dear
oo	ooze, tool, crew	s	sell, castle, pass
oo	look, pull, moor	t	top, cattle, hat
yoo	use, cute, few	v	vat, hovel, have
yoo	united, cure, globule	w	will, always, swear
		y	yet, onion, yard
oi	oil, point, toy	z	zebra, dazzle, haze
ou	out, crowd, plow		
u	up, cut, color	ch	chin, catcher, arch
ur	urn, fur, deter	sh	she, cushion, dash
ə	a in ago		
	e in agent	th	thin, nothing, truth
	i in sanity	zh	azure, leisure
	o in comply	ŋ	ring, anger, drink
	u in focus	′	able (ā′ b'l)
ər	perhaps, murder	′′	expedition (ek′ spə dish′ ən)

Inventory Test

These are all the target words in the book. Why not see how many you think you already know . . . or don't know?

- If you're sure *you know the word, mark the* **Y** *("yes") circle.*
- If you think you *might know it, mark the* **?** *(question mark) circle.*
- If you have *no idea what it means, mark the* **N** *("no") circle.*

Y	?	N		Y	?	N		Y	?	N	
O	O	O	abstract	O	O	O	condense	O	O	O	enhance
O	O	O	accessibility	O	O	O	conform	O	O	O	enigma
O	O	O	adapt	O	O	O	confrontation	O	O	O	ensure
O	O	O	adjacent	O	O	O	consent	O	O	O	enterprise
O	O	O	agency	O	O	O	considerable	O	O	O	entice
O	O	O	agitate	O	O	O	conspicuous	O	O	O	erode
O	O	O	alien	O	O	O	constituency	O	O	O	esoteric
O	O	O	allegedly	O	O	O	constitute	O	O	O	estate
O	O	O	allot	O	O	O	contemporary	O	O	O	estrangement
O	O	O	alter ego	O	O	O	conversion	O	O	O	estuary
O	O	O	ambiguity	O	O	O	conviction	O	O	O	ethnic
O	O	O	analytical	O	O	O	convulsive	O	O	O	evoke
O	O	O	appallingly	O	O	O	cower	O	O	O	export
O	O	O	apprehension	O	O	O	crystallize	O	O	O	exquisite
O	O	O	arbitrary	O	O	O	cycle	O	O	O	facility
O	O	O	array	O	O	O	cynic	O	O	O	fermentation
O	O	O	ascetic	O	O	O	defiance	O	O	O	fleeting
O	O	O	associate	O	O	O	deft	O	O	O	forerunner
O	O	O	assumption	O	O	O	derive	O	O	O	formally
O	O	O	attainment	O	O	O	despondent	O	O	O	formidable
O	O	O	authority				*You're making progress.*	O	O	O	formulate
O	O	O	baffle	O	O	O	despotism	O	O	O	fragility
O	O	O	benign	O	O	O	diffuse	O	O	O	frigid
O	O	O	bewilderment	O	O	O	dilemma	O	O	O	functional
O	O	O	bleak	O	O	O	dimension	O	O	O	gloat
O	O	O	brood	O	O	O	diminutive	O	O	O	grotesque
O	O	O	bulbous	O	O	O	disadvantaged	O	O	O	heritage
O	O	O	capacity	O	O	O	disconsolately	O	O	O	homogeneity
O	O	O	chaos	O	O	O	disdainful	O	O	O	hostility
O	O	O	circumstance	O	O	O	dismiss	O	O	O	hydrological
O	O	O	classic	O	O	O	dispose	O	O	O	idol
O	O	O	classify	O	O	O	disquieting	O	O	O	illiterate
O	O	O	code	O	O	O	distinguished	O	O	O	illusion
O	O	O	commitment	O	O	O	diverse	O	O	O	imperceptible
O	O	O	communal	O	O	O	dominate	O	O	O	impose
O	O	O	compensate	O	O	O	dynamic	O	O	O	impregnable
O	O	O	component	O	O	O	effect	O	O	O	incessant
O	O	O	comprehend	O	O	O	elaborate	O	O	O	infinite
O	O	O	concede	O	O	O	embrace	O	O	O	initial
O	O	O	concentration	O	O	O	embryo	O	O	O	inquiry
			That's the first 40.	O	O	O	enduring				*Take a break!*

234

Y	?	N	
○	○	○	instinctively
○	○	○	integral
○	○	○	intellectual
○	○	○	interior
○	○	○	interminable
○	○	○	introvert
○	○	○	invalid
○	○	○	isolate
○	○	○	laborious
○	○	○	lax
○	○	○	liberation
○	○	○	luminous
○	○	○	malformation
○	○	○	masochist
○	○	○	meditative
○	○	○	memorable
○	○	○	mentor
○	○	○	merge
○	○	○	metaphor
○	○	○	mettlesome
○	○	○	mindless
○	○	○	mingle
○	○	○	mutable
○	○	○	mystic
○	○	○	mythological

Half the alphabet.

Y	?	N	
○	○	○	naive
○	○	○	nautical
○	○	○	nonchalant
○	○	○	nutrient
○	○	○	obligate
○	○	○	oppression
○	○	○	optimistic
○	○	○	original
○	○	○	ostentatious
○	○	○	pacific
○	○	○	paradoxical
○	○	○	paragon
○	○	○	parasite
○	○	○	paternalism
○	○	○	perceptive

Y	?	N	
○	○	○	perennial
○	○	○	persistent
○	○	○	personify
○	○	○	phenomenon
○	○	○	physiology
○	○	○	placid
○	○	○	posterity
○	○	○	precede
○	○	○	precursor
○	○	○	predominantly
○	○	○	prejudicial
○	○	○	prerequisite
○	○	○	primitive
○	○	○	proclaim
○	○	○	prolong
○	○	○	prone
○	○	○	prospect
○	○	○	quota
○	○	○	recurrence
○	○	○	refined
○	○	○	reflexive
○	○	○	reform
○	○	○	regard
○	○	○	rejection
○	○	○	relentless
○	○	○	relic
○	○	○	repression
○	○	○	resentment
○	○	○	resilient
○	○	○	restoration
○	○	○	retain
○	○	○	rigorous
○	○	○	score
○	○	○	sector
○	○	○	sediment
○	○	○	serenity
○	○	○	simultaneous

This list will end soon.

Y	?	N	
○	○	○	somber
○	○	○	specter
○	○	○	spirit

Y	?	N	
○	○	○	spontaneity
○	○	○	sprawl
○	○	○	spurious
○	○	○	stimulate
○	○	○	stunted
○	○	○	subdivision
○	○	○	sublime
○	○	○	subsequent
○	○	○	substantive
○	○	○	subtle
○	○	○	summarily
○	○	○	superciliously
○	○	○	supernatural
○	○	○	susceptible
○	○	○	sustain
○	○	○	swoon
○	○	○	taunt
○	○	○	taut
○	○	○	tendency
○	○	○	tenuous

Only 20 more.

Y	?	N	
○	○	○	theory
○	○	○	thesis
○	○	○	timorously
○	○	○	tolerant
○	○	○	transient
○	○	○	tributary
○	○	○	turmoil
○	○	○	tyranny
○	○	○	ultimately
○	○	○	unalterable
○	○	○	uncompromising
○	○	○	undulate
○	○	○	uniform
○	○	○	unpretentious
○	○	○	unrestrained
○	○	○	velocity
○	○	○	virtue
○	○	○	voluptuous
○	○	○	wary
○	○	○	watershed

Congratulations! That was 240 words. How many of them *don't* you know? Highlight any words you marked **N**, and pay special attention to them as you work through the book. You'll soon know them all!

Strategies *for Discovering Word Meaning*

Use What You Already Know

There are many ways to get information about what an unfamiliar word might mean.

- It may contain a familiar **whole word**.
- It may be a **compound** of familiar words put together.
- You may recognize the **root**.
- You may recognize a **prefix** or **suffix**.
- There may be **context clues** to the meaning.

Try Everything

When you see an unfamiliar word, use every trick you can think of. You may be surprised to discover how useful what you already know can be. Take a look at how this can work with the word *enfeeblement* in the sentence, "She resented her enfeeblement."

	THOUGHT PROCESS	
enfeeblement	Since *resent* means "to feel hurt about," *enfeeblement* seems to be something bad.	**a context clue**
en • feeble • ment	I see *feeble* in there. Doesn't it mean "weak"?	**a whole word**
en• feeblement	Hmm . . . *en-* like in *endear, enlarge, enrage.* So it means something like "to make" or "to cause."	**a familiar prefix**
enfeeble • ment	That ending is common . . . *enjoy, enjoyment . . . measure, measurement.* It creates nouns.	**a familiar suffix**
	Noun. Feeble. To make. . . . So, she resented being made weak!	

Try It Yourself

_____ 1. disquietude (think about *disagreement, quiet,* and *altitude*)
   a. silence   b. sophistication   c. uneasiness

_____ 2. quadruped (think about *quadruple* and *pedestrian*)
   a. four-footed   b. four-sided   c. rectangular

_____ 3. preferential (think about *prefer* and *confidential*)
   a. publicized   b. favoring   c. before choosing

_____ 4. proximity (think about *approximate* and *humidity*)
   a. success   b. nearness   c. accuracy

_____ 5. overlay (think about *over* and *lay*)
   a. to cover   b. to notice   c. to return

UNIT 1   Test Yourself

Part A   Applying Meaning
Write the letter of the best answer.

_____ 1. A <u>concentration</u> of soldiers would be where the soldiers had
   a. died.   b. gathered.   c. hidden.   d. been defeated.

_____ 2. When we refer to our <u>posterity</u>, we are talking about
   a. the past.   b. the present.   c. our belongings.   d. future generations.

_____ 3. A person who <u>conforms</u> to the laws is someone who
   a. obeys them.   b. makes them.   c. breaks them.   d. enforces them.

_____ 4. <u>Tyranny</u> refers to a situation in which someone has an overabundance of, and misuses,
   a. power.   b. wealth.   c. intelligence.   d. natural resources.

_____ 5. If you need someone's <u>consent</u> in order to do something, you need that person's
   a. help.   b. silence.   c. permission.   d. participation.

_____ 6. If you are <u>obligated</u> to do something, you are likely to think of it as a
   a. treat.   b. danger.   c. duty.   d. goal.

_____ 7. A person who is <u>susceptible</u> to flattery is one who
   a. uses it.   b. ignores it.   c. is embarrassed by it.   d. is influenced by it.

_____ 8. <u>Uniform</u> laws would be ones that were
   a. voted on.   b. very strict.   c. never broken.   d. the same everywhere.

_____ 9. A person will be <u>prone</u> to injuries if he or she
   a. is careful.   b. is clumsy.   c. is a bully.   d. studies medicine.

_____ 10. What <u>precedes</u> turning 17?
   a. voting   b. being 16   c. being 17   d. turning 18

Part B   Matching Definitions
Match each word on the left with its definition on the right. Write the letter of the definition in the blank.

_____ 11. circumstance   a. to understand fully

_____ 12. subsequent   b. unchangeable; firm

_____ 13. constitute   c. to announce or declare publicly

_____ 14. proclaim   d. government under an absolute ruler

_____ 15. arbitrary   e. a detail, incident, or fact

_____ 16. diffuse   f. to scatter; spread out

_____ 17. unalterable   g. following; coming after

_____ 18. comprehend   h. to set up; establish; make up or form

_____ 19. subdivision   i. the dividing of parts into smaller parts

_____ 20. despotism   j. made without considering all the facts or the wishes of others

---

Score Yourself!   _The answers are on page 249._   Number correct: _____   Part A: _____   Part B: _____

UNIT 2   Test Yourself

Part A   Synonyms

Write the letter of the word that is closest in meaning to the capitalized word.

_____ 1. TENUOUS: (A) cowardly   (B) tilted   (C) shaky   (D) determined

_____ 2. MINGLE: (A) giggle   (B) confuse   (C) beat   (D) blend

_____ 3. DIMINUTIVE: (A) polite   (B) tiny   (C) pretty   (D) shadowy

_____ 4. INTERIOR: (A) inner   (B) hidden   (C) worse   (D) strong

_____ 5. ENIGMA: (A) puzzle   (B) poison   (C) insult   (D) collection

_____ 6. PERENNIAL: (A) bordering   (B) spreading   (C) lasting   (D) strict

_____ 7. ALIEN: (A) creative   (B) dangerous   (C) foreign   (D) incorrect

_____ 8. INFINITE: (A) delightful   (B) exhausting   (C) illegal   (D) unending

Part B   Recognizing Meaning

Write the letter of the word or phrase that is closest in meaning to the word or words in italics.

_____ 9. to *undulate* across the room
- a. hurry
- b. call out
- c. crawl slowly
- d. move in waves

_____ 10. a *frigid* day
- a. lucky
- b. very cold
- c. peculiar
- d. frightening

_____ 11. to *merge* slowly
- a. combine
- b. gather up
- c. awaken
- d. remember

_____ 12. to *classify* pictures
- a. label
- b. complete
- c. make available
- d. put into groups

_____ 13. its *stunted* growth
- a. slow
- b. limited
- c. twisted
- d. spreading

_____ 14. an odd *array* of stones
- a. heap
- b. structure
- c. arrangement
- d. broken section

_____ 15. to *adapt* to cold
- a. adjust to
- b. treat with
- c. react to
- d. retreat from

_____ 16. to *sprawl* on the floor
- a. relax
- b. lie still
- c. stretch out
- d. trip or stumble

_____ 17. his *persistent* interruptions
- a. rude
- b. continuing
- c. humorous
- d. not successful

_____ 18. to *evoke* an answer
- a. dislike
- b. call forth
- c. require
- d. not allow

_____ 19. the *fragility* of the bowl
- a. delicacy
- b. high value
- c. elegance
- d. unusual design

_____ 20. to be known as *parasites*
- a. followers
- b. important people
- c. habitual liars
- d. ones who live off others

Score Yourself!   *The answers are on page 249.*   Number correct: _____   Part A: _____   Part B: _____

238

UNIT 3 Test Yourself

Part A Matching Definitions

Match each word on the left with its definition on the right. Write the letter of the definition in the blank.

_____ 1. code   a. puzzling, full of contradictions

_____ 2. naive   b. another side of oneself; second self

_____ 3. formally   c. a fault-finding critic of human nature

_____ 4. authority   d. a separation based on lack of affection

_____ 5. cynic   e. a set of principles or laws; rules

_____ 6. dilemma   f. in a way that follows a fixed custom, ceremony, or rule

_____ 7. paradoxical   g. simple and innocent; overly trusting; unsophisticated

_____ 8. estrangement   h. people represented by an elected official; voters

_____ 9. alter ego   i. a situation requiring a choice between equally unpleasant things

_____ 10. constituency   j. the power or right to give commands or influence behavior

Part B Recognizing Meaning

Write the letter of the word or phrase that is closest in meaning to the word or words in italics.

_____ 11. those who will *ultimately* decide
  a. fairly   c. hastily
  b. too slowly   d. in the end

_____ 12. a feeling of *hostility*
  a. fear   c. envy
  b. unfriendliness   d. glad welcome

_____ 13. a *considerable* problem
  a. risky   c. fairly large
  b. puzzling   d. not solvable

_____ 14. to avoid *ambiguity*
  a. dishonesty   c. lack of progress
  b. lack of clarity   d. a sudden attack

_____ 15. an odd *enterprise*
  a. project   c. reaction
  b. request   d. surrounding

_____ 16. a new *dimension*
  a. rule   c. size
  b. brightness   d. success

_____ 17. a rather *mindless* activity
  a. impolite   c. disobedient
  b. imaginative   d. stupid or foolish

_____ 18. to *agitate* the crowd
  a. stir up   c. ignore
  b. speak to   d. move through

_____ 19. a group of *diverse* people
  a. angry   c. fortunate
  b. not alike   d. kept apart

_____ 20. her *reflexive* response
  a. latest   c. slow
  b. thoughtful   d. automatic

Score Yourself!   *The answers are on page 249.*   Number correct: _____   Part A: _____   Part B: _____

239

UNIT 5   Test Yourself

Part A   Synonyms
Write the letter of the word that is closest in meaning to the capitalized word.

_____ 1. BENIGN: (A) useless   (B) harmless   (C) helpful   (D) dangerous

_____ 2. PLACID: (A) calm   (B) dull   (C) friendly   (D) hidden

_____ 3. INTERMINABLE: (A) blended   (B) puzzling   (C) endless   (D) exhausting

_____ 4. IMPERCEPTIBLE: (A) unneeded   (B) unnoticeable (C) unkind   (D) hard

_____ 5. LUMINOUS: (A) clumsy   (B) expensive   (C) glowing   (D) meaningful

_____ 6. SERENITY: (A) friendliness (B) loneliness   (C) enthusiasm (D) peacefulness

_____ 7. EXQUISITE: (A) rare   (B) beautiful   (C) complicated (D) pure

_____ 8. SOMBER: (A) careful   (B) incomplete   (C) silent   (D) serious

_____ 9. PACIFIC: (A) peaceful   (B) large   (C) deep   (D) well-meaning

_____ 10. TOLERANT: (A) helpful   (B) cheerful   (C) accepting   (D) unusual

Part B   Matching Definitions
Match each word on the left with its definition on the right. Write the letter of the definition in the blank.

_____ 11. condense   a. a strong belief

_____ 12. ascetic   b. a worshiped object

_____ 13. virtue   c. filled with deep and serious thought

_____ 14. personify   d. the place where a river joins a sea

_____ 15. conviction   e. a good quality; morality

_____ 16. estuary   f. to give an animal or object human characteristics

_____ 17. brood   g. self-denying; allowing oneself few pleasures

_____ 18. idol   h. to make smaller; say in fewer words

_____ 19. meditative   i. having to do with water, sailors, or ships

_____ 20. nautical   j. to think in an anxious way; worry

UNIT 6   *Test Yourself*

Part A   *Synonyms*

Write the letter of the word that is closest in meaning to the capitalized word.

_____ 1. LAX: (A) main   (B) loose   (C) delicate   (D) straight

_____ 2. ENSURE: (A) guarantee   (B) pay   (C) contain   (D) claim

_____ 3. PREREQUISITE: (A) law   (B) plea   (C) guess   (D) requirement

_____ 4. METTLESOME: (A) brave   (B) pushy   (C) irritating   (D) careless

_____ 5. INITIAL: (A) same   (B) first   (C) partial   (D) identifying

_____ 6. TAUT: (A) curved   (B) short   (C) lasting   (D) tight

_____ 7. RELENTLESS: (A) unyielding   (B) merciful   (C) bored   (D) competitive

_____ 8. SUSTAIN: (A) remember   (B) restrict   (C) increase   (D) support

_____ 9. DERIVE: (A) get   (B) change   (C) scorn   (D) leave

_____ 10. SWOON: (A) spin   (B) bend   (C) faint   (D) die

_____ 11. CAPACITY: (A) ability   (B) likelihood (C) reluctance   (D) enthusiasm

_____ 12. TENDENCY: (A) enclosure   (B) leaning   (C) suggestion   (D) skill

Part B   *Applying Meaning*

Write the letter of the best answer.

_____ 13. One example of an action that is usually <u>convulsive</u> is a
          a. hug.   b. sneeze.   c. wink.   d. leap.

_____ 14. Something meant to <u>enhance</u> one's appearance is
          a. a mirror.   b. a disguise.   c. bright light.   d. make-up.

_____ 15. If you want to <u>prolong</u> an experience, you want it to
          a. last.   b. be remembered.   c. get better.   d. be over with.

_____ 16. An example of a <u>resilient</u> material is
          a. satin.   b. rubber.   c. iron.   d. chalk.

_____ 17. A <u>masochist</u> is someone who enjoys
          a. eating.   b. conversation.   c. pain.   d. excitement.

_____ 18. One person who must be able to create <u>illusions</u> is
          a. a doctor.   b. an inventor.   c. a magician.   d. a photographer.

_____ 19. A basketball player might <u>compensate</u> for being short by
          a. quitting.   b. making jokes.   c. growing taller.   d. jumping high.

_____ 20. A <u>malformation</u> in a body or body part is something that is
          a. not normal.   b. needed for survival.   c. slow to develop.   d. not useful.

Score Yourself!   *The answers are on page 249.*   Number correct: _____   Part A: _____   Part B: _____

UNIT 7 Test Yourself

Part A Matching Definitions

Match each word on the left with its definition on the right. Write the letter of the definition in the blank.

_____ 1. relic   a. to look at steadily

_____ 2. regard   b. disturbing; unsettling

_____ 3. grotesque   c. a throwing away or refusal

_____ 4. disquieting   d. a face-to-face meeting

_____ 5. instinctively   e. an object associated with a saint

_____ 6. rejection   f. not showy; not marked by unnecessary display

_____ 7. impregnable   g. without having to be learned; naturally

_____ 8. unpretentious   h. having a strange, bizarre experience

_____ 9. confrontation   i. a feeling of ill will in response to injury or insult

_____ 10. resentment   j. not capable of being penetrated or entered by force

Part B Recognizing Meaning

Write the letter of the word or phrase that is closest in meaning to the word or words in italics.

_____ 11. a *bleak* room
    a. small   c. peaceful
    b. cheerless   d. crowded

_____ 12. a *fleeting* feeling
    a. sad   c. passing quickly
    b. mild   d. not enthusiastic

_____ 13. his *ostentatious* gesture
    a. barely seen   c. coldly polite
    b. friendly   d. showy

_____ 14. in a state of *turmoil*
    a. upset   c. insecurity
    b. violence   d. deep worry

_____ 15. her *spurious* statements
    a. untrue   c. hopeful
    b. wicked   d. bitter and angry

_____ 16. *transient* sensations
    a. strong   c. temporary
    b. confusing d. unpleasant

_____ 17. to be *disposed* there
    a. left   c. learned
    b. positioned d. encouraged

_____ 18. a sense of *apprehension*
    a. terror   c. regret
    b. worry   d. unfriendliness

_____ 19. to take part in a *conversion*
    a. journey   c. major change
    b. discussion d. brief experience

_____ 20. one *memorable* experience
    a. lucky   c. recalled
    b. painful   d. easy to
                 remember

UNIT 9   Test Yourself

Part A   Matching Definitions

Match each word on the left with its definition on the right. Write the letter of the
definition in the blank.

_____ 1. esoteric   a. understood by only a few

_____ 2. thesis   b. of the first or earliest times

_____ 3. allegedly   c. a fatherlike system of control

_____ 4. classic   d. the harsh, unjust use of power

_____ 5. primitive   e. in a way that is stated but unproved; supposedly

_____ 6. oppression   f. a statement or idea defended in an argument

_____ 7. assumption   g. of the highest quality, class, or rank

_____ 8. paternalism   h. something thought but not known to be true; a
                              taking for granted

Part B   Recognizing Meaning

Write the letter of the word or phrase that is closest in meaning to the word or words
in italics.

_____ 9. such *abstract* concepts
   a. general   c. common
   b. ridiculous   d. extraordinary

_____ 10. *mythological* animals
   a. useful   c. not real
   b. untamed   d. endangered

_____ 11. her *theory* about it
   a. feeling   c. unproven idea
   b. misery   d. incorrect belief

_____ 12. to be *predominantly* middle-class
   a. mainly   c. proudly
   b. hopelessly   d. definitely

_____ 13. a *contemporary* Canadian
   a. scornful   c. complete
   b. modern-day   d. struggling

_____ 14. his *dynamic* speech
   a. royal   c. firm
   b. overly long   d. energetic

_____ 15. his *conspicuous* movements
   a. obvious   c. respectful
   b. uninterrupted d. wickedly secret

_____ 16. this surprising *attainment*
   a. quality   c. strong affection
   b. use of force   d. accomplishment

_____ 17. to *dominate* the conversation
   a. steer   c. rule or control
   b. take part in   d. keep records of

_____ 18. to keep my *commitment*
   a. secret   c. close attention
   b. pledge   d. polite concern

_____ 19. in charge of the *estate*
   a. sale   c. workplace
   b. property   d. estimation

_____ 20. just one *sector*
   a. part   c. time period
   b. colony   d. side or view

Score Yourself!   *The answers are on page 249.*   Number correct: _____   Part A: _____   Part B: _____

UNIT 10 Test Yourself

Part A Applying Meaning
Write the letter of the best answer.

_____ 1. The <u>watershed</u> of a particular river is the area that
   a. forms its banks.   b. it floods.   c. drains into it.   d. can be dammed up.

_____ 2. Someone who experienced a <u>recurrence</u> of an illness would be
   a. cured.   b. sick again.   c. near death.   d. only mildly ill.

_____ 3. A <u>tributary</u> of a river is
   a. the sea.   b. a boat.   c. the river's source.   d. a smaller river.

_____ 4. One example of a natural <u>cycle</u> is
   a. the seasons.   b. roots and branches.   c. a bird's nest.   d. thunder and
                                                                       lightning.

_____ 5. A common <u>sediment</u> in bathtubs is
   a. dirt.   b. bubbles.   c. a bar of soap.   d. a nonslip mat.

_____ 6. <u>Simultaneous</u> basketball games cannot occur
   a. indoors.   b. in bad weather.   c. on the same court.   d. with professionals.

_____ 7. The <u>restoration</u> of a building, a prairie, or a river is undertaken to make it
   a. as it once was.   b. larger or grander.   c. more useful.   d. more profitable.

_____ 8. <u>Hydrological</u> surveys and research deal with the study of
   a. fish.   b. water.   c. shipping.   d. infections.

_____ 9. One example of a <u>nutrient</u> is
   a. love.   b. mathematics.   c. vitamin C.   d. income tax.

_____ 10. One thing that the United States <u>exports</u> is
   a. tourists.   b. American cars.   c. foreign money.   d. Lake Michigan.

Part B Synonyms
Write the letter of the word that is closest in meaning to the capitalized word.

_____ 11. INTEGRAL: (A) small   (B) normal   (C) necessary   (D) measurable

_____ 12. STIMULATE: (A) hurt   (B) arouse   (C) change   (D) discourage

_____ 13. COMPONENT: (A) part   (B) gathering   (C) payment   (D) enclosure

_____ 14. EFFECT: (A) quality   (B) result   (C) attempt   (D) use

_____ 15. VELOCITY: (A) heat   (B) strength   (C) truth   (D) speed

_____ 16. SUBTLE: (A) buried   (B) delicate   (C) flexible   (D) surprising

_____ 17. INCESSANT: (A) clear   (B) thoughtless   (C) unending   (D) gleaming

_____ 18. ADJACENT: (A) bordering   (B) temporary   (C) helpful   (D) additional

_____ 19. ASSOCIATE: (A) confuse   (B) quicken   (C) absorb   (D) connect

_____ 20. RETAIN: (A) keep   (B) need   (C) sell   (D) decide

---

Score Yourself!   *The answers are on page 249.*   Number correct: _____   Part A: _____   Part B: _____

244

UNIT 11 Test Yourself

Part A Matching Definitions

Match each word on the left with its definition on the right. Write the letter of the definition in the blank.

_____ 1. gloat   a. proudly and scornfully

_____ 2. deft   b. having proper, good manners; well-bred

_____ 3. refined   c. skillful in a quick and easy way

_____ 4. embryo   d. to react with great satisfaction, especially mean satisfaction

_____ 5. defiance   e. having to do with the pleasures of the senses

_____ 6. bulbous   f. an animal in an early stage of development

_____ 7. formidable   g. causing fear or awe; difficult to overcome

_____ 8. distinguished   h. a show of disregard for, or scorn of, authority

_____ 9. voluptuous   i. round and swollen in appearance; like a bulb

_____ 10. superciliously   j. having qualities that seem superior; famous

Part B Recognizing Meaning

Write the letter of the word or phrase that is closest in meaning to the word or words in italics.

_____ 11. a quick *embrace*
     a. hug   c. change
     b. glance   d. feeling of relief

_____ 12. a *score* of children
     a. team   c. twenty
     b. common fear   d. lifelike picture

_____ 13. to react *timorously*
     a. with haste   c. loudly
     b. thoughtfully   d. without courage

_____ 14. a *paragon* of friendliness
     a. sign   c. perfect example
     b. refusal   d. recommendation

_____ 15. to speak *disconsolately*
     a. shyly   c. cruelly
     b. sadly   d. senselessly

_____ 16. with *nonchalant* attitudes
     a. rude   c. unconcerned
     b. stuck-up   d. very worried

_____ 17. their *appallingly* bad manners
     a. terribly   c. thoughtlessly
     b. surprisingly   d. newly learned

_____ 18. a *communal* kitchen
     a. large   c. very ordinary
     b. shared   d. well-equipped

_____ 19. a rather *disdainful* statement
     a. scolding   c. scornful
     b. insincere   d. enthusiastic

_____ 20. his *despondent* manner
     a. clumsy   c. unsympathetic
     b. questioning   d. discouraged

UNIT 13 Test Yourself

Part A Matching Definitions
Match each word on the left with its definition on the right. Write the letter of the definition in the blank.

_____ 1. uncompromising   a. first; earliest

_____ 2. mystic   b. complete disorder and confusion

_____ 3. spirit   c. able to understand quickly and easily; insightful

_____ 4. forerunner   d. one who claims to have spiritual experiences that reveal truth

_____ 5. agency   e. a main principle, quality, frame of mind, or inclination

_____ 6. chaos   f. able to break up a whole into its parts in order to understand

_____ 7. formulate   g. refusing to yield or to modify one's ideas

_____ 8. perceptive   h. the means by which something can be done; ability or skill

_____ 9. original   i. to identify by separating from others; to set apart

_____ 10. analytical   j. someone or something that comes before another

_____ 11. facility   k. the work of a person or group authorized to act for another

_____ 12. isolate   l. to express in an organized way; develop

Part B Applying Meaning
Write the letter of the best answer.

_____ 13. An example of a <u>supernatural</u> being would be
    a. an eagle.   b. a ghost.   c. a hero.   d. a weightlifter.

_____ 14. If you felt <u>sublime</u>, you might say that you felt as if you were walking on
    a. air.   b. eggshells.   c. thin ice.   d. hot coals.

_____ 15. A person eating in an <u>unrestrained</u> way would
    a. nibble.   b. gnaw.   c. munch.   d. gobble.

_____ 16. A <u>rigorous</u> test would be one that was
    a. unfair.   b. thorough.   c. easy to pass.   d. important.

_____ 17. Any <u>inquiry</u> involves
    a. questions.   b. accusations.   c. threats.   d. lawyers.

_____ 18. During a course in <u>physiology</u>, one would be most likely to study
    a. rock formations.   b. prehistoric times.   c. the brain.   d. the solar system.

_____ 19. One thing that can cause <u>fermentation</u> is
    a. yeast.   b. freezing temperatures.   c. dampness.   d. crime.

_____ 20. A <u>precursor</u> of the compact disk player was the
    a. light bulb.   b. record player.   c. VCR.   d. electronics industry.

Part A   Recognizing Meaning

Write the letter of the word or phrase that is closest in meaning to the word or words in italics.

_____ 1. to *erode* the shore
    a. go along   c. cover over
    b. wear away   d. separate from

_____ 2. to await *liberation*
    a. generosity   c. a freeing
    b. permission   d. relief from pain

_____ 3. a shocking *specter*
    a. prediction   c. rate of change
    b. sort or kind   d. object of dread

_____ 4. in a *wary* manner
    a. tired   c. skillful
    b. cautious   d. sympathetic

_____ 5. the group's *homogeneity*
    a. loyalty   c. truthfulness
    b. sameness   d. shared feeling

_____ 6. to *taunt* the stranger
    a. mock   c. avoid
    b. notice   d. welcome

_____ 7. to *concede* a right
    a. claim   c. fight for
    b. give up   d. take away

_____ 8. the *mutable* conditions
    a. difficult   c. risky
    b. peaceful   d. changeable

_____ 9. due to the *quota*
    a. gathering   c. share or limit
    b. disagreement d. stated purpose

_____ 10. a look of *bewilderment*
    a. fierceness   c. deep confusion
    b. determination d. patient suffering

Part B   Matching Definitions

Match each word on the left with its definition on the right. Write the letter of the definition in the blank.

_____ 11. impose   a. unsound or untrue; not effective

_____ 12. heritage   b. the act of holding back by force

_____ 13. ethnic   c. anything observable; anything extremely unusual

_____ 14. invalid   d. to place or force on another

_____ 15. metaphor   e. to take shape; cause to form

_____ 16. repression   f. something passed down over time

_____ 17. prejudicial   g. the state of being easy to reach

_____ 18. phenomenon   h. having to do with a group's customs, language, or religion

_____ 19. crystallize   i. a figure of speech that speaks of one thing as if it were another

_____ 20. accessibility   j. having to do with a favoring or dislike without good reason; biased

---

Score Yourself!   *The answers are on page 249.*   Number correct: _____   Part A: _____   Part B: _____

UNIT 15 Test Yourself

Part A   Synonyms

Write the letter of the word that is closest in meaning to the capitalized word.

_____ 1. ENTICE: (A) threaten   (B) confuse   (C) tempt   (D) thrill

_____ 2. LABORIOUS: (A) careful   (B) difficult (C) scientific (D) risky

_____ 3. ELABORATE: (A) expensive   (B) permanent (C) charming (D) complicated

_____ 4. DISADVANTAGED: (A) poor   (B) fair   (C) indecent (D) useless

_____ 5. MENTOR: (A) boss   (B) advisor   (C) prophet   (D) genius

_____ 6. ALLOT: (A) soothe   (B) increase   (C) request   (D) assign

_____ 7. FUNCTIONAL: (A) useful   (B) amusing   (C) necessary (D) sufficient

_____ 8. OPTIMISTIC: (A) cautious   (B) complete   (C) hopeful   (D) reasonable

_____ 9. ENDURING: (A) cheerful   (B) solid   (C) distressing (D) lasting

_____ 10. SUBSTANTIVE: (A) challenging (B) misleading (C) inferior (D) basic

_____ 11. REFORM: (A) improve   (B) replace   (C) criticize (D) forgive

_____ 12. DISMISS: (A) support   (B) ignore   (C) reject   (D) avoid

Part B   Applying Meaning

Write the letter of the best answer.

_____ 13. An illiterate person needs a
        a. doctor.   b. teacher.   c. meal.   d. map.

_____ 14. Introverts are people who are concerned mainly with
        a. spiritual affairs.   b. wealth and fame.   c. their own thoughts.   d. social success.

_____ 15. Something might be done summarily if one's major concern were
        a. haste.   b. fairness.   c. profit.   d. thoroughness.

_____ 16. The emotion that would lead one to cower is
        a. pride.   b. fury.   c. fear.   d. eagerness.

_____ 17. Which of the following is most likely to baffle someone?
        a. a vicious dog   b. a mystery   c. a compliment   d. a good joke

_____ 18. If you want to know what your prospects are, you are concerned about your
        a. ancestors.   b. future.   c. immediate needs.   d. friends.

_____ 19. Spontaneity occurs when people act without
        a. plans.   b. fear.   c. consequences.   d. concern for others.

_____ 20. One example of an intellectual activity is
        a. playing tag.   b. eating fine food.   c. parachuting.   d. problem-solving.

Score Yourself!   The answers are on page 249.   Number correct: _____   Part A: _____   Part B: _____

248

Score Yourself!

Unit 1	Unit 2	Unit 3	Unit 5	Unit 6	Unit 7
Part A	*Part A*	*Part A*	*Part A*	*Part A*	*Part A*
1. b	1. C	1. e	1. B	1. B	1. e
2. d	2. D	2. g	2. A	2. A	2. a
3. a	3. B	3. f	3. C	3. D	3. h
4. a	4. A	4. j	4. B	4. A	4. b
5. c	5. A	5. c	5. C	5. B	5. g
6. c	6. C	6. i	6. D	6. D	6. c
7. d	7. C	7. a	7. B	7. A	7. j
8. d	8. D	8. d	8. D	8. D	8. f
9. b	*Part B*	9. b	9. A	9. A	9. d
10. b	9. d	10. h	10. C	10. C	10. i
Part B	10. b	*Part B*	*Part B*	11. A	*Part B*
11. e	11. a	11. d	11. h	12. B	11. b
12. g	12. d	12. b	12. g	*Part B*	12. c
13. h	13. b	13. c	13. e	13. b	13. d
14. c	14. c	14. b	14. f	14. d	14. a
15. j	15. a	15. a	15. a	15. a	15. a
16. f	16. c	16. c	16. d	16. b	16. c
17. b	17. b	17. d	17. j	17. c	17. b
18. a	18. b	18. a	18. b	18. c	18. b
19. i	19. a	19. b	19. c	19. d	19. c
20. d	20. d	20. d	20. i	20. a	20. d

Unit 9	Unit 10	Unit 11	Unit 13	Unit 14	Unit 15
Part A	*Part A*	*Part A*	*Part A*	*Part A*	*Part A*
1. a	1. c	1. d	1. g	1. b	1. C
2. f	2. b	2. c	2. d	2. c	2. B
3. e	3. d	3. b	3. e	3. d	3. D
4. g	4. a	4. f	4. j	4. b	4. A
5. b	5. a	5. h	5. k	5. b	5. B
6. d	6. c	6. i	6. b	6. a	6. D
7. h	7. a	7. g	7. l	7. b	7. A
8. c	8. b	8. j	8. c	8. d	8. C
Part B	9. c	9. e	9. a	9. c	9. D
9. a	10. b	10. a	10. f	10. c	10. D
10. c	*Part B*	*Part B*	11. h	*Part B*	11. A
11. c	11. C	11. a	12. i	11. d	12. C
12. a	12. B	12. c	*Part B*	12. f	*Part B*
13. b	13. A	13. d	13. b	13. h	13. b
14. d	14. B	14. c	14. a	14. a	14. c
15. a	15. D	15. b	15. d	15. i	15. a
16. d	16. B	16. c	16. b	16. b	16. c
17. c	17. C	17. a	17. a	17. j	17. b
18. b	18. A	18. b	18. c	18. c	18. b
19. b	19. D	19. c	19. a	19. e	19. a
20. a	20. A	20. d	20. b	20. g	20. d

Acknowledgments

- City News Publishing Co.: For an abridgement of "Our Basic Liberties: Freedom of the Individual" by Sam J. Ervin, Jr., from *Vital Speeches of the Day*, Vol. 40, May 15, 1974.

- Imperial Oil Company: For an abridged version of "Tundra" by Rachel Kilsdonk, from *Imperial Oil Review*, © Imperial Oil Ltd., Toronto, Ontario, Canada.

- Time, Inc.: For excerpts from "Don't Love The Press, But Understand It" by Henry Grunwald, from *Time*, July 8, 1974; reprinted by permission of Time, The Weekly Newsmagazine; copyright Time, Inc., 1974

- Prentice-Hall, Inc.: For an abridged version of Joseph Conrad's *Heart of Darkness: With Backgrounds and Criticisms*, edited by Leonard F. Dean; copyright © 1960 by Prentice-Hall, Inc.

- Harold Ober Associates: For an excerpt from "Decision," from *Dance to the Piper* by Agnes de Mille; copyright 1951, 1952 by Agnes de Mille; copyright © renewed 1979, 1980 by Agnes de Mille.

- Macmillan Publishing Company, Inc.: For an excerpt from *Innocent Blood* by P.D. James; copyright © 1980 by P.D. James. Charles Scribner's Sons, an imprint of Macmillan Publishing Company.

- Macmillan Publishing Company, Inc.: For an excerpt from *Custer Died for Your Sins* by Vine Deloria, Jr.; copyright © 1969 by Vine Deloria, Jr.

- Harcourt Brace Jovanovich, Inc.: For an excerpt from *Arrowsmith* by Sinclair Lewis.

- Doubleday & Company, Inc.: For an excerpt from *Chemicals from the Atmosphere* by Charles H. Simpson; copyright © 1969 by the Air Reduction Company, Inc.

- Time, Inc.: For excerpts from "Climbing All Over the Family Trees" by Stefan Kanfer, from *Time*, March 28, 1977; reprinted by permission of Time, The Weekly Newsmagazine; copyright Time, Inc., 1977.

- Mara Wolynski: for an excerpt from "Confessions of a Misspent Youth" by Mara Wolynski, from *Newsweek*, August 30, 1976, by permission of the author.

- Simon & Schuster: For definition of *walk* from *Webster's New World Dictionary*, Students Edition; copyright © 1981, 1976.

Every effort has been made to trace the ownership of all copyrighted materials and to obtain permission.

Cover Art

Puddle (detail), 1952, M.C. Escher. National Gallery of Art, Washington, D.C., Rosenwald Collection.

Photographs

Leo Choplin/Black Star: 16; W. Perry Conway/Tom Stack & Associates: 25; UPI/Bettman: 36; The Bettmann Archive: 42; AP/Wide World Photos: 106; James L. Bixby Collections, courtesy of Northwestern University Archives: 128; Collection of the International Museum of Photography, George Eastman House: 164.

Illustrations

Tom Dunnington: 58; Diane Magnuson: 70; Suzanne Snider: 79; David Cunningham: 118; George Suyeoka: 152.

Personal Vocabulary Log

Use the following pages to keep track of the unfamiliar words you encounter in your reading. Write brief definitions and pronunciations for each word. This will make the words part of your permanent vocabulary.

_____

_____

_____

_____

_____

_____

_____

_____

_____

_____

_____

_____

_____

_____

_____

_____

_____

_____

_____

_____

_____

_____

_____

Personal Vocabulary Log

Personal Vocabulary Log

Personal Vocabulary Log

Personal Vocabulary Log